Rioting in the UK and France

Rioting in the UK and France
A comparative analysis

Edited by
David Waddington, Fabien Jobard and Mike King

WILLAN
PUBLISHING

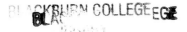

Published by

Willan Publishing
Culmcott House
Mill Street, Uffculme
Cullompton, Devon
EX15 3AT, UK
Tel: +44(0)1884 840337
Fax: +44(0)1884 840251
e-mail: info@willanpublishing.co.uk
website: www.willanpublishing.co.uk

Published simultaneously in the USA and Canada by

Willan Publishing
c/o ISBS, 920 NE 58th Ave, Suite 300,
Portland, Oregon 97213-3786, USA
Tel: +001(0)503 287 3093
Fax: +001(0)503 280 8832
e-mail: info@isbs.com
website: www.isbs.com

First published 2009

ISBN   978-1-84392-504-0 hardback

British Library Cataloguing-in-Publication Data

A catalogue record for this book is available from the British Library

FSC
Mixed Sources
Product group from well-managed
forests and other controlled sources

Cert no. SGS-COC-2482
www.fsc.org
© 1996 Forest Stewardship Council

Project managed by Deer Park Productions, Tavistock, Devon
Typeset by GCS, Leighton Buzzard, Bedfordshire
Printed and bound by T.J. International Ltd, Padstow, Cornwall

Contents

Part IV Other International Comparisons

Part V Conclusions

Tables and figures

Acknowledgements

This book draws on academic contributions to a series of three workshops on 'A Comparative Analysis of Recent French and British Riots', which took place between February and October 2007. The series formed part of a Franco-British Collaborative Workshop Scheme, jointly established by the British Arts and Humanities Research Council (AHRC) and Economic and Social Research Council (ESRC), and the French *Agence Nationale de la Recherche* (ANR). Our workshops were funded on the basis of a grant awarded to David Waddington and Mike King by the ESRC (Grant Reference: RES-170-250001) and a related award to Fabien Jobard by the ANR (Grant Reference: FrBr-05-001). We are grateful to each of these agencies for allowing us the opportunity to exchange relevant experiences and ideas with a view to enhancing knowledge and informing social policy.

The 'core' group of participants in the workshops comprised eight British and eight French academics. Also involved were a number of relevant practitioners and a pair of overseas academics (one Dutch, the other German) whose occasional attendance brought additional vitality and specialist expertise to our discussions. Among such individuals were: Edward van der Torre, senior researcher in Public Administration, Leiden University, The Netherlands; PC Zoe George and Inspector Mark Leighton of West Yorkshire Police; Liz Hanney of the Bradford-based Diversity Exchange; Manawar Jan-Kahn, a community activist from the Manningham area of Bradford; Raja Mia, MBE, of the Oldham-based Peacemaker group; Olau Thomassen, Project Manager of Bradford's Community Accord organisation; Bertrand Vallet, *Direction Générale de l'Urbanisme, de l'Habitat et de la*

Construction; and Pierre Willem of the French National Police Union, *UNSA Police*. The contributions made to the workshops by these occasional speakers were truly invaluable and have greatly informed our written efforts.

Separate contributors to this volume would also like to register their indebtedness to particular individuals and funding agencies. Janet Bujra and Jenny Pearce are grateful to the Safer Communities Partnership of Bradford Vision, which funded the research on which their chapter is based. They also wish to recognise the assistance provided by three local auxiliaries on the project (Altaf Arif, Abbas Ali and Baasit Arif) and the co-operation given by West Yorkshire Police. Janet and Jenny do emphasise, however, that they accept sole responsibility for any views and analysis appearing in their chapter. Likewise, Mike King would like to thank his West Midlands Police interviewees for their participation. Paul Bagguley and Yasmin Hussain are eager to acknowledge the financial support of the British Academy (Grant number: SG-35152) which enabled them to carry out the research reported in their chapter. These colleagues also wish to emphasise that the Census output referred to in their chapter is Crown copyright and is produced with the permission of the Controller of HMSO and the Queen's printer for Scotland. Finally, Tim Lukas's participation in the workshop series was made possible by the financial support of the *Laboratoire européen associé 'Délinquance'* (CNRS-MPG).

We, as editors, would like to express our appreciation to our administrative colleagues and/or research assistants, Clare Garrett and Kerry McSeveny (of the Cultural, Communication and Computing Research Institute, Sheffield Hallam University), Bessie Leconte (CNRS-GERN) and Isabelle Pénin (CNRS-CESDIP), for their vital and much needed support in helping us to edit our texts and prepare the final manuscript. We are further grateful to Peter Haegel, Caroline Lemerle, Jennifer Merchant and Priya Vari Sen for their help in translating the French contributions into English. Last, but not least, we would like to thank our partners in life, Joanna Waddington, Eve Plenel and Wibke Rickers-King, for all their patience, encouragement and support while we were working on this volume.

David Waddington
Fabien Jobard and
Mike King

Notes on contributors

Paul Bagguley is Senior Lecturer in Sociology at the University of Leeds. His main interests are protest, social movements, racism and ethnicity. He is the author of *From Protest to Acquiescence? Political Movements of the Unemployed* (Macmillan 1991) and co-author, of *Riotous Citizens: Ethnic Conflict in Multicultural Britain* (with Y. Hussain, Ashgate 2008).

Janet Bujra is an Honorary Reader and Senior Research Associate in the Department of Peace Studies at the University of Bradford. Her research concerns encompass class and gender relations, the political economy of development, and the state and political participation. She has worked both in Africa and in the UK and is currently exploring the political context of rioting as well as the politicisation of people living with HIV/AIDS in Tanzania. Her publications include *Sexuality and Gender in Africa* (with C. Baylies, Routledge 2001) and *Serving Class: Masculinity and the Feminisation of Domestic Service in Tanzania* (Edinburgh Press 2001).

Renaud Epstein is Post-doctoral Researcher at the Institut des Sciences sociales du Politique (CNRS-ENS Cachan) and teaches at Sciences-Po in Paris. His main research interests are urban policies and administrative and decentralisation reforms. He has recently published 'L'éphémère retour des villes. L'autonomie locale à l'épreuve des recompositions de l'Etat', *Esprit*, February 2008, and (with J. Donzelot) 'Démocratie et participation. L'exemple de la rénovation urbaine', *Esprit*, July 2006.

Christine Fauvelle-Aymar is Associate Professor of Economics at Addis-Ababa University in Ethiopia and at the University of Tours in France (on leave). Her main research interests are electoral turnout in different electoral contexts and voting behaviour in French deprived areas. She has recently co-authored publications on parliamentary election turnouts in Europe and South Africa in the *Electoral Studies* and *Transformations* journals.

Abel François is Associate Professor of Economics at Strasbourg University and Associate Researcher at Telecom ParisTech. His current research interests focus on issues around electoral behaviour (e.g. the financing of electoral campaigns and voter turnout activity). His articles have been published in such journals as *Public Choice*, the *Journal of European Public Policy, French Politics*, and *Revue Française de Science Politique*.

Camille Hamidi is Lecturer in Political Science at Lyon II University and an Associate Researcher at CNRS-Triangle. Her main research interests are race and immigration, politicisation processes, collective action of migrants and minorities, social movements and voluntary associations. Her publications on the organisation and politicisation of French migrants have recently appeared, or are scheduled to appear, in such journals as *Migrants and Minorities, Revue Française de Science Politique* and *Revue Française de Sociologie.*

Yasmin Hussain is Lecturer in Sociology at the University of Leeds. Her main research interests are ethnicity, racism and gender. She is the author of *Writing Diaspora: South Asian Women, Culture and Ethnicity* (Ashgate 2005) and co-author of *Moving On Up: South Asian Women and Higher Education* (Trentham 2007).

Fabien Jobard is Permanent Researcher at the CNRS, Centre de recherches sociologiques sur le droit et les institutions pénales, France. His main research interests are race and criminal justice, police use of force, and policing and public disorder. He is author of *Bavures Policières? La force publique et ses usages* (La Découverte 2002). His other recent publications have appeared in such journals as *Revue Française de Sociologie, English Annual Supplement, Policing & Society, Berliner Journal für Soziologie, Swiss Journal of Sociology* and *Compass Sociology.*

Virinder Kalra is Senior Lecturer in Sociology at the University of Manchester. His main research interests are racism and ethnicity diaspora and popular culture and South Asian religious practices. He is author of *From Textile Mills to Taxi Ranks: Experiences of Migration, Labour and Social Change* (Ashgate 2000), and co-author of *Hybridity and Diaspora* (Sage 2006).

Mike King is Research Professor of Criminal Justice Policy at the Centre for Criminal Justice Policy and Research, Birmingham City University. His primary research interests are public order policing, comparative policing and policing and social change. He is co-author, with N. Brearley, of *Public Order Policing: Contemporary Perspectives on Strategy and Tactics* (Perpetuity/Palgrave Macmillan 1996). His recent publications on these topics have appeared in such journals as *Policing and Society, Policing: A Journal of Policy & Practice*, and *Mobilization: An International Journal.*

Michel Kokoreff is a Lecturer (maître de conférences) at Paris Sorbonne University (Paris 5, CESAMES-CNRS). As a sociologist, his works deal with the new urban features of juvenile delinquency, with social practises linked with drugs traffic and use, and with transformations of poor urban areas in the French *banlieues*. He has recently published *Sociologie de l'émeute* (Payot 2008) and *La Force des quartiers. De la délinquance à l'engagement politique* (Payot 2003).

Hugues Lagrange is Permanent Senior Researcher at CNRS and works at Observatoire sociologique du changement (CNRS, Sciences-po, Paris), where he has been working on crime prevention in impoverished areas of French towns. He is currently involved in a comparative study of school dropouts and high achievers in three cities. He has recently co-edited, with M. Oberti, *Emeutes urbaines et protestations* (Presses de Sciences-po 2006).

Tim Lukas is a sociologist and researcher at the Max Planck Institute for Foreign and International Criminal Law in Freiburg, Germany. His research interests range from money laundering and police-minority relations to urban regeneration and crime prevention. He is co-author of *Gefährdung von Rechtsanwälten, Steuerberatern, Notaren und Wirtschaftsprüfern durch Geldwäsche* (with M. Kilchling, Forum Verlag 2005), and has recently edited *Crime Prevention in High-Rise Housing* (Duncker and Humblot 2007).

Marwan Mohammed is Postdoctoral Researcher at the CNRS, Centre de recherches sociologiques sur le droit et les institutions pénales, France. His main research interest is that of youth gangs and delinquent behaviour in France. He is the recent co-editor, with L. Mucchielli, of *Les bandes de jeunes* (La Découverte 2007) and sole author of the article 'Les voies de la colère: Violences urbaines ou révolte politique?', appearing the same year in *Socio-Logos*.

Christian Mouhanna is Permanent Researcher at the CNRS, Centre de recherches sociologiques sur le droit et les institutions pénales, France. His main research interests are police organisation and cultures, relationships between police officers and the public, public policies on policing, and police-court relations. He has recently co-written books on the subjects of *Police: des chiffres et des doutes* (with J-H. Matelly, Michalon 2007) and *Une justice dans l'urgence* (with B. Bastard, PUF 2007).

Jenny Pearce is Professor of Latin American Politics and Director of the International Centre for Participation Studies. Her main recent research focus is on new forms of participation in the city, and she is just completing an ESRC-funded project which explored this theme in three cities in the UK and three in Latin America. Her publications include: *Gender Socialisation and the Transmission of Violence Through Time and Space: Global Civil Society* (Sage 2007) and *Civil Society and Development: A Critical Exploration* (with J. Howell and L. Reinner 2001).

James Rhodes is an ESRC Postdoctoral Research Fellow in the School of Sociology and Social Policy, University of Leeds. His main research interests are white racisms; the politics of 'race'; 'race', class and understandings of place; de-industrialisation and accounts of social change; and urban sociology.

Paul Thomas is Senior Lecturer in Youth and Community Work in the School of Education and Professional Development, University of Huddersfield. His main research interests are around community cohesion, multiculturalism and anti-racism, and issues of racial tension and segregation involving young people. He is currently working on an empirical project investigating young people's experiences of 'identity', segregation and cohesion in Oldham and Rochdale, Greater Manchester. His recent publications on the subject of 'community cohesion' have appeared in *Youth and Policy* and the *Journal of Social Policy*.

Patricia Vornetti is Associate Professor of Economics and Director of the MBA Programme 'Local development and urban planning' at the University of Paris 1 – Panthéon-Sorbonne. Her research primarily focuses on public policies and their local impacts. A recently submitted chapter, 'La présidentielle 2007 dans les zones urbaines sensibles de PACA', co-writtten with C. Fauvelle-Aymar and A. François, is due to appear in *Vote en PACA 2007* (edited by J. Gombin and P. Mayance, L'Harmattan 2009).

David Waddington is Professor of Communications and Head of the Communication and Computing Research Centre at Sheffield Hallam University. His main research interests are industrial relations, the sociology of mining communities, and policing and public disorder. He is author of *Contemporary Issues in Public Disorder: A Comparative and Historical Approach* (Routledge 1992), and *Policing Public Disorder: Theory and Practice* (Willan 2007). He is also co-author of *Flashpoints: Studies in Public Disorder* (with C. Critcher and K. Jones, Routledge 1989).

Glossary

This section comprises a series of definitions of key French terms as well as references to key politicians and political organisations that will be repeatedly mentioned in the course of this volume.

ANRU The *Agence nationale pour la renovation urbaine* ('National Urban Renewal Agency') was created in 2003 with the objective of demolishing 250,000 apartments, rehabilitating 400,000 rental-housing units, and upgrading a further 250,000 other residential quarters.

Banlieue A widely used term designating an urbanised area on the outskirts of a large town. Literally, *'banlieue'* means 'banned location': in the Middle Ages, such areas were under the control of the main town and did not enjoy the rights and freedoms enjoyed by corresponding local authorities in other towns. From the end of the 19th century onwards, industry and its workers gravitated to the *banlieues* in response to the low ground and property rentals being asked of them. The French economic growth of the 1950s and 1960s and the need for a foreign workforce, combined with the diverse political immigration waves following the latter country's declaration of independence in 1962, produced a massive increase in the ethnic minority population residing in the *banlieues*. Huge social housing estates (*cités*) were raised to accommodate this influx. Such locations were placed firmly under the spotlight when the first wave of French rioting occurred in 1981. Progressively, the word *'banlieue'* has become synonymous in the public imagination with a swathe of social problems such as urban deprivation and degeneration, illiteracy, drug abuse, and criminality and violence. Among the more recent issues associated with these areas are inter-racial conflict, increased electoral success on the part of the Far Right *Front National*, Islamic Fundamentalism, violence against women, police brutality and, of course, riots or urban disorders.

Brigade anti-criminalité (BAC)   These 'anti-crime units' consist of specially selected plain-clothed police officers whose duty it is to catch out individuals or groups who are in the act of committing crimes. These units are a source of constant resentment as far as *banlieues* youths are concerned.

Chirac, Jacques   Conservative Prime Minister in 1974–76 and 1986–88, *Président de la République* from 1995 to 2007. His defeat at the parliamentary election in 1997 forced him to occupy a less conspicuous role in French politics from 1997 to 2002.

Cité   This word describes the housing estates erected in the 1950s, 1960s and 1970s to accommodate, among others, France's newly arriving migrant workers. The slowdown in their construction in the early 1970s coincided with the growing salience of the type of social problems referred to above (see *banlieues*). Names like Les 300 (Aulnay-sous-Bois, 93rd Dept) or Les 4000 (La Courneuve, 93rd Dept) sometimes refer to the number of apartments constituting the *cités*. Others refer to the former rural status of such localities (e.g. La Plaine du Lys in Dammarie-lès-Lys, a *banlieue* on the eastern edge of Paris) or, perhaps, betray a political or artistic heritage (Cité Nelson Mandela, Cité Pablo Picasso, Cité Lénine, etc.). In recent years, a fiercely parochial territorialism has become more evident, characterised by conflict between youths groups from rival *cités*.

Commune/Municipality (or 'Town')   The *commune* is the most basic unit of French administration, of which there are no fewer than 36,000. It has no real equivalent in England, though it approximates most closely to the English 'district'. Each *commune* is led by an elected mayor who, in half of the cases involved, presides over populations of fewer than 380 inhabitants. *Communes* in urban areas tend to be referred to as 'municipalities'. For the sake of simplicity, we shall be using the word 'town' as a synonym for municipality.

Conseil   Représentatif   des   Associations   Noires   CRAN ('Representative Council of Black Associations') was founded in the days following the end of the nationwide riots in November 2005. CRAN promotes an active policy shift regarding minorities, notably encompassing a US-like affirmative action policy and the introduction of racial statistics into the national census.

CPE The *Contrat Première Embauche* (CPE or 'First Job Contract') is a major legislative measure brought into discussion in January 2006 by the French Prime Minister, Dominique de Villepin, with the intention of ensuring more jobs for socially disadvantaged youth in the aftermath of the 2005 riots. However, due to a provision allowing employers the freedom to fire their new employees without any obligation to pay them the usual separation costs, the proposed measure was abandoned amidst massive student protests.

de Villepin, Dominique Jacques Chirac's conservative Prime Minister from 2005 to 2007.

Département and Conseil Général Ever since the French Revolution, France has been divided up into 100 départements, which are numbered according to alphabetical occurrence. Paris constitutes a single *département*. Along with all the others, it has its own elected assembly in the form of a *Conseil Général* (general council), which is accountable for local social policy, including such issues as urban development and education and social work provision. The 93rd *département* (Seine-Saint-Denis) warrants a special mention in this book, since it was the very epicentre of the riots that occurred in 2005. The 93rd is one of the three most densely populated *départements* in France. It is also among the country's most urbanised and socially deprived locations and accommodates one of its largest migrant populations.

Front National This party of the Far Right has been prominent in French elections since 1983. Its crowning achievement occurred in 2002 when its founder, Jean-Marie Le Pen, benefited from a low electoral turnout to outscore Lionel Jospin in the first stage of the presidential election, only to be eventually defeated by Jacques Chirac.

Gendarmerie nationale This is the second-largest police organisation in France and it is characterised by the military status of its officers. *Gendarmerie nationale* officers are mainly deployed in rural or low-urbanised areas. However, also within their ranks is the *Gendarmerie mobile* (founded in 1921) which is similar in purpose and orientation to the *Police nationale's* CRS unit.

Île-de-France   Île-de-France is the administrative region embracing the municipality of Paris and the seven *départements* which surround it. Taken as a whole, the region constitutes one fifth of France's entire population and contains both the poorest and the richest sections of French society.

'Immigrant' and 'race'   French law defines an immigrant as 'any person residing in France who was born in a foreign country and who declares foreign citizenship or has acquired French citizenship' (INSEE, 'National Institute for Statistics and Economics'). According to the 1999 census, there were 2.4 million non-European immigrants residing in France. There are no racial categories in use in official census statistics in France and people born and raised in France are considered as French. Public policies bypass this difficulty in dealing with territories rather than with populations (see *politique de la ville*). However, French common language uses the terms *'Français/ Jeunes issus de l'immigration'* ('French/Youths of immigrant origin') to designate what would be named 'non-white populations' in English-speaking countries.

Jospin, Lionel   A socialist Prime Minister at the time of the Jacques Chirac's presidency (1997–2002).

Marche des Beurs   The 'Beurs Movement' (*'beur'* is a slang word for 'Arab') was the largest political movement ever stemming from French second-generation immigrant youth. It originated in an outer Lyons *cité* as a protest against the Summer 1983 wave of hate crimes and police killings. Young Arabs initiated a march from Lyons to Paris, passing by numerous French *cités*. The march arrived in Paris in 1984 where President François Mitterrand gave a welcome reception at the Elysée Palace. The *Marche's* leaders suffered from a dramatic lack of personal resources and strategic experience and the movement quickly came to an end.

Mayor   Mayors are elected every six years. They deal at *commune* level with such fundamentally local issues as the provision and maintenance of housing, roads and basic utilities. The mayor has no jurisdiction over the police.

Mitterrand, François   Leader of the *Parti Socialiste* (PS) from 1971 onwards and *Président de la République* from 1981 to 1995. His parliamentary election defeats of 1986 and 1993 resulted in his consignment in 1986–88 and 1993–95 to minor political roles on the French scene (and sharing his foreign policy powers).

Mouvement des Indigènes de la République MIR ('The Republic's Natives Movement') was founded in January 2005 by French Arabs and French Africans. They stand for an official condemnation of France's colonial past, and denounce French state and society for their alleged inability to consider French immigrants and their descendants other than as second-class citizens caught in a humiliating *de facto* status between citizens and foreigners (i.e. 'Natives'). They also display a constant hostility towards NPNS.

Mouvement Immigration Banlieue MIB ('Immigration and *Banlieue* Movement') was founded in 1995 as a network of several *banlieue* grassroots associations principally focused on police abuse and criminal justice issues. Marked by lasting financial deprivation and recruitment among the most deprived *banlieues* youths, they have strong connections with radical rap bands and promote disruptive modes of action. They once shared MIR's political orientations, but finally rejected MIR's focus on post-colonial grievances.

Ni Putes Ni Soumises NPNS (Neither Whores, Nor Submissive') was founded in 2002 as a reaction to the murder of a young French Arab woman by French Arab men from the same *cité*. Led by PS members, NPNS set up a 'Women's march against the ghettos and for equal treatment' – between men and women and between French and immigrants – that received extensive media coverage. Promoting a very offensive stance against sexism in the *banlieues*, they are often perceived by other activists as favouring hostility towards Arab men and boys or even supporting racist-oriented policies, for instance the law banning headscarves in schools. Their leader Fadela Amara, a former PS member, was appointed as the member of government in charge of *politique de la ville* by Nicolas Sarkozy in 2007.

Parti Communiste The Communist Party has long played a significant role in the political life of the working-class *banlieues*. However, since the 1970s its political influence has seriously declined relative to that of the *Parti Socialiste*.

Parti Socialiste (PS) The main French left-wing political party. It was founded in 1920. Its leaders have included François Mitterrand and (from November 2006 onwards) Ségolène Royal.

Police de proximité 'PolProx' is best characterised as a French version of neighbourhood policing, first implemented by Prime

Minister Lionel Jospin's Socialist government of 1997–2002. This initiative, which was always largely opposed by *Police nationale* directors, was terminated in 2003 by the minister of the Interior, Nicolas Sarkozy, as part of his campaign to toughen up the policing of the *banlieues*.

Police nationale   Unlike the situation existing in the UK, the French police system is based on different forces united under the sole Ministry of the Interior. *Police nationale* is the main police force in France, incorporating around 130,000 armed officers. It comprises various specialist units under the leadership of the *Direction Générale de la Police Nationale*. These include: urban police units (*Sécurité publique*), riot police (the CRS, founded in 1944), criminal investigation units (*Police judiciaire*) and intelligence gathering units (*Renseignements généraux*, which were most recently reorganised in 2008). Such units are chiefly deployed in urban areas, placing them on the 'front line' insofar as policing the *banlieues* is concerned. The *Police nationale* reputation became tarnished in the 1990s, following condemnations by such bodies as the Council of Europe (European Committee for the Prevention of Torture) and the European Court of Human Rights, associating French police officers with acts of torture.

Politique de la Ville   This refers to a policy framework implemented from the late 1970s onwards with the objective of reversing the social and economic problems inherent to France's most seriously deprived *cités*. Given the high concentration of immigrants in such localities, *politique de la ville* is generally regarded as the *de facto* set of policies for dealing with the range of problems besetting France's non-white urban populations. *Politique de la ville* embodies the French policy doctrine that the state should focus on territories and not on racial groups.

Préfet   Each *département* has its own *préfet*, who is the plenipotentiary of the central government. The *préfets* have overall responsibility for the local allocation of central state finances. This allocation is made on the basis of negotiations with the different elected authorities at department and *commune* level (i.e. the Conseil Général and Mayor, respectively). The *préfet* leads the police and is accountable for anything that has to do with public order.

Royal, Ségolène   A socialist Minister in Jospin's government and main opponent of Nicolas Sarkozy for the 2007 presidential race which she lost in the second ballot by gaining a vote of 47 per cent against Sarkozy's 53 per cent.

Sarkozy, Nicolas   Jacques Chirac's Minister of Interior (from 2002 to 2004 and from 2005 to 2007), he was elected *Président de la République* in 2007.

Town   (see *Commune/Municipality*)

Union pour la Majorité Présidentielle (UMP)   France's foremost Conservative party. Its leaders have included Jacques Chirac and Nicolas Sarkozy.

ZEP   The French concept of the *Zone d'éducation prioritaire* ('priority education zone') was coined in 1982 to refer to areas prioritised by the state for the targeting of school resources. The ZEP programme was further enhanced in 1989 and now encompasses some 9 per cent of all French schoolchildren aged 3 to 18 years.

ZFU   Forty-four of France's *Zones franches urbaines* ('tax/duty free zones') were created by the 1996 French law concerning 'urban policy recovery', which was designed to target public resources in those areas most requiring support, and a further 41 by a 2003 law focusing on urban development and renewal. Such zones encourage economic development by enabling companies and/or small enterprises to settle within ZUSs without any obligation to pay taxes or duties for specified periods of time.

ZUS   The 751 *Zones urbaines sensibles* ('sensitive urban areas') were also created by the 1996 French law concerning 'urban policy recovery'. The ZUSs were designated according to such statistical criteria as local employment rates, skill levels and the ratio of the population under 25 years old. They account for some 4.7 million inhabitants and are entitled to a raft of administrative, fiscal and economic advantages, all designed to stimulate greater economic and social well-being. Within everyday French discourse, the term 'ZUS' has become interchangeable with that of 'deprived *banlieue* area'.

Part I

Setting the Scene

Chapter 1

Introduction and overview: the British and French riots

David Waddington, Mike King and Fabien Jobard

The French riots and their predecessors

Academics and journalists have resorted to various forms of metaphor in attempting to characterise and explain the French riots of October to November 2005, which saw youths and police confronting one another nationwide against a seemingly constant backdrop of blazing cars and buildings. Some commentators alluded to natural or even *supernatural* phenomena in order to capture the essence of such drama. Schneider (2008), for example, likened the disorders to a 'maelstrom', while Wallerstein (2005) described them as exploding 'like a phoenix'. Others evoked unsettling comparisons with recent natural disasters – describing the disorders as 'France's Hurricane Katrina' (Murray 2006) and a 'tsunami of inchoate youth rebellion' (Ireland 2005). Like countless other riots in history, they were triggered off by a 'banal confrontation' (Brown 2007) on the afternoon of 27 October when police officers intercepted nine male youths thought to have been involved in the break-in of a shed on a housing estate in the Parisian town of Clichy-sous-Bois.

What transformed this innocuous affair into an incident of such international significance was the tragedy befalling a trio of the youths who had become unwittingly implicated in the encounter with the police. The three teenagers concerned (one of Turkish descent, the other two of African heritage) had been returning home from playing football in their school holidays when they were apprehended along with the other youths. Evidently fearing capture, or desperate at least to avoid the regular rigmarole of having their identity papers checked, the youths fled and took refuge in an electricity substation located to the rear of a nearby cemetery. This intensely dangerous environment quickly took its toll: the two Africans were fatally electrocuted, though the Turk somehow survived while still incurring extremely serious burns.

Rumours of this incident rapidly circulated the neighbourhood and, inside two hours, around 100 local youths embarked on a highly destructive 'rampage', setting fire to 23 vehicles in the process (Brown 2007). This action, and the two further nights of intermittent rioting that followed, occurred amidst a highly charged political atmosphere:

> During the hours following the incident the Minister of Interior, Nicolas Sarkozy, accused the three youngsters of involvement in a burglary but denied that they had been chased. Three days earlier, visiting Argenteuil, another town of the *banlieue*, he had declared he would 'rid them of the *racaille'* (riff-raff), employing a term youths would use to insult each other. A few months before, commenting on the death of a child shot dead by a youth in the infamous Cité de 4000 in La Courneuve, Sarkozy had brutally announced that he would 'cleanse the neighbourhood with a Kärcher' (high-pressure hose) … Neither the government nor the police made any gesture of compassion or respect towards the grieving parents and relatives of the boys. (Fassin 2006: 1)

It seems probable that a widely reported secondary incident was responsible for spreading the conflagration. Reports emphasise that the rioting had actually been calming down by the night of 29/30 October following a silent march by 500 mourners and protesters, many of whom wore t-shirts proclaiming 'Dead for nothing' in honour of the two dead boys (Mucchielli 2009). However, on the evening of 30/31 October, police officers pursuing a group of local youths fired a tear gas grenade into a local mosque where worshippers were saying prayers for Ramadan. Scores of those present were asphyxiated but Mr Sarkozy denied that the police had been guilty of any wrongdoing (Schneider 2008). This incident and Sarkozy's denial had a catalytic effect, causing rioting to spread initially to other ZUSs (sensitive urban areas) in the 93rd Department of Seine-Saint-Denis. Its subsequent progress was inexorable. By 7 November, conflict had spread to some

280 cities nationwide, causing the French Prime Minister to declare a state of emergency. The rioting continued with decreasing levels of intensity until 17 November, by which time it petered out.

The 20-day period of disorder resulted in no further loss of life immediately linked to the collective violence – indeed, the only serious injuries sustained were those caused to a disabled woman who was severely burned when the bus she had boarded in Seine-Saint-Denis was petrol-bombed by youths. There were few reports of looting, either. Nevertheless, the physical damage done was far from insignificant: a reported 201 police and 26 firefighters were injured in the riots, and as many as 10,000 private vehicles and 30,000 rubbish bins were deliberately ignited. Further damage was done to 250 public buildings, raising the total cost of urban destruction to an estimated €200 million. The legal consequences of the rioting were equally far-reaching: 5,200 people were arrested, of whom 4,800 were placed in police custody and 600 subsequently imprisoned (Jobard 2008; Mucchielli 2009). Since the disorders of 2005, France has experienced further occasional instances of rioting, as in the Parisian *banlieue* of Villiers-le-Bel in November 2007, Grigny in May 2007, and little-known small towns such as Saint-Dizier (in October 2007) and Vitry-le-François and Romans-sur-Isère (in June and October 2008, respectively).

Though certainly unprecedented in scope and duration, the French riots are a far from novel phenomenon. In the quarter of a decade predating the 2005 riots, French society was affected by a catalogue of major urban disorders (e.g. Bonelli 2007; Oberti 2008). Zauberman and Levy (2003: 1073) note how, even by the late 1990s, a particular pattern had emerged:

> These incidents may result from police shootings – whether lawful, unlawful or accidental. More often, they result from lethal traffic accidents occurring during a police chase of youth trying to escape an arrest in a stolen vehicle. Riots are also triggered by the outcomes of judicial investigations or trials, when local youth feel that the police officers involved have been unjustly cleared or too leniently sentenced.

It is evident that the incident that first triggered the 2005 riots was entirely consistent with this recent French tradition.

Making sense of the riots

During the 2005 riot period and in its aftermath, numerous possible explanations were put forward for the violence and destruction. Some political and media pundits argued that the disorders had been deliberately provoked by 'Islamic fundamentalist extremists', were the consequence of provocative hip-hop lyrics, or were a by-product either of the dysfunctionally polygamus Muslim families or inherent criminality of the 'riff-raff' inhabiting the French *banlieues* (Laachir 2007; Mucchielli 2009; Waddington 2008). The view that the allegedly 'contagious' dispersal of the riots was due to the 'copycat' effect of television coverage also gained widespread political currency (Waddington op. cit.).

On the opposite side, it was generally asserted that the riots (*émutes*) constituted a nationwide *révolte* (or 'rebellion') by the socially disaffected youth residents of the *banlieues*. There was little here to distinguish the views of such diverse organs as the pro-Sarkozy French weekly newspaper, *Le Journal du Dimanche*, whose editorial of 6 November 2005 spoke of 'forgotten generations' of geographically concentrated youths telling of their 'hatred' and 'despair' towards French society, and the left-leaning British daily, the *Guardian*, whose feature writer, Jonathan Freedland, expressed the opinion that:

> The riots themselves are not hard to fathom; several French commentators have said the only mystery is why they didn't break out 15 years earlier. If you corral hundreds of thousands of the poor and disadvantaged into sink estates and suburbs in a misery doughnut around the city, expose them to unemployment rates of up to 40%, and then subject them to daily racial discrimination at the hands of employers and the police, you can hardly expect peace and tranquillity. Cut public spending on social programmes by 20% and you will guarantee an explosion. All you have to do is light the fuse. (9 November 2005)

Political and media debate also focused in part on the relative merits of the British and French approaches to incorporating ethnic diversity (*Guardian*, 12 November 2005). The British model of *multiculturalism* is supposed to encourage diverse communities to develop semi-autonomously while preserving their own, unique identities. The corresponding French *assimilatory* model demands, as its name suggests, the incorporation of its migrant populations into a French way of life in which everyone is accepted as 'equal and the same' as soon as French citizenship and nationality have been conferred upon them (Favell 1998; Garbaye 2005; Weil and Crowley 1994).

Murray (2006: 37) points out that the French and British appear to harbour a mutual disdain for each other's primary model of society. He maintains that the French are apt to perceive the British model as a 'multitude of ethnic and religious ghettos'. In the wake of the London bombings of July 2005, French newspapers like *Le Monde* asserted that it was due to the robustness of the French model that there had been no such terrorist attacks in France (Laachir 2007: 50). British commentators reacted just as censoriously to the events of November 2005. For instance, the Chair of the British Commission for Racial Equality (CRE) graphically asserted how: 'The hundreds of cars that have now been burnt in French streets are pyres that mark the passing of a French delusion – that the incantation of *"liberté, égalité, fraternité"* would somehow mask the *réalité* of life for non-white French men and women: repression, discrimination, segregation' (*Observer*, 6 November 2005).

What is certainly evident, even from this brief review, is that more systematic and considered sociological analysis is required of such matters as the social profiles of the rioters and the precise nature of their grievances; the background conditions against which the riots occurred; the manner in which they broke out and spread across the 300 towns that were eventually involved; the possible roles in all this of authoritative institutions like the police and media; and the possible importance of race and ethnicity. It is on these and related issues that contributors to this book will be focusing their attention.

The British riots, 1980–2005

British observers of the French riots already had the benefit of a 35-year experience of recent rioting in their own country on which to formulate their ideas. In the early and mid-1980s, there were recurring confrontations in crumbling UK inner-city areas involving police and, predominantly, African-Caribbean youths. First to appear was the 1980 St Paul's (Bristol) riot where, 'Greatly outnumbered and unprepared for the anger of the community, the police were forced to withdraw, after attempting to confront the youth with military-style tactics for two hours. For four hours while the police awaited reinforcements, St Paul's was a "no-go" area' (Muncie 1984: 85). Though initially dismissed as a 'social aberration', the Bristol riot was actually a portent of the more widespread rioting occurring one year later in major inner-city areas like Brixton (London), Moss Side (Manchester), Handsworth (Birmingham), Toxteth (Liverpool) and Chapeltown (Leeds). The earliest and most serious of these was the Brixton riot of 10 to 12 April 1981, which saw black youths overturning cars and using petrol bombs against the police. Twenty-eight buildings were set alight and a total of 279 police officers reported injured (Lea 2004).

In 1991 and again in 1992, it was the turn of white working-class youths on the run-down and heavily stigmatised council housing estates of places like Cardiff, Oxford, Coventry and Newcastle to run riot in their localities. Such disorders constituted 'street battles' between youth and local police officers intervening in response to various forms of 'car crime', such as 'hotting' (performing acrobatic stunt driving on local streets) or 'joyriding' stolen cars (Campbell 1993; Lea 2004; Power and Tunstall 1997). There were four confrontations of this nature in 1991 and a further nine one year later.

Closest in similarity to the French disorders were the riots occurring in a handful of former mill towns and cities in West Yorkshire and East Lancashire in the spring and early summer of 2001. Following a minor disturbance in Bradford (West Yorkshire) on 14–15 April, more serious disorders occurred in Oldham (Greater Manchester), Burnley (Lancashire) and then in Bradford once again. The central participants in each of these riots were the police and British-born youths of Pakistani and Bangladeshi origin. In all cases the disorder broke out in close proximity to areas chiefly occupied by Asian Muslims, following the trouble-causing activities of white racists (Kalra 2002). To briefly summarise,

> In Oldham on 26–29 May around 500 people were involved, injuring 2 police officers and 3 members of the public with damage estimated at £1.4 million. In Burnley about 400 were involved on 24–26 June, with 83 police officers and 28 members of the public injured, and damage estimated at over £0.5 million. Finally, in Bradford up to 500 people were involved in 'riots' over the weekend of 7–9 July. The injured included 326 police officers and 14 members of the public with estimates of damage to property ranging up to £10 million … Around 400 people have been arrested in relation to the disturbances in Bradford, Burnley and Oldham. (Bagguley and Hussain 2003: 1)

The Oldham riot occurred when, following an argument between a 36-year-old white woman and pair of Asian youths, members of a white racist organisation (Combat 18 or C18) carried out retributive attacks on nearby Asian residents and their properties. Thereafter, a more serious and prolonged confrontation developed between the police and Asian young men who accused the former, not only of failing to adequately respond to the fascist attacks, but of actually providing protection to the white assailants (Waddington 2007).

A more complicated series of events in Burnley began with a late-night assault on an Asian taxi driver – answered later the following day by a retaliatory attack involving 70 Asian men on a public house frequented by members of the Far Right. Hostilities resumed on the day after that, when Asian youths fought with police officers struggling to separate them from white racists staging an impromptu march within the boundaries of an Asian residential area (King and Waddington 2004).

Finally, the Bradford riot occurred in the context of an anti-fascist rally called in response to rumours of an impending appearance in the city centre by members of the Far Right British National Party (BNP). Heightened tension apparently resulting from a series of minor altercations and abusive behaviour involving BNP activists developed into a confrontation between police and demonstrators. Such conflict was exacerbated following a police strategy of pushing Asian participants away from the city centre towards the Asian-dominated residential area of Manningham (Hussain and Bagguley 2005).

A succession of official reports soon appeared, with each one setting out the possible causes of the riots and making associated policy recommendations (Cantle 2001; Clarke 2001; Denham 2002; Ritchie 2001). These tended to highlight the significance of such factors as the 'self exclusion' of Asian Muslims from British society, the absence of credible political leadership within their ranks, and the growing criminality of Asian youth. Corresponding academic research and analysis shifted the focus of discussion onto such issues as social disadvantage and deprivation, political marginalisation and disaffection, youth alienation and deviance, and the possible contributing roles of the police and media (e.g. Amin 2002; Kalra 2002; Kundnani 2001; Lea 2004). Such debates were given further impetus and significance following rioting (on 22–23 October 2005) in the Lozells area of Birmingham, where clashes between Asian and African-Caribbean youths were precipitated by a rumour that a 14-year-old African girl had been 'gang raped' by a youths of Asian heritage (*Guardian*, 29 November 2005).

The origins and focus of the book

It soon became apparent to the editors of this volume that British attempts to analyse and remedy the underlying causes of the 2001 riots might constitute a potentially valuable resource to French academics, practitioners and policy makers currently striving to make sense of and formulate reactions to the recent disorders. We likewise considered that the French experience could provide a fertile basis for re-applying, testing and enhancing existing British theory and policy. Hence, we successfully applied to the British Economic and Social Research Council (ESRC) and French *Agence nationale de la recherche* (ANR) to undertake a series of exploratory workshops, geared to exchanging information, developing theory and formulating recommendations for just and sensible social policy.

The core (permanent) group of participants in these workshops comprised eight British and eight French academics with interests in the UK and/or French riots. Included in this group were one British and two French doctoral students. The British participants were drawn from a range of separate disciplines, encompassing communication studies, criminology, peace studies, youth work, sociology and urban regeneration. French colleagues exhibited similar diversity, coming from such disciplines as criminology, police studies, politics, sociology and urban studies. In addition to this permanent group, the workshops incorporated an equally diverse collection of one-off ('occasional') guest speakers, both academics and practitioners (ranging from police personnel to community workers and housing officers).

Following a preliminary planning meeting of the grant holders in Paris in December 2006, a series of three two-day workshops took place in 2007. These were held in Sheffield (on 14–16 February), Paris (17–19 June) and Birmingham (24–26 October). The first workshop was primarily concerned with the description and analysis of the English riots of April to July 2001. The second workshop placed corresponding descriptive and analytical emphasis on the French riots of October to November 2005. The final workshop paid particular attention to policy initiatives implemented in the wake of the British disorders. Part of this final session was also devoted to ensuring the widest possible dissemination of our conclusions and policy recommendations. It was with this objective in mind that the idea of creating this volume was conceived and has since achieved fruition.

The book's contents and scope

The book is presented in four parts. Part I comprises our attempt to 'set the scene' by placing the British riots of 2001 and French riots of 2005 and after in their appropriate historical and theoretical contexts. Thus, in Chapter 2, David Waddington and Mike King provide an overview of the British disorders of the 1980s and 1990s, and of attempted academic explanations. Chapter 3 constitutes a corresponding overview by Fabien Jobard of the French riots of 1981–2004. The purpose of these preliminary chapters is to outline theoretical constructs and insights that are potentially capable of informing our analyses of the most recent riots in each country.

The five chapters comprising Part II of the book focus primarily on the British riots of 2001 and 2005. In the first of these (Chapter 4), Virinder Kalra and Chris Rhodes identify the significance of the 'local histories' underpinning the 'identity politics' of the riot-affected areas of Oldham and Burnley. They argue that conflict in these towns was facilitated and encouraged by such crucial 'technologies of information flow' as the manipulation of the local media and internet, and the 'calling to arms' of riot participants via taxi radio networks and use of the mobile phone.

Janet Bujra and Jenny Pearce's analysis of the police's experience of the Bradford riot (Chapter 5) highlights the subjective and operational tensions involved in the management of inter-ethnic conflict. A corresponding analysis of civilian participation in the Bradford riot by Paul Bagguley and Yasmin Hussain in Chapter 6 emphasises not only the wide variation of underlying motives for engaging in disorder, but also the extent to which individual orientations towards the police and violence were anything but constant or consistent.

There is a shift of focus in Chapter 7, in which Paul Thomas uses a case study of youth work in Oldham to test out the implications of the UK Government's post-riot policy emphasis on 'Community Cohesion'. Sceptics of such policy had made dire predictions of it leading to the 'death of multiculturalism' but Thomas suggests that its accent on prejudice reduction and relationship building has enabled ethnic diversity to flourish. Mike King's equally singular discussion (in Chapter 8) traces the background to and genesis of the 2005 riot in the Lozells district of Birmingham, which was unusual for the involvement of rival factions of Asians and African-Caribbeans.

The change of emphasis in Part III onto the French riots of 2005–2008 begins with Hugues Lagrange's discussion, in Chapter 9, of some of the key structural variables (e.g. housing, population segregation, employment, ethnicity and family size) underlying riot propensity. One of these themes – exploring the relationship between rioting and the recent instigation of particular French housing and urban regeneration programmes – is taken up by Renaud Epstein in Chapter 10. This is followed by Camille Hamidi's discussion, in Chapter 11, of the possible influence on the rioting of the historically poor political representation of migrant workers in French society.

The next three chapters represent counterparts to our earlier Chapters 5 and 6. Thus, in Chapter 12, Michel Kokoreff explores the experiences and political belief systems of those youths who participated or, conversely, refrained from engaging, in the riots. Following this, Marwan Mohammed outlines (in Chapter 13) his in-depth field study of youth gangs from one particular *cité* involved in the 2005 riots. Specific emphasis is placed on the relationships existing between the youths and local politicians, and of the routine role of violence in everyday political affairs. Christian Mouhanna then speculates (in Chapter 14) in terms of those characteristics of the French policing system which helped to give rise to eventual confrontation. The final chapter of this Part, by Christine Fauvelle-Aymar, Abel François and Patricia Vornetti, then considers the impact of the French riots in terms of their possible influence on voting patterns and other forms of political behaviour.

In Part IV, we briefly divert our attention onto rioting (or the absence of such conduct) in other major western societies. In Chapter 16, David Waddington investigates the possible causes of the only major instance of rioting to occur in the United States of America in the new millennium by focusing on the 2001 Cincinnati riot and subsequent attempts by local actors to avoid a repetition. Tim Lukas then concentrates (in Chapter 17) on those aspects of German police policy towards ethnic minorities which he considers to have been instrumental in ensuring an absence of rioting in that nation.

The final chapter of the book draws both the lessons to be learned from these earlier contributions and insights from the wider literature into a comparative discussion of the main causes of the rioting in the United Kingdom and France. Such discussion is then used as a springboard for evaluating current policies aimed at alleviating social problems and preventing future disorder.

Chapter 2

Theoretical orientations: lessons of the UK riots of the 1980s and 1990s

David Waddington and Mike King

Introduction

The following two chapters of this book are devoted to trying to understand the underlying causes of the French riots. We aim to uncover relevant insights by: (a) using descriptions and analyses of the 2001 UK riots as a possible basis of enlightenment; and (b) employing recent studies by French scholars of possible reasons for the conflict that occurred. Before embarking on this agenda, we are pausing in this chapter to reflect on the main characteristics of two previous 'riot eras' occurring in recent British history: the inner-city riots of the 1980s and the 1990s disorders on white-dominated, working-class housing estates. This review is undertaken in the belief that the theories and ideas already expounded in relation to these riots have much to contribute to our understanding of the French disorders. In each case, we present an overview of events, followed by an outline of relevant lay and academic theories. The corresponding purpose of Chapter 2 is to provide an overview and analytical discussion of French riots occurring two decades prior to the disorders of 2005.

The 1980s inner-city riots

An overview of events

The 1980s UK riots occurred in major inner-city areas containing relatively compact and highly segregated African-Caribbean populations, each the product of post-war immigration which saw thousands of West Indians encouraged to join the UK workforce, albeit in the lower-paid and more menial employment sectors (Waddington 1992). The first of these riots, in St Paul's (Bristol) in April 1980, established a clear causal precedent. A crowd gathering in response to a police raid on the locally based 'Black and White' café reacted angrily to the arrest of its popular African-Caribbean proprietor and a second African-Caribbean man on charges related to drug use and the sale of illicit beer. As the prisoners were being escorted from the premises, the police and their vehicles were bombarded with bricks and bottles by waiting youths. A two-hour confrontation ensued as a consequence of which the police, though heavily reinforced, were driven from St Paul's, turning it temporarily into a 'no-go' area (Reicher 1984).

Establishment claims that the Bristol riot was a 'social aberration' (Benyon and Solomos 1987) were resoundingly discredited by the Brixton disorder of April 1981. The area had recently been subjected to a police policy known as 'Swamp 81', which involved 'saturating' the locality with uniformed and undercover police, stopping and searching 'suspects' by the hundred and raiding homes and cafés in a drive to eliminate 'muggings' (violent street robberies). Growing community tension escalated on 10 April when police, wrongly perceived to be obstructing a 19-year-old black stab-wound victim from going to hospital, engaged in an 80-minute confrontation with African-Caribbean youths.

The police presence was stepped up on the following day, whereupon an even more serious incident took place with dire repercussions:

On 11 April two 'SWAMP' officers searched a 'mini-cab' (taxi) driver (outside the S and M Car Hire office) after seeing him push something into his socks which they suspected was drugs. In fact it was a number of bank notes but the police went on to search the car. A crowd of about 30 people had gathered, which soon increased to about 150. One person was arrested for [obstruction], and back-up was called for after an officer was erroneously thought to have been stabbed. The crowd then started a missile attack. Eventually a police van was set alight and there were a number of police charges. Looting took place and for the first time in mainland Britain petrol bombs were thrown at the police. In 4 days the toll of the rioting amounted to 145 buildings damaged; 207 vehicles damaged or destroyed; and 450 people reported injured. (King and Brearley 1996: 55)

Major riots followed thereafter in the major inner-city areas of Moss Side (Manchester), Toxteth (Liverpool), Handsworth (Birmingham), Chapeltown (Leeds) and in Brixton once again. Hundreds of smaller riots were also reported, spanning the length and breadth of the UK. Major rioting then resumed in 1985, with the most spectacular disorders occurring at Handsworth, where two Asian civilians died of asphyxiation, and on Tottenham's Broadwater Farm Estate (London), where a police officer was stabbed to death and gunshots were fired at his colleagues. As in 1981, each riot was triggered by a preliminary altercation between police officers and one or more black civilians amidst worsening police-community relations (Benyon and Solomos 1987).

Lay and academic explanations

As in the French riots, media representations of the 1981 disorders emphasised the roles of 'wanton criminality' and outside agitators (Murdock 1984; Tumber 1982). The idea that 'media contagion' may have played its part was given credence by Lord Scarman, who in his official report of inquiry blamed the broadcasting media's coverage of the April 1981 Brixton disorder for generating the 'copycat element' which resulted in further rioting elsewhere in the country as the summer wore on (Scarman 1981).

This 'copycat theory' of rioting was rejected by the senior police officers and media reporters approached by Tumber (1982). These practitioners maintained that participants had mobilised primarily as a consequence of 'word of mouth'. Murdock (1984: 87) is nevertheless receptive to the notion that media coverage *did* play a role in the rioting:

> Some observers have argued that this kind of coverage raised the consciousness of inner city youth and increased their readiness to take on the police. This is a possibility, but the coverage also had lessons for the police. It primed them to expect major trouble in the cities and strengthened their resolve to crack down on it early by stepping up their activities in inner city areas. This in turn cemented youth resentment at police behaviour and fed local rumours that a riot was imminent. As a result, both sides 'tooled up' for trouble, so that eventually it only took a minor incident on the streets to trigger a confrontation.

By and large, the Scarman report was scornful of conspiracy or riff-raff explanations of the violence, preferring to focus instead on larger sociological issues. Scarman concluded that the disorders had arisen due to a 'complex political, social and economic situation' (involving high unemployment, poor housing, economic deprivation, a lack of amenities and 'heavy policing'); he maintained that the disorders were 'neither premeditated nor planned'; rather, they amounted to 'the spontaneous reaction of angry young men, most of whom were black, against what they saw as a hostile police force' (Scarman 1981: 45).

Many official reactions to the riots of 1985 clearly sought to discredit and condemn the participants and their actions. Thus,

> Conservative politicians, newspapers and police officers adopted riff-raff explanations and ascribed the riots to criminality and greed, hooliganism and 'mindless violence', extremists and subversives, imitation, base impulses in human nature and general evil, or to a failure in education and a breakdown in family life and proper values ... A number of senior police officers said that the riots were planned, either by political extremists ... or by drug dealers. The media seized on both these propositions and, on 8 October 1985 in its 'Tottenham Riot Special' edition, the *Daily Express* led with a story of how 'a hand-picked death squad' which had been 'trained in Moscow and Libya', acted on the orders of 'crazed Left-wing extremists'. (Benyon 1987: 32)

Not all right-wing politicians, senior police and newspaper columnists were so committed to these perspectives. Many such individuals aligned themselves with left-wing politicians and spokespersons for the black communities in maintaining that high unemployment, poor housing, political exclusion and alienation, and negative police-community relations were all major ingredients in the riots (ibid.: 32–3). Variables of this nature have figured prominently in attempts by British academics to explain the precise causes of the 1980s' riots.

Like numerous commentators on the American urban disorders of the 1960s (e.g. Hundley 1968), Benyon (1987) distinguishes between the *trigger* event responsible for 'sparking off' each riot and the underlying social conditions that provided the *tinder* required for a major conflagration. Benyon maintains that, insofar as the 1980s' riots were concerned, 'The *immediate precipitants* or *trigger events* in each case involved police officers and black people' (ibid.: 33). The tinder comprised five social characteristics common to each riot, namely:

(i) racial disadvantage and discrimination; (ii) high unemployment, especially among young African-Caribbean males; (iii) widespread deprivation, including substandard housing, environmental decay, high crime, and inadequate educational and social service provision; (iv) political exclusion and powerlessness (a lack of political 'voice' resulting from an absence of 'institutions, opportunities and resources for articulating grievances and bringing pressure to bear on those with political power'); and (v) extensive mistrust of, and hostility to, the police, especially among young people regularly subjected to 'stop-and-search' procedures and related forms of harassment and abuse (ibid.: 33–4).

Benyon's 'five common characteristics' provide a useful basis for understanding the 1980s riots. Nevertheless, related research highlights the need to recognise the significance of such additional variables as cultural differences between black youths and the police, the ideological vilification of African-Caribbean youth, the historical and symbolic significance of the locations where the rioting occurred, and the particular dynamics of the daily police-civilian encounters which culminated in disorder.

There is substantial overlap between Benyon's approach and the explanation of the 1980s disorders proffered by Lea and Young (1982, 1993; Kinsey et al. 1986). Like Benyon, these authors also recognise the importance of relative deprivation, especially in terms of its impact on *second-generation, British-born*, African-Caribbean youth, raised to expect social equality with their white peers. These authors also concur with Benyon that an absence of representative political organisations and/or 'any viable tradition of ethnic politics' had left the youths hopelessly politically marginalised (Lea and Young 1982: 15).

In extending Benyon's argument, Lea and Young maintain that black youths adapted to this predicament by fashioning a *subcultural* solution, incorporating elements of the rastafarian and 'rude boy' cultures originating from the West Indies. Lea and Young paint a decidedly unromantic picture of this development, emphasising how:

> Cultures which grow out of adversity and oppression are as likely to be predatory as progressive. Crime abounds in such communities and whereas most of it is of no significance (e.g. cannabis smoking) other elements such as street robbery and interpersonal violence are seriously anti-social. It is a common mistake on the left to imagine that street criminals are a

species of inner-city Robin Hoods. In reality the victims of such crimes are usually poor and otherwise ill capable of defending themselves. (ibid.: 8–9)

Indeed, they reckon that it was in response to a resulting proliferation of street crime – especially robbery with violence (or 'muggings') – that the police were eventually pushed into using more desperate measures, such as covert community surveillance and random stop-and-search procedures. The inherent danger of adopting such a 'dragnet' approach is that police actions can soon appear indiscriminate and turn whole communities against them. In such a context, the arrest of one individual can be the spark for an upsurge of collective resentment and resistance – as occurred, for example, in Brixton.

While such an explanation is to be applauded for having outlined some of the key social conditions, mediating cultural variables and social dynamics which contributed to the riots, it arguably displays a tendency to underplay police culpability in the riots. Numerous studies have emphasised that many of the sentiments, beliefs and recipes of action embodied in the police occupational culture are fundamental to explaining the negative and often confrontational relationships between the police and ethnic minorities. According to such authorities as Holdaway (1983) and Reiner (1992), rank-and-file officers are invariably conservative in outlook, harbouring highly suspicious and prejudicial attitudes towards blacks and Asians. Additionally, these lower ranks tend to place a high value on action, challenge and excitement, relishing the opportunity for a car chase or confrontation. This view is consistent with the revelation that:

> The prospect of a violent disturbance or a riot is something that is certainly found interesting and exciting by many police officers, though if they are in small groups they may not look forward to it through finding it too frightening. However, larger groups such as immediate response units certainly look forward to disturbances and, in fact, tend to find anything else boring by comparison. (Smith and Gray 1985: 341)

Lea and Young's analysis has been directly criticised by Scraton (1985: 98–9) for having shown 'no conception of the ways in which black communities have been discriminated against by the police, no reference to the strategies of selective law enforcement and the targeting of particular groups'. Part of this missing theoretical link is provided by Jefferson and Grimshaw (1984: ch. 4), who set out a detailed explanation of 'the extraordinary mobilisation of attention and resources' used to combat 'street crime' in the build-up to the 1981 Brixton riot.

These authors maintain that the 'militaristic' style of policing framing the 1981 Brixton riot was encouraged by a combination of three important factors: rising crime figures, the attitudes of the courts in dealing with offenders, and indicators of the prevailing 'public opinion'. They agree with Lea and Young that street crime figures for the Brixton area had recently been increasing. However, they insist that, since such figures had been showing an upward trend for some time without provoking a particular strategic response, it is clear that other factors helped to shape the ultimate nature of the police operation:

> What was also critical in this instance was the role of the media in representing public opinion in a particular form on the issue of street crime, and the attitude of the courts. It was this *combination* of rising crime statistics, the construction of public opinion as 'anxious and concerned' on the matter, and the tough, uncompromising attitude of the courts to the offenders unlucky enough to be labelled as part of the street crime problem, which has to be understood as the essential backcloth for the development of a distinctive police strategy. (Jefferson and Grimshaw 1984: 89, original emphasis)

In the face of this apparent mounting public disquiet, the Metropolitan police implemented a proactive, clear-up strategy, based largely on the use of stop-and-search powers and the periodical deployment of mobile response units, notably the Special Patrol Group. Jefferson and Grimshaw emphasise how this 'crude blunderbuss' of a strategy served to alienate every section of the Brixton community, making day-to-day relations profoundly problematic.

The importance of this work lies in its ability to illustrate the relationship between the prevailing ideological climate and face-to-face relations between the police and members of black communities. Such commitment to producing a model of disorder capable of analysing both the underlying social factors and interactional dynamics which contribute to rioting is evident in one of the present authors' studies of 'flashpoints' of public disorder (e.g. Waddington 1992; Waddington *et al.* 1989). As Waddington *et al.* (1989: 1) explain, the impetus for their research on 'flashpoints' was provided by Lord Scarman's report on the Brixton riots, in which he stated:

The incident which sparked off the disorder on Saturday was nothing unusual on the streets of Brixton ... Why, on this occasion, did the incident escalate into major disorder culminating in arson and a full-scale battle with the police? ... The tinder for a major conflagration was there: the arrest outside the S & M car hire office was undoubtedly the spark which set it ablaze ... Deeper causes undoubtedly existed, and must be probed; but the immediate cause of Saturday's events was a spontaneous combustion set off by the spark of a single incident. (Scarman 1981: 37)

Waddington (1992: 82–9) applies the flashpoints model to the Brixton riot. The disturbance is analysed in terms of the model's six levels: structural, political/ideological, cultural, contextual, situational and interactional. The resulting explanation incorporates all of the variables reviewed above. Thus, at his *structural* level, Waddington emphasises the relative deprivation, discrimination, police harassment and political powerlessness endured by Brixton blacks. The *political/ideological* level highlights the nature and impact of the muggings moral panic analysed by Jefferson and Grimshaw, while the *cultural level* reiterates the importance of the subcultural discrepancies inherent in the police and black youth subcultures, also just referred to.

Waddington's *contextual* level deals with both the long- and short-term aspects of the breakdown of relations between the police and the Brixton community. Attention is focused, for example, on the collapse of a police-community liaison committeee, which was set up by the police and the Council for Community Relations in Lambeth (CCRL) in 1978 to improve the area's policing problems:

Three days after their first meeting, the SPG [police Special Patrol Group] were brought in without any prior warning to the committee. Liaison immediately collapsed. Then, in February 1979, three members of the CCRL were arrested at their office and taken to Brixton police station in connection with an incident at a local club where two plain-clothed officers and a bar staff member were stabbed. The only obvious link between them and the person suspected of the stabbing was that they wore sheepskin coats. (ibid.: 85–6)

Corresponding attention is paid at this level to more recent police activities, notably the implementation of Swamp 81 and the accelerating build-up of tension which reached boiling point when police intervened to investigate the stabbing of the local black youth. Great significance is also attached to the role of rumour (e.g. that hospital casualty departments had been warned to be 'on standby' by the police well before any disturbance had occurred) in generating a tense and hostile environment.

The model's *situational* level explores the 'spatial and symbolic significance' of Brixton's Railton Road, the community's 'front-line' meeting place and hive of cultural activity. It was here, of course, that the main rioting broke out. Its causal significance lay in the fact that, being popularly frequented, it not only provided the sufficient number of people (a 'critical mass') required to engage in rioting, but also symbolic 'turf' to be defended by local people or seized by the police (see also Keith 1993).

Finally, the *interactional* level emphasises the problematic nature of key police interventions. For example, Waddington (1992: 86–7) reviews evidence to suggest that the 'final spark' for Saturday's riot, the incident in which police officers apprehended the taxi driver outside the S & M car hire, was unnecessarily prolonged and involved a 'needless display of authority' on their part. Waddington also refers to the police's unwillingness to negotiate or compromise at key stages in the development of disorder. When four credible intermediaries (including two local councillors and a vicar) approached the senior officer on the spot to discuss a negotiated withdrawal, he emphatically refused on the grounds that the disturbance might spread. Waddington notes how, as in the American riots of the 1960s, there appeared to be a logic to the pattern of arson and destruction that occurred: 'Those businesses with a reputation for exploiting black people or treating them with incivility were the principal targets of attack' (ibid.: 87). Equally, the prevailing 'carnival type' atmosphere – suggesting an extreme collective euphoria – was seen as resulting from acquisition of a temporary political 'voice' by community members and an equally ephemeral liberation from the repressive policing that generally governed their lives.

The riots of the 1990s

An overview of events

A decade on from the inner-city riots, Britain witnessed fresh rounds of rioting in 1991 and 1992. There were five such disorders in 1991 and a further eight one year later. In contrast to the 1980s riots, the disturbances occurring in the 1990s primarily involved white youths from working-class council estates and generally resulted from police operations instigated in response to the theft of motor vehicles for the purpose of 'joyriding' (driving at high speeds for the 'thrill' of it), 'hotting' (performing 'acrobatic stunts', such as skids and 'hand-brake turns' in the road), and 'ram-raiding' (crashing into shop-fronts with the intention of looting the premises). The televisual impact of these riots was spectacular:

> Bombed, blazing neighbourhoods and automobile acrobatics, much of it the work of young masked men, appeared on nationwide television. The stars of the riots were boys. Lads who rarely travelled more than a mile or so from home were suddenly globalised, became international icons, were seen on television screens from Toulouse to Tokyo. They achieved not just Andy Warhol's fifteen minutes of fame, but a fortnight of it. (Campbell 1993: 3)

Two contrasting examples from 1991 are typical of these riots.

The trigger for the four successive nights of rioting on the Blackbird Leys estate in Oxford was a police clamp down following a series of hotting displays regularly attended by audiences of up to 250 local residents, who would gather by night on the estate's central shopping square, known as the 'Arena'. Police had been systematically monitoring this activity for several nights. Then, on 29 August, they struck in determined manner, only to precipitate four nights of rioting in which petrol bombs were thrown at police donning riot gear.

As in Oxford, the Meadow Well disorder was the direct result of a police crackdown on car theft and the related activities of ram-raiding and joyriding. As Campbell says of this phenomenon:

> The incidence of car crime rocketed during the summer. In July the corpses of forty-seven stolen cars ended up at Meadow Well. In August the total reached fifty-two. A battalion of boys were recruits to the circuit and at the beginning of September two of them died in a gruesome clash; their deaths started the countdown to the riot. On Friday, 6 September, twenty-one-year-old Colin Atkins and seventeen-year-old Dale Robson were being followed by police when they raced eastwards along one of the coast roads in a red Renault turbo hatchback they had stolen in Newcastle. They were consumed in flames when their car

crashed into a lamppost at around 130 m.p.h. and immediately blew up. Their identities could be traced only through the teeth, keys and jewellery found among their remains. (ibid.: 54–5)

Graffiti immediately appearing on local garden walls accused the police of having murdered the two young men. On 9 September, youths set fire to an electricity sub station as a calculated strategy to pitch the estate into darkness. Hundreds of them then ran amok, looting shops and leaving burnt down properties (including a school and community centre) in their wake.

Lay and theoretical explanations

It was impossible, of course, to analyse the 1990s' riots within discourses of race and racism. Some sections of the media, certain politicians and a handful of senior police officers endeavoured to explain the 1991 riots in terms of boredom, drunkenness or the prevailingly hot weather (Waddington 1992: 198). Others, like the Home Office Minister, John Patten, sought to pathologise this behaviour as 'mindless hooliganism and yobbery' while the shadow Home Secretary, Roy Hattersley, appealed for 'exemplary sentences' to be doled out to the ringleaders (ibid.: 198). Following the occurrence of the 1992 disorders, right-wing politicians and newspaper editorials generally maintained that lack of parental discipline on estates characterised by high proportions of single-parent families was largely to blame for the riots (Campbell 1993). This was to seriously disregard the presence of numerous contributing social and political factors.

Power and Tunstall's (1997) report into the nature and causality of the riots observes how they invariably occurred on huge, geographically isolated council estates, the majority of which had been built as part of slum clearance projects in the pre- and post-Second World War eras. These authors proffered the more specific conclusion that:

The places where disorders happened in the early 1990s were most often large, marginal and low-income council estates with a poor reputation, high unemployment and extremely large populations of children and young people, often with lone parents ... They were well-built, physically attractive areas of houses with gardens. They housed a mainly British white population. But they were stigmatised and unpopular. Boys in particular were harshly affected by loss of industrial jobs and poor educational performance. (ibid.: 12)

Campbell makes the complementary observation that loss of local industry and cutbacks in local authority expenditure had intensified the 'economic emergency' affecting these locations. Equally, such neighbourhoods had found themselves 'largely abandoned by the main political parties [and, therefore] left without representation' (1993: xi).

Both Campbell and Power and Tunstall are united in explaining the causation of the riots in terms of the differing ways in which local young men and women responded and adapted to the onset of such crisis. Without disputing the fact that local women may have occasionally tried to restrain their men-folk, or attempted to protect certain local buildings (such as schools or community centres) from destruction, it was mainly their male peers who participated in the riots. The above authors begin their attempts to interpret this discrepancy in behaviour by pointing out that, in addition to doing better at school and acquiring superior employment prospects, the young women often drew on an alternative source of esteem – young motherhood – that was unavailable to their masculine counterparts (Power and Tunstall 1997: 51).

One particular manifestation of the predicament confronting local young men was their attempt to find alternative ways of expressing a positive self-identity in the absence of paid work. Campbell maintains that in days of fuller employment these youths would have fashioned secure occupational identities as the basis of self-esteem, while their wage status would have enabled them to monopolise the community's leisure spaces while women dependants were relegated to the home. According to her, the acquisition and flaunting of high-performance cars that immediately predated the riots represented a masculine reassertion of power and status involving the appropriation and domination of community space: 'According to a youth worker who had, himself, been one of the lads, their culture was about proving themselves by having bottle, being good drivers, getting into places, looking for fights all the time, getting a bit crazier than everybody else, being able to get control of other people' (Campbell 1993: 201). Such reputation was sustained by other illicit activities, such as burglary, shoplifting and drug-dealing, and the direct intimidation of anyone threatening to report them to the police.

Police attempts to impose the rule of law on such neighbourhoods were allegedly hampered by their limited powers of intervention. In any case, the use of cautions and the prospect of court appearances served only to reinforce the notoriety of young men hell-bent on impressing their peers: 'At best, court became part of the young men's social life, part of the circuit of visibility from the street to the court house, another public appearance where what mattered to them was not that their behaviour was perceived as wrong but that it was seen as *important*' (ibid.: 266).

Power and Tunstall regard the absence of a sustained, community-oriented police presence in these neighbourhoods as a key ingredient in the rioting that eventually ensued:

> It was a symptom of wider policing difficulties and weak enforcement that incidents of violence, law-breaking and criminal damage rumbled on over years in areas of weak control, until they finally boiled over ... Tension between older residents and groups of law-breaking youths built up to a point where eventually residents demanded police action to suppress behaviour they themselves could not control. (Power and Tunstall 1997: 15)

Sudden and uncompromising police intervention was responded to as 'a challenge' by the youths of these areas. In Campbell's view, the violent reaction was all the more inevitable due to the fact that the police and young men constituted rival cultures that 'needed' each other to endorse their own avowedly masculine self-images (1993: 190). To the outside onlooker, the youths' behaviour may well have appeared 'ugly, irrational or short-term, but from a perspective which sees no exit and no future it may have offered some immediate relief of inexpressible feelings' (Power and Tunstall 1997: 53).

Conclusion

In this preliminary chapter, we have emphasised how the lay and political discourses attributing the 2005 French riots to the rabble-rousing activities of outside agitators and political extremists, to the criminal motives of local 'riff-raff', or to 'copycat' behaviour encouraged by the media were equally evident in the UK disorders of the 1980s and 1990s.

Our overviews of attempts by UK academics to theorise these riots suggest that it would be sensible to explore the relevance to our understanding of the French riots of such contingent variables as:

- social segregation
- deprivation and disadvantage
- unemployment
- political powerlessness and marginalisation
- ideological vilification
- cultural difference and adaptation
- spatial and territorial symbolism
- police strategic decision-making
- police-community interaction.

In the following chapters, we shall be exploring the possible utility of such variables in our attempts to achieve a better understanding of the French disorders. First, however, we shall turn to a corresponding overview of preceding French riots of the past three decades.

Chapter 3

An overview of French riots, 1981–2004

Fabien Jobard

Introduction

In contemporary France, 'riots'[1] refer to urban disorders mainly, if not exclusively, located in urban areas called *banlieues**. The aim of this chapter is to provide an overview of such events in the two decades or more leading up to the most recent French riots of 2005–7. It will soon become evident that there is no recent French academic tradition devoted to theoretically explaining these preceding riots to rank alongside the British literature alluded to in the previous chapter. Here, our contribution will trace the historical evolution of the riots and their consequences in two areas: the policies that were implemented as a response to those urban disorders, and the influence of the riots on political representations in France.

Riots in contemporary France

Riots involving sections of France's immigrant population and/or the inhabitants of deprived urban areas were not, strictly speaking, a new phenomenon at the beginning of the 1980s, specifically in Paris and its immediate outskirts where many low-scale insurgencies of Algerian workers and activists against the police had occurred during the Algerian War of Independence 1954–62 (Blanchard 2007). But the events that took place in several of Lyon's *cités* in 1981 did not involve Algerian activists; rather, they were engaged in by French citizens of Arabic descent. Moreover, they did not occur amidst stereotypically wretched shantytowns, but in recently erected housing estates. As we shall see, the disorders of 1981 were much smaller in scale than those of the following decade. However, their impact was sufficiently profound to ignite decades of concern and fear about what the French habitually refer to as the *problème des banlieues* or the *violence urbaine*.

L'été chaud, Minguettes estates, 1981

The 'Minguettes Hot Summer' of 1981 is the term used to designate a series of urban disorders occurring during the extended French summer school vacation in the 'Minguettes' housing estates, located in the *banlieue*-town of Vénissieux in the Eastern outskirts of Lyon. The disorders consisted of joyriding activities by local adolescents, who were apt to steal expensive, high-performance cars in the centre of Lyon, bring them up to the Minguettes *cité* and engage in chases (either between themselves or with police traffic patrols), before setting the vehicles on fire. From this point on, vandalism, nihilism and life-risking activities were the undisputed hallmarks of the *banlieues* crisis in France.

By the end of the '*été chaud*' ('hot summer'), around 250 cars had been destroyed. These events were comparable in nature with the wave of 'ram-raiding' thefts and 'hotting' cars events that took place on white, English working-class estates at the beginning of the 1990s. The main difference between them resided in the fact that the Minguettes were housing estates built-up in the mid-1960s in order to locate the huge strain of immigrant workers recruited from former French colonies in northern-Saharan Africa. The Minguettes are an urban area made up of almost 40 towers encompassing 10,000 apartments, or 35,000 inhabitants, with 55 per cent of the relocated population from 1975 to 1982 being foreigners or of foreign descent (Jazouli 1993: 20). In the wake of the Lyon area riots, there were numerous attempts by factions of immigrant youth to mobilise in pursuit of beneficial changes in policy on the part of the Mitterrand government that came to power in 1981. But these movements (most notably the '*Marche des Beurs*' – see Hamidi, this volume) experienced blatant failure, due to the political inexperience of the young *banlieues* leaders, who found themselves detached from older and more experienced first-generation movements, and marginalised by the hegemonic *Parti Socialiste*, whose short-sighted tactics stymied the development of an institutionalised immigrant elite on the left of French politics (Garbaye 2005). As Garbaye puts it, 'The failure of the Beurs movement alone is responsible for the lingering crisis of confidence among many second-generation Maghrebis in French institutions, and, to a large extent, for 20 years of political exclusion' (2005: 216). This period of missed political opportunities was brought to a close by a particularly intense riot in 1990 in another *cité*, Mas du Taureau, on the outskirts of Lyon, which opened the floodgates on several years of urban disorder.

The 'riots decade' of the 1990s

The disorders that hit the Mas du Taureau estates involved three nights of confrontations between the police and local youths, in which looting and the torching of cars were equally prevalent activities. These events were of significance to both past and the future developments. Concerning the former, the riots took place in a freshly renewed urban area, governed by a Communist mayor actively involved in many actions undertaken under the auspices of what was known as the *politique de la ville* policy (to be explained in more detail below). Thus, this particular riot (which consisted of torching cars, confronting the police for a two-day period and looting the local department store) was deciphered as a blatant failure of the policies targeted towards the *banlieue* during the first Mitterrand presidency.

With regard to the future, the riot sequence observed at Mas du Taureau was soon established as a prototype for subsequent disorders of the 1990s, especially those occurring in the first half of the decade at the rate of 10 to 15 conflicts, both large and small, each year (Lagrange 2006a: 44). Mantes-la-Jolie 1991, Sartrouville 1992, Melun 1993, Paris 1993, Dammarie-lès-Lys 1997, Toulouse 1998, Lille 2001, Clichy-sous-Bois 2004, Villiers-le-Bel 2007 are among the locations where deadly encounters with the police[2] led to (in)famous unrests.

From the Mas du Taureau events onwards, the labels *'violence urbaine'* or *'crise des banlieues'* became synonymous with social concern and fears of crime stoked up by intense press coverage (Body-Gendrot 2000: 93–96; Bonelli 2007; Tissot 2008). By looking more closely into the details of these events, as Hugues Lagrange recently did (2006a: 44–5), one can distinguish two kinds of riot-like events. In a first period (1992 to 1996), unrests consisted for the main part in confrontations between the youths and the police (32 per cent) or between the youths and civil servants like bus drivers or fire officers (40 per cent of the cases).[3] Fights between youth groups or gangs represented only a fifth of all these incidents reported in the national press (28 per cent). But in a second period, from 1997 to 2004 (no major incidents having occurred in 1995 and 1996), such inter-group confrontations rose to more than one half of these events. This shift in forms of collective violence in the *banlieues* is explained by Lagrange as a sign of worsening employment and living conditions, which produced such consequences as the radicalisation of inter-neighbourhoods confrontations, a rise of neighbourhood-related identities and pride and/or inter-racial fights, and a rise of routine violent or sexual crimes committed by the *banlieue* youths.

One of the most remarkable features of the 2005 French riots is that excluded from the litany of disorderly locations were many of the sites of the first unrests in the 1980s and 1990s, specifically in Lyon's *banlieues*. These seem to remain untouched by the latest waves of disorders. What is indisputable, however, is that France's turbulent *banlieues* are now back to the same social and violence-prone state as at the beginning of the 1990s. Does this mean that nothing has changed since the first uprisings in 1981? In order to answer such a question, we now need to shift our attention to the policies implemented in different attempts to deal with the *crise des banlieues* in France.

Politics and policies in the French *banlieues*: the growth of authoritarian powerlessness

It would be disingenuous to pretend that that nothing has been done to cope with the riots and their underlying causes. Such a clichéd proposition (while quite prominent in the current English-speaking literature) overlooks the fact that the Minguettes uprisings of 1981 led to the instigation of real reformative measures on the part of the French state. The problem was that, not only were such measures incompletely implemented, but the urban and social trends they were designed to tackle head on were too profoundly irresistible to be successfully reined in. This state of affairs led to a kind of conservative backlash from the mid-1990s onwards, aimed at bringing the central state back in – not only in relation to the police and criminal justice system, but also in respect of other urban policies.

The Minguettes disorders and the birth of the politique de la ville

The Minguettes outbreak, in conjunction with the election of President François Mitterrand in May 1981 and his strong 'decentralisation' policy (involving the allocation of more power to local authorities), opened a large policy window concerning the so-called 'urban issue' (Body-Gendrot 2000: 71–9; Le Galès 2008: 163–9; Le Galès and Mawson 1995).

The first policy measure undertaken after the Minguettes events was the bluntly-named *operation anti-été chauds* ('anti-hot summers operation'), which was aimed at cooling down the potential for social disorder by using such devices as out-of-town vacations or on-the-spot 'recreation' or 'entertainment' schemes (*anti-été chauds* programmes - see Juhem 2000: 65) whose primary goal was to engage up to 100,000 youths in activities that might deter them from otherwise rioting.[4] The very low-cost and apparent effectiveness of these programmes ('evidenced' by the fact that there was no duplication of a large-scale collective disorder during any further summer of the 1980s) made them one of the pillars of public policies in France during the 1980s and after.

Besides these reactive programmes, a much more ambitious policy framework, known as *politique de la ville*, was also implemented. *Politique de la ville* is based on numerous programmes aimed at the revitalisation of deprived urban areas and at substantial investment in the poor *banlieues*. It must be seen as a 'national umbrella policy' (see Epstein, this volume), which represented a break with the usual French centralised and top-down policy-making approach. It is a policy framework that encompassed measures passed at the beginning of the 1980s in different policy sectors, namely:

- **education** with the creation of *Zones d'Education Prioritaire* (ZEP or 'education priority areas') in some *banlieues*, encompassing more than 10 per cent of all pupils in today's France (Benabou, Kramarz and Prost 2005);

- **housing, urban planning and development** with the creation of a *Développement Social des Quartiers* programme (DSQ or 'Neighbourhood Social Development'), implemented in more than 400 localities in 1988, which consists of special resource allocation programmes from the central state with regard to 'bottom-up' projects; and

- **employment policy** with the creation of new job centres in numerous urban areas.

From a public policy perspective, the consequences of urban disorders, as exemplified by the Minguettes episode, are of two kinds, the first one breaking with French policy traditions, the second one a continuation of them.

First, the *politique de la ville* broke with the lasting centralisation of French policy-making (Damamme and Jobert 1995; Linhart 1992). For the first time ever in French administrative history, the central state gave more power to local authorities. This policy shift was facilitated by the fact that the new Mitterrand government could rely on a very active network of Leftist mayors. Many of them were defeated in the municipal elections of 1983, but the conservative municipal teams that succeeded them continued to fit their local agenda under the policy umbrella set up by the *politique de la ville*.

Second, the *politique de la ville* appears to be a set of policies based on territorial units (i.e. towns or neighbourhoods), thus avoiding policies based on populations defined by racial or migration-related characteristics (Weil 2001). Policies do not target specific racial groups, but territorial units (in which such groups are over-represented), not only to conform to the republican-egalitarian French tradition, but also to avoid any resentment possibly linked to any kind of affirmative action. In this, one can see a strong continuity from the Left at the beginning of the 1980s to the conservative governments in the 1990s.

Accordingly, as Damamme and Jobert point out, the word *ville* rapidly became

> the place for political and policy-related overinvestment ... a way to point to the weight of the world and, at the same time, to put a veil on it. DSQ, DSU[5], Ville, these are new words and new and easy ways to address the *banlieues* and deprivation (and immigration, school drop, joblessness ...) issue without even mentioning them, or to mention it without daring to name it. (1995: 10)

It is indisputable that initiatives undertaken as part of the *politique de la ville* framework have generally failed in their objectives, especially since no policy was able to reverse the slow but inevitable effects of deindustrialisation or bridge the growing gap between the fresh needs of a more demanding labour market and the unsuitability of the growing number of unskilled *banlieue* working-class young males. But is the efficiency issue of any relevance here? Very ironically, the riot that symbolically opened the 1990s' riot decade in France occurred in a neighbourhood which could not have been more advantaged by all kinds of *politique de la ville* related operations (see above). This led to (sincere or opportunistic) calls for an abrogation of these policies, which, since they corresponded to social and political changes in French society, resonated profoundly among politicians and policy makers.

Politics in the 1980s: radicalisation of the banlieue issue

Since the end of the 1970s, French society seems to have become more and more polarised by the *banlieue* issue. The growing economic deprivation after 1974 and the rapid deindustrialisation hit primarily the unskilled workers gathered in the *cités* and, more so, the immigrant families in their midst (Bonelli 2007; Zauberman and Lévy 2003). *Banlieue* areas came to host a generation of sons of unskilled and increasingly unemployed immigrant blue-collar families who were not able to overcome their disadvantaged legacy through education. At the same time, the need for the organisation of the rising heroin market, the dramatic under-deployment of police forces in the *banlieue* towns[6], and the massive proliferation of available goods due to the growth of the consumer's society encouraged a growing part of the *banlieue* youths to become involved in crime and delinquency. As a matter of fact, crime rose dramatically from the 1970s onwards, particularly acquisitive criminality (Robert 1991).

This situation led the conservative President, Giscard d'Estaing, to pass a 'Security and Liberty' law in February 1981, a few months prior to the election of Mitterrand. This law had been preceded by a three-year long conference on crime and security issues, which placed 'law and order' the top of the public agenda. Consequently, the 1980s were characterised by a long-term alignment shift in French political culture (Robert and Pottier 2006). In response to the rise of crime against property, alongside which we can point to a rise of violent crime from the mid-1980s (Robert 2008), press coverage, political parties and opinion makers focused ever increasingly on law and order issues.

Within this political climate, the electoral success story of the Far Right leader Jean-Marie Le Pen is quite typical: it started in one of the three most deprived precincts of inner Paris in 1983, and ended with Nicolas Sarkozy's election as President in 2007 (Evans and Mayer 2005; Mayer and Tiberj 2002)[7]. Le Pen's successes embody the rise of a conservative and fear-driven political culture in France, which focused on the *banlieues* and started to generate clear policy responses at the beginning of the 1990s. The blatant failure of conservative Jacques Chirac against François Mitterrand in 1988 (an election marked by a 14 per cent score for Le Pen) served only to stall the repressive policies that would be implemented later on. Finally, one could state with Romain Garbaye that, from 1983 onwards, 'the strength of the FN effectively brought the issue of immigration to the forefront of the electoral debate and kept it there ... Because (the other) parties on the whole clung to the consensual policy, they effectively cleared the way for the FN' (2005: 81), the consensual policy being characterised by the 'republican integration model (used) as an apparatus for legitimating the defensive status quo' concerning the implications of immigration for French political life.

Policies in the 1990s and 2000s: political authoritarianism and policy path dependence

With their return to power in 1993, the Conservatives, led by Chirac, implemented a resolute law-and-order policy, which mainly consisted of getting tougher on juvenile delinquency and violent crime (Mucchielli 2004). This led to a permanent deterioration in the quality of encounters between young males from the *cités* and the police, the police being used as metonymical symbol for a hostile society in the eyes of the youths, who felt more and more justified in considering the police as their sole enemy (see Bonelli 2007; Mouhanna, this volume). In this regard, the various provisions introduced by Home Minister Nicolas Sarkozy, in 2002 and after, only perpetuated the 1990s legacy, to which he added a permanent state of verbal warfare against the *racaille* ('riff-raff'), designed to lure *Front National* voters back into the electoral mainstream. Contrary to what can be read in the literature on law and order policies in France, there has been neither a real shift nor a real radicalisation of those policies under Sarkozy's tenure as Home Minister or President (Monjardet 2008). This holds true despite the symbolic ending, pronounced in 2003 by Sarkozy, of any form of neighbourhood policing, which increased the militarisation process that we have already evoked, the latter being reinforced again on the occasion and in the aftermath of the 2005 riots, and the deep hate that Sarkozy inspired among the youths in the *cités*. All these development can be seen as *a continuation of the general tightening of law and order* against any form of disorder in the *banlieues*.

Does this mean that the *politique de la ville* policies have been replaced in France by a 'penalisation of poverty' process, as deplored by some sociologists? Before answering this question, it must be noted that one of the effects of the riots and, more generally, of the concern about the deterioration of police-youths relationships in the 1990s, has been a change introduced in police powers comparable to the Police and Criminal Evidence Act 1984 (PACE) in the United Kingdom. Two days after its defeat in the parliamentary election of 1986, Mitterrand's government enacted an order creating a *Police Nationale* Code of Ethics; and a few months before a further parliamentary election defeat, Mitterrand passed a law in 1993 that offered a person detained in a police cell the opportunity to be visited by a lawyer and a doctor. This was directly linked to the Spring 1991 riots occurring in Mantes-la-Jolie, following the death of a young male diabetic while in police custody. Finally, in 2000, Lionel Jospin passed a law which saw the inception of a civilian complaints authority (Body-Gendrot 2010) This development was a consequence of criticisms of the police appearing in reports adopted by the European Council's Committee for the Prevention of Torture, and of allegations of police 'torture' brought before the European Court for Human Rights (Jobard 2003).

The deterioration of relations between the police and urban male youth in the context of a harsher 'law and order' climate was accompanied by a growing legal and media scrutiny of possible police abuses of force. It should be pointed out, however, that such concern has never reached the height of the public controversy surrounding the corresponding treatment by British police of ethnic minority populations.[8]

In addition to these ambivalent developments, policies launched in the 1980s continued to be implemented, following two major policy shifts. The first one is the attempt to substitute the direct transfer of resources by the central state with a policy of fiscal support for enterprises and administrations to settle in specific *banlieue* territories. This has involved the creation, in 1996, of 751 *Zones urbaines sensibles* (ZUS, sensitive urban areas) in different *banlieue* towns, in which 80 *Zones franches urbaines* (ZFU or tax/duty free zones) were also established on the basis of tax exemptions for local enterprises (see chapters by Lagrange and Epstein, this volume). This zoning of the *banlieues* is not a simple shift towards free market policies because ZUS territories also benefit from different tax re-allocation resources thanks to an 'urban solidarity' law passed by the *Parti Socialiste* in 2000 (under Lionel Jospin's government).

The second and most important shift may be characterised as an authoritarian-style return of the central state in the policy game. *Politique de la ville* policies were a set of countless local agreements between the *préfets* and the local authorities, which encompassed aspects of social policy, urban renewal and urban development.

From 1997 onwards, these policies could take a new breath with the help of a national policy geared towards economic growth and state-sustained jobs ('*emplois jeunes*'), implemented by Jospin's government, which was able to supply these programmes with a tax free workforce mainly constituted of *banlieue* youths. The conservative government that succeeded Jospin after his defeat in 2002 abruptly ended these employment programmes, and reorganised the allocation of the state subsidies to voluntary associations in the *banlieues*.[9] Moreover, the government passed the 2003 law 'for the town and urban renewal' that led to the creation of the ANRU (National Urban Renewal Agency), which allowed the central state to centralise all *politique de la ville*-related financial resources in order to focus them all on one sole objective: urban renewal – in concrete terms, the destruction of 250,000 dwellings and the construction of 400,000 new ones (see Epstein, this volume).

In the final analysis, a kind of authoritarian powerlessness can be observed today, incorporating an insistence on militarised forms of policing (at the expense of neighbourhood policing and other forms of citizen-oriented policing), a recentralisation of decisions and resources in the hands of the central state, and a policy path dependence that maintains the *politique de la ville* as a political slogan, even though it has been reduced from 2002 onwards to a mere urban destruction/reconstruction programme.

Conclusion

By the eve of the 2005 nationwide upsurges, '*banlieue*' had long been synonymous with urban disorders, fear of crime, racial issues and deindustrialisation. The Summer 1981 disorders on the Les Minguettes estates, and the sudden media interest generated towards hate crime and allegations of police abuse, initially led to a national political organisation formed by second-generation immigrants, mostly of North African descent, and to remarkable shifts in central state policy. However, the onset of economic crisis, growing delinquency and fear of crime, combined with changing electoral trends occurring at the start of the 1990s, produced a two-step transformation in the way that 'urban crisis' was handled by public authorities, the main thrust of which has been consistently applied, bar a partial suspension during the period spent in office by Lionel Jospin's government of 1997 to 2002.

First, there was the development of a law-and-order approach introduced by new legal provisions from 1993 onwards to deterring juvenile crime. This reinforced the rise in urban disorders observed from 1990 onwards – producing, in turn, the proliferation of paramilitary police units in the *cités* and a radicalisation of the nature of confrontations between the youths and the law enforcement forces. The beginning of the 2000s was then marked by the transformation of public policies towards an emphasis on urban renewal. This gave rise to a troubled era in which poor urban residents found themselves uprooted and disconcerted by change – and this at a time when sudden cutbacks in state-subsidised employment schemes which had operated from 1997 to 2002 also served to heighten tensions in the *cités*.

Any suggestion that successive French governments may have neglected or abandoned the *banlieues* is not based on reality. In contrast to, say, the American situation of the 1960s, the French state has striven to implement policies devoted to the deterrence of rioting in its urban areas. It is also fair to say, however, that the impact of such policies has been marginal at best and, in some important respects, extremely counterproductive. While much closer in comparison with other European countries than the USA according to such indicators as police use of deadly force and ratios of juvenile imprisonment, French society is undoubtedly exceptional in terms of the negativity of contemporary relations between its police and urban youth. Indeed, having considered the state of tension that had existed for several months in the build up to the eventual riots, it is reasonable to ask why such a large-scale conflictual reaction had not arrived sooner.

Notes

1 I will use the term 'riot' in this chapter, since it is the term in use in France (*'émeute'*), despite all the problems raised by the polemic content of the word and, above all, its disputed sociological accuracy (Marx 1970: 24; Tilly 2003: 18).
2 With a private security agent in Sartrouville.
3 These numbers come from a systematic collection of violent events that occurred in Paris and its *banlieue* cities, covered by the national press from 1990 to 2004 (n=160). A comparison with other kinds of sources, such as the police, would give similar results (Lagrange 2006a: 44).
4 Some summer camps were then created, which were called 'Trigano-Defferre' camps, named after Gilbert Trigano (the founding leader of Club Med) and Gaston Defferre (the then Minister of Interior).

5   Another kind of urban policy.

6   *Police nationale* and *gendarmerie* forces have never been displayed on the French territory according to the new demography and the booming of French *banlieues*, mainly due to refusals by local elected authorities to let the government remove the police forces from their declining territories off to the *banlieues*.

7   The highest score reached by Le Pen has been during the 2002 presidential election when he received 17% in the first round and could get access to the second round (there being defeated by Jacques Chirac with 82%). In 2007 presidential election, Le Pen only reached 10% of the votes and could not qualify for the second ballot: his electoral support had been 'siphoned off' (Mayer 2007: 429) by Sarkozy's candidacy.

8   For further discussions of French and British police conduct in relation to ethnic minorities see Bleich (2007) for a comparison on stop-and-search in France and in the UK and Pager (2008) or Jobard and Névanen (2009) for statistical studies on race and sentencing in France.

9   We shall see how, according to Lagrange (this volume), *banlieues* towns where these subsidies were still allocated or where municipalities could take charge of them were less hit by riots in 2005 – this could be the main explanatory factor for a low riot level in the deprived east and south-east Paris *banlieues*. But other authors (Epstein 2008) show that the conservative government elected after 2002 did not so much cut the subsidies as reorganise their allocation system.

Part II

The British Riots, 2001–2005

Chapter 4

Local events, national implications: riots in Oldham and Burnley 2001

Virinder Kalra and James Rhodes

Introduction

The localised civil disturbances of the summer of 2001 in the northern textile towns of Oldham, Burnley and Bradford quickly assumed a national importance within politics and academia. For New Labour, the response was to pursue an aggressive 'integrationism' (Kundnani 2007), in which 'immigrants' and racialised others, particularly South Asians, were expected to demonstrate their commitment to the nation, and adherence to its, as yet, unsystematically defined values. Such a response emerged from an understanding that the riots resulted from the self-segregation of a singular and homogeneous 'Asian Muslim' community, who had failed to adequately integrate into British society (Cantle 2001; Denham 2002). At the other extreme, much of the academic literature has sought to view the riots as an assertion of British citizenship. 'Asian' communities mobilised not to *reject* national values or citizenship but instead to stake claims for *a more equitable position* within a society laced with racialised inequalities (Amin 2002; Bagguley and Hussain 2003; Hussain and Bagguley 2005; Kundnani 2001). These insightful and strident academic critiques of the way in which the riots were understood have often made the jump from the local stage to the national arena in a seamless fashion. Our intention here is to try and avoid a view that reads the riot as simply an indicator of the state of British multiculturalism but rather to relate the events to broader social trends, while also not losing sight of the details of the riot events themselves.

The aim of this chapter, therefore, is to consider in more depth the 2001 disturbances in Burnley and Oldham – locations that have received less attention than the unrest in Bradford. The theoretical approach taken here is informed by the work of Keith (1993) into the riots in London during the 1980s. Keith calls for a recovery of local histories and 'spatiality' in accounts of urban disorder. He suggests that in the contest over the significance and meaning of such events, the particularity of riots is lost in favour of generalisations which present overly simplistic treatments of events, devoid of historicity, and failing to engage with the complexity of both disorder and its participants. It can be argued that Keith's own work, however, loses sight of broader implications in the density of the micro-details presented. However, the theoretical apparatus that is brought to work by Keith, we would argue, is absent in much explaining of the 2001 disturbances.

Theorising the 2001 riots

In Feldman's study of violence within Northern Ireland, he states that a linear model is often applied in the wake of violent disorder, where: 'Aberrant (cause) leads to pathological symptom (violence) which requires a potential cure (elimination of cause)' (1991: 19). Feldman rejects the idea that there exist 'relations of uninterrupted linearity between the conditions of political antagonism and the relational practices of antagonism' (ibid.: 4). However, this is precisely the normative mode in which riots are viewed. In January 2007, at a conference on integration and cohesion in London, John Denham MP, the author of the government's response to the independent inquiries into the 2001 riots (Denham 2002), talked of how Peacemaker, an Oldham-based youth organisation, had predicted the riots because of work they were conducting with young people, and their 'knowledge' of the street.

In Burnley, too, there is evidence of individuals resorting to an 'insider' account of the disturbances, and their predictability. The month before the unrest in Burnley, the home of a Kosovan asylum-seeker was petrol bombed on a council estate. A local resident stated how, 'You can feel the tension. It is going to explode. I am just afraid the situation could get out of control' (*Burnley Express* 4 May 2001). Similarly following the riots, another resident claimed that, 'What happened was no surprise to me and should not have been a surprise to anyone else with their finger on the pulse of the town'

(*Burnley Express* 6 July 2001). These notions of knc
this formulaic response to violence; yet this belies
that is central to the riot itself and it is incumbent
take the explanation of the event as a substitute for
processes that may have led to it. In other words, i
problems cause the riots, does that mean that in the ~~absence of riots,~~
the problems that are predictable and knowable disappear?

The micro-details of why a riot starts, such as the stories about
pregnant women being attacked in Oldham, or the rumours of
extreme-right incursion in Bradford, and the subsequent movements
of people and acts of violence, are not necessarily related to the
reasons or even to those most affected by the array of factors that
are implicated in the lead up to these events or that subsequently
emerge within causal analysis. A number of factors were identified
in relation to the 2001 riots:

- socio-economic deprivation
- the presence of Far Right organisations
- poor police-community relations
- competition for scarce resources
- white victimisation
- young male alienation/frustration
- yob culture
- criminal gangs.

Each of these factors gets emphasised or de-emphasised according
to the particular viewpoint of the commentator or policy maker,
with the crudest division often being between those who see the
events solely as an issue of law and order and those who see it as
a manifestation of acute social and economic deprivation. For Keith,
the central problem with this type of approach is the way in which
a desire to 'blame' leads to a deterministic form of analysis (1993:
77). He criticises accounts that seek to identify a 'recipe of "causes"
... varying principally in the causal significance attributed to each of
a list of component "ingredients"' (ibid.). Such notions are formed
around a problematic linkage which posits a 'false equivalence
between cause and blame' (ibid.: 78).

What an emphasis on the 'cause and blame' of the riot also fails
to do is to place the disturbances within a historical context. For
example, the 1981 and 1985 riots in various cities throughout the
UK, most notably London, Birmingham and Liverpool, involved
racialised others in urban protest and were explained with recourse

racialised discourses. This is not to suggest that the 2001 riots were simply a replication of these earlier forms of unrest; rather, they should alert us to changes which are less about the discursive terrain of 'race' than wider societal issues – something we shall return to later. As stated above, a problem that appears to exist is that the absence of violent conflict on a serious scale has historically been taken as evidence of good 'community relations' between racialised others and white communities and the police. The 1980 riots in St Paul's in Bristol and the 1985 disturbances in Handsworth were both viewed as 'surprising', at least by those with little local knowledge (Keith 1993).

Similar notions were apparent in response to the 2001 riots, particularly within the media. A pair of articles appearing in the *Daily Mail*'s 26 June 2001 edition described how, 'After years of living side by side in relative harmony the streets of Burnley erupted into violence', presenting an account of how, 'for many years, Burnley was among the most racially tolerant areas in Britain. Then mobs went on the rampage and the barricades went up.' An article in the *Guardian* in response to the riots in Burnley bore the headline, 'Years of harmony wrecked in days' (26 June 2001). As will be argued below, such responses demonstrate an ignorance, or denial, on behalf of the media and politicians of the local political contexts within both Burnley and Oldham. Keith identifies a similar lack of historical knowledge in the coverage of the 1981 riots in London:

> The context in which police/Black antagonism briefly flowered in 1981 was unremarkable if the *spatialities* of the specific locations are understood. This conflict itself was a historical product, accessible to most of the Black community as a form of 'local knowledge', violence only one of many manifestations of it ... In this sense, conflict is not synonymous with confrontation. (1993: 169; emphasis in original)

Keith suggests that it was not unrest itself but the 'qualitative and quantitative scale of seriousness of disorder' that distinguished the 1981 London riots (ibid.: 70). Beyond this, 'the forms of collective behaviour that were seen in the summer of 1981 were not new to the streets of London, or novel in the recent past' (ibid.). Rather, past incidences had been largely ignored or under-reported within the media. It is important instead to view the riots as a point of intensity within the routine of daily lives which are marred by omnipresent conflict of varying degrees. In this sense, the disturbances need to be situated within a context of annual summer disturbances between the police and younger urban males. In Glodwick, the scene of the unrest in Oldham in 2001, only the previous year a double-decker bus was stolen and used to barricade the main road. Indeed, it is the persistence and continuities of everyday racialised tension that are rarely mentioned within media coverage or governmental discourses, which present an ongoing backdrop to *normal* life in these areas. It is a recognition of this which can then help us to understand the trigger of the riots in Oldham and Burnley. Keith observes the need to recognise both the contingency involved in disorder and the social context in which this disorder is located (ibid.: 94). It is important to disentangle notions of contingency from ideas of exceptionality and aberrancy, something with which it often appears to be conflated.

A question that emerges here then is why the events of 2001 received the media and governmental attention that previous forms of unrest have failed to garner. As mentioned, on the one hand, it was the scale and intensity of the 2001 riots that granted them additional importance. However, if the particularities and reasons for the formation of the violent incidences in Oldham and Burnley show marked similarities to other disturbances, what is particular about the historical moment that renders the riot possible? Our contention is that two interlinked processes that are ongoing and wider to the context of the riots appeared to have a role to play. The first is the role of identity politics in the context of the local state and the fraught relationship between place and identification; and second, the role of technologies of information flow. How these two broader processes interact with local incidents and politics forms the remainder of this chapter.

Place and identification

In examining local racist expressions and contestations of community within the Isle of Dogs at a time of active BNP presence, Back and Keith (1999) observed the existence of what they termed 'narrative harmony', as the discourses proffered by the BNP entered into synergy with local debates around belonging and entitlement. This notion of narrative harmony is an interesting concept that can allow us to consider the relationship between localised events and their broader resonance. In the contemporary period, the shifting relationship between the 'local' and the 'global' has been a source of much contention and debate. It has been suggested that the 'global' and the 'local' have become increasingly intertwined, as the 'local' comes to bear traces of global events, and can be viewed as itself an 'aspect of globalization' (Robertson 1995: 30). For Bauman (2004), the uncertainty associated with globalisation means that the 'local' arena assumes a new importance, as global events can no longer be simplistically detached from localised contexts.

It is clear that the resonance of the 2001 riots in the UK extended well beyond the areas of Bradford, Burnley and Oldham. The disorders were interpreted and represented with recourse to events and discourses that were not exclusive to these three northern towns. By the time the government issued its official response to the 2001 riots, the events of 9/11 had occurred, and the UK had already become the principal supporting actor in the US-led 'War on Terror'. The attacks in New York had stimulated debates of belonging and entitlement within Britain where, since the Rushdie Affair in particular, anxieties were articulated regarding Britain's Muslim 'community' and its perceived lack of adherence to national values. In the wake of the 2001 riots, it was argued that multiculturalism in Britain had failed, that diversity had its limits which, if not managed correctly, could lead to a breakdown in social stability and order as witnessed in places such as Oldham. This jump from the local to the global and back again requires a concept such as narrative harmony to provide the substance between these various events. Clearly, the material distance between New York City and Oldham is bridged in the discursive terrain of the insults hurled at Muslim young people in the aftermath of the 9/11 events, but their link to the previous insults requires further contextualisation. Deploying narrative harmony enables us to link with national narratives but also to retain the independence of local claims and disputes without subsumption.

During the 1980s and 1990s, in deprived former industrial towns such as Oldham, Burnley and Bradford, local white and predominantly Muslim Pakistani and Bangladeshi populations had been engaged in conflicts over belonging and entitlement, within a political context in which national narratives of 'undeserving' recipients of benefits, most notably asylum seekers, resonated with local discourses regarding the allocation of resources. White resentment became articulated through the banal processes of government funding which allocates resources according to ward level indices of multiple deprivation. It is important to recognise that in Oldham and Burnley a situation emerged in which areas have become codified in terms of 'race'. Cohen (1996) has suggested that places really come to life within the narratives, the 'popular poetics of place', used to describe them, as they reveal the nature of social relations within a particular locale. In London's East End, Cohen found that 'these narratives mapped out a *symbolic landscape* of shared and contested territories ... it is through this grid of symbolic representation that struggles over access and entitlement to public amenity and resources – housing, education, jobs, leisure facilities, transport – are largely articulated and racialised' (ibid.: 171–2).

What has occurred in Oldham and Burnley is that areas have come to be seen as either homogeneously 'white' or 'Asian'. In Burnley, for example, the 'Asian' population, which consists primarily of those with a Pakistani or Bangladeshi heritage, makes up two thirds of the Daneshouse and Stoneyholme area, around which much of the disturbances centred. This has led to the area being viewed as an 'Asian' 'enclave', 'ghetto' and a 'no-go area' for whites. Just two of the town's other 15 wards, Bank Hall and Queensgate, have 'Asian' population exceeding five per cent of the total, and both areas neighbour Daneshouse and Stoneyholme. This has facilitated a territorial demarcation in which, for British National Party (BNP) voters especially, the location of certain public facilities in the 'Asian' area of town was seen, not only to benefit the 'Asian' community alone, but to exclude white residents from using them. Interviews conducted with BNP voters in Burnley neatly illustrate this point, as the following quote from a middle-aged female voter living in a predominantly 'white' area demonstrates:

> There's a new gym opened ... a gym and a swimming pool ... all fantastic from the outside from what we can see, well to me it's all very elegant, it's cost a lot of money but *it's for Asians.* (Rhodes 2006: 10, emphasis added)

Similarly, the allocation of funding to the 'Asian' area was viewed by BNP voters as a form of positive discrimination in which they had been abandoned by their traditional representatives. This was despite the fact that approximately one third of the Daneshouse and Stoneyholme area consists of white residents. Again the following quote from a BNP voter, a male in his twenties, living on a deprived, almost exclusively white, estate demonstrates this:

> They put all new lights up outside and they had all new streets put in, all new [flagstones], all new bloody windows, they all got security gates put in and it's like well hang on a minute, *why've they got it and we haven't?* (ibid.: emphasis added)

This development of racialised symbolic landscapes in both towns can be traced back to the collapse of the textile industry and the housing markets. Kundnani (2001: 107) suggests that former sites of interaction have been reduced as a result of the different positions occupied by white and Asian communities within the emergent service-based economy and developing patterns of residence. Within this context, 'the geography of the balkanized northern towns became a chessboard of mutually exclusive areas'. This notion of 'no-go' areas is symptomatic of this shift and racialised notions of place 'heighten imagined geographies of fear, ethnic conflict and resentment' (Webster 2003: 96).

This was clearly evident in Oldham, where the riots were precipitated by a number of violent confrontations that occurred between March and May 2001, and were focused upon Glodwick, the symbolically 'Asian' area of Oldham which was increasingly popularised as a no-go area through the coverage of racist attacks on whites in particular. The march organised by the BNP and the National Front (NF) on 26 May which was largely seen as leading to the rioting was in fact the third such demonstration involving white racists that year (Lowles 2001; Renton 2003; Webster 2003). On 28 April, following a match between Stoke City and Oldham Athletic, 450 Stoke City hooligans, interestingly a town which has registered significant levels of BNP support in recent years, marched through Glodwick in an attempt to incite the local 'Asian' community (Copsey 2004: 127). The riots in Oldham, therefore, must be seen within a context of repeated incursions instigated by the BNP, NF and C18, involving both local white racists and activists from Birmingham and London. What is interesting in relation to the symbolic landscapes and racialised geographies of each town is that the disorder was focused primarily within or around these perceived 'Asian' areas. As mentioned, it was the march through Glodwick on 26 May that sparked the disorder in Oldham as, following the march, 'far-right gangs refused to disperse, but congregated in Oldham's pubs waiting for trouble. When white crowds gathered, the police allowed them to march through Asian areas. When Asian crowds gathered the police acted to disperse them. Finally, areas such as Glodwick erupted with anger' (Renton 2003: 79). Similarly, in Burnley, as mentioned above, the key event in the unrest was the attack by white youths on an Asian taxi-driver within the Stoneyholme and Daneshouse ward.

In both instances disorder soon converged on the contested territories on the margins of 'Asian' and the surrounding 'whiter' areas. In Burnley, on the Saturday night, following the attack on the Asian taxi-driver earlier that day, the Duke of York pub in Duke Bar, with a predominantly white clientele, was attacked by Asian youths and windows were smashed (King and Waddington 2004: 125). The following day the same pub shut early on the advice of the police and regulars gathered outside the nearby Baltic Fleet, with a group of people including known white racists (ibid.: 126). Following the abuse of a number of Asian motorists and damages to local taxis, surrounding Asian communities began to mobilise. At the same time, white males within the crowd at the Baltic Fleet 'set off with the intention of *penetrating* the Daneshouse area' (ibid., emphasis added). The men were intercepted by the police who tried to separate the growing crowds of both 'whites' and 'Asians'; 'from this point on, the disorder escalated as both ethnic groups briefly retrenched in their own areas before commencing to attack places owned or frequented by their rivals' (ibid.). There was significant unrest in the predominantly white Burnley Wood area, a ward for which Councillor Brooks stood and had consistently suggested was losing out in funding to Asian communities. Here Asian-owned property was attacked. The report recognised that in general the attacks on white-owned property by Asians were 'primarily retributive' (ibid.). In Oldham, similar dynamics of place and identity were at play. Following attacks on Asian property within Glodwick, Asian communities mobilised in response and the Live and Let Live pub was targeted, as were other public houses and the police.

In some senses this competition for local resources is similar to the competition for jobs that marked the rhetoric of racist mobilisation in the 1970s, but here the difference was that there were two groups defending territory. In this sense there is a distinction to be made between the Burnley case and that of Oldham and Bradford. In Burnley, there was much greater direct confrontation between gangs of white and Asian youth, reflecting the actual small size numerically of that population, but also that this is the first time in a long while that confrontation was enabled through the lack of police resources. There is also a need to consider the way in which the police not only respond to the racialised symbolic landscapes within Burnley and Oldham, but also help to produce them (Kalra 2003; Keith 1993). As will be discussed in more detail below, the police were involved in this production via the release of statistics of racist attacks in Oldham. In both instances there was within the 'Asian' community a perceived failure of the police to tackle the incursion of white racists. Members of the Asian community in both Oldham and Burnley registered high levels of disaffection with the police, and the inaction of the police leading up to and during the riots. In this way, there are resentments towards the police similar to that which existed during the 1981 riots (ibid.).

The police submission following the Burnley riots is criticised by King and Waddington, who argue that repeated attacks on Asian taxi-drivers were not granted as much attention as drink-related violent crime; 'this exclusive concentration serves to place in the foreground "criminality" and de-emphasize racism as a key issue in the town' (2004: 124). This emphasis manifested itself when the police presence outside the Baltic Fleet pub where whites were hurling racist abuse was weakened in an attempt to defuse tension by deploying police in surrounding areas in the hope of being able to respond to any further outbreaks (ibid.: 131). For King and Waddington, such a response inevitably heightened Asian disaffection towards the police at a time of perceived vulnerability (ibid.: 132). The police failed, too, to reflect the ethnic diversity of the community in which they operated. In Oldham, for example, just 12 of 402 police officers were drawn from minority ethnic communities (Oldham Independent Review 2001: 45).

Demarcation of territories was therefore not combated at the institutional level, with local government and police failing to provide institutional spaces in which mundane interactions between racialised groups could take place. In its place policies were established that reinforced the perception of territories as white and Asian, even though we are clear that the idea of self-segregation is itself a false understanding of the geography of these areas (Phillips 2006; Simpson 2007). In this context, it is the perceptions of territory and their defence which is of most concern. The irony of Asian Muslims defending their local turf against white incursions is clear when the BNP base their ideas in autochthonous notions of territory. Nonetheless, the fraught relationship between place and identity was clearly played out in the lead up to the riots in Oldham and Burnley.

Technologies of information flow

If we are to take seriously the need to historicise the 2001 riots and not fall into a glib racialising discourse, which begins with the 1958 Notting Hill riots and ends in Bradford in 2001, it is necessary to pay attention not to the ethnicity of the rioters but to the role of wider social changes that impinge upon, control and trigger these events. It is clear from our understanding of the events in Oldham and Burnley that information technologies played a crucial role in the build-up to the riot events, during the proceedings themselves and afterwards in subsequent court cases. The use of mobile telephones to spread rumours, the police use of video surveillance in court cases and the role of the local print/radio media all played new and incisive roles in these riot events. While our consideration here is limited to a detailed analysis of the print media, these other technologies played an equally significant role and it is possible that all future riot events will be fully videoed given the prevalence of CCTV cameras in Britain's urban landscapes.

Something that has received scant attention in the academic coverage of the 2001 riots is the role played by the local media in managing the racial landscape in Oldham and Burnley. In Burnley, for instance, the most popular local paper, the *Burnley Express*, was criticised by the inquiry into the disturbances there for 'biased news reporting', which had 'led to an exacerbation in the levels of distrust and misunderstanding between Burnley communities' (Clarke 2001: 55). Indeed, the role of the paper cannot be underestimated when considering the spread of racist sentiments in the town. During the 1990s, Harry Brooks, a local Independent councillor, consistently attacked the Labour council for what he perceived to be 'positive discrimination' in the allocation of resources. He argued that poor white areas were being neglected as funds were directed to 'Asian' communities in order to attract votes. The *Express* consistently granted Brooks a forum for his views, and the Labour Group complained that the local press had led him to be 'elevated to almost cult status' (ibid.: appendix 2c). The paper also appeared to confirm Brooks' views regarding the destination of council monies. In the month after the 2001 riots, a resident criticised the paper for an article regarding housing in which two photographs appeared: one depicted a terraced house in the predominantly 'Asian' area of Burnley following a regeneration project, while the other showed decaying property within a deprived white area. It failed to mention that these properties had in actuality been demolished. The resident concluded that such a 'juxtaposition…[would] only add more fuel to the arguments that incite hatred' (*Burnley Express* 20 July 2001). In Oldham also, the *Chronicle* had questioned the allocation of funding to Asian communities while its letters pages were consistently airing the views of local British National Party candidates.

This focus on the role of technology and information flow also allows us to consider the role of the British National Party in the 2001 riots in both Oldham and Burnley. Following the implosion of

Brooks' Independent Group following the 2000 local elections, the BNP was able to assume ownership of this racist political agenda in Burnley, again emphasising the extent to which the council was favouring 'Asian' communities in the allocation of resources. The party targeted the letters pages of the local paper in an attempt to popularise its racialised political agenda and increase its own legitimacy. In this sense, the *Express* once again proved to be a willing accomplice. Steven Smith, the leading BNP activist in the town during this period, suggests that the local paper published 80 per cent of the letters sent in by the party (Smith 2004). The *Oldham Chronicle* had also been a key player in the rise of the BNP, questioning the equity of the allocation of funds. Furthermore, 'its letters pages were replete with correspondence, often anonymous, that expressed frank opinions about Asian attacks on whites, and about the Asian community in general. History informs us that where readers' letters disseminate racist opinions, they can help set local agendas' (Copsey 2004: 128).

In Oldham, the *Chronicle* newspaper was targeted during the riots, and its offices were petrol-bombed, which indicates a certain amount of political targeting. In January 2001, the Chief Superintendent of Oldham, Eric Hewitt, reported to the media his concern about the increase of racist attacks by gangs of young Pakistani and Bangladeshi men (BBC News, 19 April 2001). Quoting statistics compiled by the police, he argued that in the previous 12 months there had been 572 racial incidents, 60 per cent of which had been committed by Asians against white men. No qualification was given to these figures. Nor was the historical under-reporting by Asian groups mentioned. In fact, Asians were still five times more likely than whites to be the victims of racist attacks (Kalra 2002: 23). Obviously, focusing solely on the raw figures gives the appearance of white people under attack or threat. The issue of racist attacks on whites was an issue that the BNP had promoted as early as 1999 (Lowles 2001), and in February 2001, under the banner 'Equal Rights for Oldham Whites', the BNP held a demonstration outside Oldham police station (Copsey 2004: 126).

These tensions were stoked further in April in response to an attack by Asian youths on 76-year-old Walter Chamberlain. The police, media, and the BNP all viewed the incident as racially motivated despite the family of the victim refusing to endorse such a position (Kalra 2002: 23). According to Renton, the paper contributed to the creation of a landscape in which, 'the mood of victimhood was an open invitation to the BNP' (2003: 79). In the same month, the *Chronicle* declared 'This has got to stop', in its reportage of an assault on a 16-year-old white youth by Asian teenagers (Copsey 2004: 127). In both towns, selective reporting of events reflected the fact that the targeted readership of both papers was implicitly white. In fact, at the time of the disturbances, the *Chronicle* drew none of its journalists from minority ethnic communities (ibid.: 128). This is also effectively demonstrated with recourse to an article which appeared in the *Burnley Express* following the 2001 riots. Under the headline 'Our night of hell', the article included pictures and quotes from white residents without reference to any Asian victims of the disturbances (26 June 2001). This created the impression that the 'riots' were something perpetrated upon the white community by Asians.

It is clear that the BNP proved adept at capitalising upon and accentuating local white narratives of resentment. In the wake of the attack on Walter Chamberlain, BNP leaflets were circulated in Oldham featuring the pensioner's badly bruised face. Similarly, on St George's Day, 'party activists flew a number of St George's flags from lampposts in the town knowing that they would be removed by the Council as a distraction to drivers. Inevitably this occasioned criticism of the Council in the letters page of the local press' (ibid.). Leaflets and even CDs were distributed in Oldham and Burnley, tailored to address the concerns and grievances of local white residents (Copsey 2004; Eatwell 2004; Lowles 2001; Smith 2004). The BNP also used the internet as a tool through which rumours were spread, enabling the party to champion local concerns. In the summer of 2001, the party introduced the *Oldham in Harmony* website which encouraged the circulation of local rumours and gossip (Eatwell 2004: 72). By the end of 2001, a similar site had been established in Burnley called *Burnley Bravepages*. Through this form of localised politics the BNP was relatively quickly able to garner significant levels of support. While there is evidence to suggest that the BNP had a branch in Oldham during the mid-1990s (Lowles 2001; Copsey 2004), it was not until summer 2000 that the unit within the town was reconstructed (Lowles 2001). Following the riots in Oldham in the 2001 General Election, the BNP leader Nick Griffin polled 16 per cent in Oldham West and Royton, while the party also received 11 per cent of the vote in Oldham East and Saddleworth. In total, the party received 13,250 votes in the town (Copsey 2004: 125).

In Burnley, prior to the disturbances there, the BNP received 11 per cent of the poll, representing over 4,000 votes (ibid.: 133). The party had contested the 1999 European Elections in the town, polling 3.7 per cent of the vote (Eatwell 2004: 74), despite the fact that a local branch had only been established in May, the month prior to the contest (Copsey 2004: 132). By December 1999, 200 people had already become registered supporters (Smith 2004: 7–8). In much of the national media coverage following the riots, the BNP and other far-right groups, such as Combat 18 (C18) and the NF, were mentioned as actors, albeit often marginally (Bagguley and Hussain 2003). However, where the influence of such groups was mentioned it was done so solely in relation to the micro-events. The longer-term presence of the BNP, for example, in Oldham, Burnley and Bradford was something on which most accounts were silent. This must be seen within an interpretative framework in which the role of white racism within the riots was de-emphasised in the response of both the media and the government (ibid.: King and Waddington 2004; McGhee 2005; Webster 2003).

The flow of information within Oldham and Burnley and the role that the media and the BNP played in moulding the racial landscape is a significant aspect of the 2001 riots. Also, for the BNP, the internet was used in order to respond to local grievances and rumour. This enabled the party to present micro-grievances to a much broader audience within Oldham, and to make them resonate with a wider set of concerns. A useful illustration of this that occurred in Oldham relates to The Owl, the centrepiece of Oldham Borough's charter mark. It sits in the centre of the town's emblem. It was also engraved into a number of bollards in the town centre, which were removed because they were not the appropriate size for the hanging baskets required for the national flower show which came to Oldham in 2001. Rumours were spread that the Owl emblem was removed because the representation of a living creature is not allowed in Islam and so it was deemed offensive to Muslims. This appeared in a local BNP paper and also on the party website and then became an issue of controversy in the letters page of the local paper.

The flow of information played a particularly important part within the riot events themselves, with the use of mobile phones being especially significant. In their analysis of the police response to the riots in Burnley, King and Waddington note the centrality of rumour in the spread of disorder in the town, as an Asian taxi-driver attacked with a hammer by white youths, an event widely recognised as being a key 'trigger' of the riots, was falsely believed to have died (2004: 125). Police attempts to counter the circulation of this proved to be unsuccessful as whites, police and Asian youths clashed later that day (ibid.). The following day reports of a group of whites outside a local pub hurling racist abuse, and known to include a number of those with 'nationalist sympathies', quickly circulated through the surrounding Asian communities, some of whom prepared for confrontation (ibid.: 126). The police submission to the Task Force report into the riots in Burnley again suggests the importance of technology and information flow, as Asian communities sought to respond to white attacks on property and individuals, having been alerted to such events by taxi radio (ibid.). Similarly, in Oldham on 26 May when a fight broke out between white and Asian youth in Glodwick, mobile phones were used to mobilise participants (Oldham Independent Review 2001: 71). While the above has enabled a consideration of the 'communicative context' (King and Waddington 2004: 129) in which the riots occurred, it also connects clearly with the first part of the discussion around issues of place and identity formation and the role that technology can play in both the management and escalation of conflict.

Conclusion

In highlighting the role played by technologies of information flow and the relationship between place and identity, we have attempted to offer an account of the 2001 riots of Oldham and Burnley that places these events within a broader set of societal concerns. This is not to distract attention from the particularity or micro-politics of the events concerned, but to problematise the too easy way in which local events become part of national discourses about 'the death of multiculturalism' or the rise of extremism. It is often the media which enables this direct jump from the local event to the national discourse and as we have highlighted the local newspapers in Oldham have often had a large role in creating the shape of the racial landscape in those towns. Nonetheless, the local media is part of a wider gamut of information flows which remain yet unexplored, the role of mobile phones for the rioters and surveillance technologies for the police is an area that requires further research.

Chapter 5

Police on the line: between control and correctness in multi-ethnic contexts of urban unrest

Janet Bujra and Jenny Pearce

Introduction

In this chapter we explore a tension in the policing of urban unrest in multi-ethnic contexts, focusing particularly on the Bradford riots of 2001. The 'politically correct' line in policing, of sensitivity to cultural difference and even to racism, defines policing as pluralistic and responsive to diversity. Conversely, 'holding the line' denotes a regime of discipline, regulation and hierarchy which demands that policing be impartial, a public service 'for all', with a singular focus on those who break the law irrespective of their backgrounds (Zedner 2006: 92). The key question is whether an institution which built its professional integrity on becoming an effective instrument of the homogenising modern state can be expected to respond to the pluralities of its postmodern successor (McLaughlin 2007: 152). Can effectiveness in responding to and preventing disorder – a priority which has always justified the police's hierarchical organisational form – be wedded to a more pluralistic police culture in tune with the society around it?

In addressing these questions, we draw on data collected between 2003 and 2005 in Bradford. Our research employed a variety of methods: interview and conversation, participant observation, social mapping, peer group work and participatory feedback. At its core were three sets of in-depth interviews with key participants in the riot: (i) a random sample of 21 adults convicted of riot and mostly interviewed in prisons scattered around the north of England; (ii) 14 'third parties' who had witnessed and/or been directly affected by the riot; and (iii) ten police officers actively involved in the riot, half of them on the 'front line', the remainder involved in the organisation and coordination of the police operation. Two of the police respondents were women, one was Asian, and four had sustained injuries in the riot. Ethnicity was not the only dimension to this riot. However, given that the rioters were overwhelmingly Pakistani Muslim male youths, in this chapter we explore the way that ethnic framing affected the way that the riot was policed and the way it was later understood.

Culturally challenged? Policing the first and second generation urban riots

In terms of public disorder and its policing, Bradford both reflects national developments and displays some unique features. The 2001 riots in Bradford were widely reported as the worst in the UK mainland for 20 years, but they formed part of a wave of unrest in that year in Northern de-industrialising cities with large ethnic minority populations.

Two decades earlier, riots in Brixton, Southall, Toxteth, Manchester Moss Side and other cities had marked a turning point in the history of urban unrest in the UK following mass immigration from the West Indies and the Indian sub-continent (Benyon 1987: 4).

During this 'long, hot summer' of 1981, rumours circulated in Bradford that the National Front (NF) was planning to attack local Asian communities. Members of the United Black Youth League (UBYL – an organisation led by Asians but including youth from diverse ethnic backgrounds) organised in defence. When a crate of homemade petrol bombs was found by police, 12 UBYL members were charged with conspiracy to cause explosion and endanger lives. The defendants won wide support and were eventually acquitted by a jury of seven white and five black people on the grounds of their right to 'defend their community' (Farrar 2004: 13; Ramamurthy 2006: 55), a claim that some of the rioters of 2001 would also make.

Between these two periods of urban unrest, policing in Bradford and elsewhere took new but potentially contradictory directions – first (reflecting national trends) towards more militarised technologies of control, and secondly towards acknowledgement of the need for pluralised policing in a multicultural society.

Police 'threat power'

Following the 1981 riots, the Police and Criminal Evidence Act 1984 gave the police wide powers of discretion to stop and search suspects, while the Public Order Act 1986 empowered them to decide the conditions and circumstances in which public protest could take place. Police riot training was also introduced following a recommendation in Scarman (1982). Fire-proofed shields and other riot gear were developed and operationalised (Waddington 1992: 85).

The danger here was that policing public disorder would entail what conflict resolution theorist Kenneth Boulding (1989) describes as simple 'threat power', rather than building community partnerships or relating to disaffected elements (Butt 2006). Waddington describes the increasing 'militarisation' of the police as tending towards provoking rather than quelling public unrest and it 'occurred without public debate or accountability' (1992: 185; see also Keith 1993: 197, 205).

After public disorders in Bradford in June 1995, following a bungled arrest in an Asian neighbourhood, a public inquiry acknowledged that the police had to protect themselves (Bradford Commission 1995: 37). But it also reported the concerns of local residents at the new style of equipment which had become available that year: 'The wearing of protective vests, and the provision of side-handled batons and rigid handcuffs, has caused adverse comment from members of the public. It is seen as offensive, not defensive, and therefore provocative.' This was a view that resurfaced in 2001.

The struggle against institutional racism

Since the 1980s, major campaigns have focused on embedded racism in the police service, culminating in the Macpherson report of 1999 which named the problem as 'institutionalised racism'. In between these two dates there were attempts to address the low recruitment of black and Asian officers and to modify police training to address prejudice and raise awareness. Such training was introduced widely, alongside the major emphasis on militaristic riot control training (Waddington 1992: 184–5).

In Bradford opinion was divided as to whether the problem was police racism or lack of appropriate cultural awareness. In 1995, a Commission of Inquiry had asserted that formal training in community and race relations in the public services including the police 'seems to be more an attempt to explain peculiar variations from the norm, to almost exclusively white trainees, rather than the building up of an intelligent team approach to working with the various groups who constitute the Bradford public' (Bradford Commission 171). Although not accusing the police of systematic racism, the Commission noted that individual officers who behave in racist ways have a negative impact on the entire police force. In a minority report, Taj (1995: 17) went further, asserting that the police force:

> must accept that the majority of its officers, however good their intentions, are insufficiently sensitive to the cultures, perception and anxieties of the Asian communities. It must accept that it contains far too few members of the Asian communities within its ranks. Most important of all, it must accept that eradicating racist behaviour, reflecting and understanding the communities that it serves is not a distraction from 'real police work' but is in fact the essential underpinning of an effective police service.

Taj's unpalatable points were repeated by many later commentaries on policing in Bradford (e.g. Ouseley 2001), despite the fact that the police introduced significant changes as a result of the Commission's report.

Meanwhile the national average of black police officers had reached only 2 per cent of the total police establishment by 1999 (Loveday 2000: 17). The West Yorkshire percentage of minority ethnic police was 2.9 per cent in 2000–2001 and 3.1 per cent a year later, but this needs to be set against a regional minority ethnic population of working age of 9 per cent (West Yorkshire Police 2002: 27). It was still the case that in 2001, predominantly Asian rioters faced an overwhelmingly white police force led by white officers.

The collapse of 'black activism'

By the 1990s social and discursive change meant that the police were no longer dealing with highly motivated and politically conscious 'black' activists (Gilroy 1992) like the UBYL, or the Asian Youth Movement (AYM) of which it was a splinter, but with diverse 'cultural communities' and with the challenge of policing multiple publics.

Economic drivers played a major role in the sidelining of anti-racist alliances in the 1980s and 1990s. De-industrialisation in the northern towns during the 1980s and 1990s eroded the class solidarity which underpinned the activism of the AYM and trade unionists in Bradford. Recession and impoverishment affected the District as a whole, but fell disproportionately on the Asian population working in the collapsing textile industry. In a report entitled *Areas of Stress within Bradford District*, 202 out of a total of 927 local Census Enumeration Districts were found to be sites of multiple deprivation measured by ten poverty indicators (City Council 1993). These sites were concentrated in ten areas of Bradford and Keighley, especially the inner city and council estates. In ethnic terms, the distribution showed 48 per cent of non-whites, but only 14 per cent of whites living in deprived areas (quoted in Bradford Commission 1995: 22).

Men who had worked for wages and been organised as workers in trade unions or in the Indian, Pakistani or Kashmiri Workers' Associations, were now increasingly unemployed. Like others in northern mill towns, some began to rebuild livelihoods around the small businesses of restaurants and taxi services, drawing on the divisive solidarities of kinship, clan and caste – what Kalra (2000) describes as a move 'from textile mills to taxi ranks'.

Some were relatively successful. But the Bradford Commission on the 1995 riots put youth unemployment in Manningham at 45 per cent (1995: 24). The report also noted a rapid recent growth in drug dealing and usage in the inner city and on the mostly white council estates. Crime statistics for Bradford as a whole stood 15 per cent higher than the West Yorkshire average and 51 per cent higher than the national average in 1998 (City of Bradford Metropolitan District Council 1998: 7), suggesting that recession and deprivation were having a wide social effect with implications for policing. While police struggled with rising crime in an impoverished city, they also faced demands for more culturally aware policing.

The local state, the police and cultural pluralism

In Bradford, the shift towards cultural representations began at least a decade before Macpherson put 'cultural issues at the heart of his recommendations' (O'Byrne 2006: 109), and it borrowed a political and religious guise. Following the 1981 riots, recognition of racial disadvantage and cultural difference generated new funding for 'deprived ethnic minority communities'. In Bradford, the Chief Executive called for a re-examination of the council's race policies in the wake of the Brixton and Toxteth riots (Greenhalf 2003: 60). The Labour Group on the Council created a Race Relations Advisory Group which focused on race equality procedures in appointments and on the appropriateness of service provision (Bradford Commission 1995: 98).

As acknowledgement of the distinct cultural and religious backgrounds of the city's minority ethnic population grew, so too did cultural claims and the public emergence of Bradford's Muslim population to press for special attention. As early as 1983, thousands of Bradford Muslims came out on the streets to demand that their children be served halal meat in schools (Greenhalf 2003). Between 1984 and 1985 the 'Honeyford affair' focused on struggles over the provision of multicultural education. An oppositional 'Black' activism was still in evidence, with the Bradford AYM organising against racism in the education system, but also defending the idea of secular education in a policy paper on religious schools (Ramamurthy 2006: 57). In 1989 Bradford was the scene of the notorious burning of Salman Rushdie's *Satanic Verses*. The 1995 disturbances were also cast in a 'cultural' light, with a claim that the police had failed to respect a Muslim woman in a house which they entered to arrest a suspect.

In recognising cultural difference, the state set cultures against one another as Ramamurthy (2006: 56–7) points out:

> Through funding criteria, the state split the communities into Asian and black and the broad-based concept of a political black identity that had been embraced by the youth movement's struggle … gave way to new identities focused on the cultural domain … In negotiating a share of the limited resources available, groups were continually identifying and arguing for their group or community's difference and distinctiveness.

For elders in the Asian community, relationships with the local state became an important mechanism for maintaining community integrity in the face of economic decline. The local state was ready to respond to the demands of a community with strong 'cultural capital' to mobilise. But this 'capital' was built on traditional social stratifications within the South Asian community, which conferred power on upper caste elders. They became the 'self-appointed community leaders' and spokespeople of their communities, an arrangement which delivered votes as well as social acquiescence to local political elites (that this was a more general pattern is suggested by Kundnani 2001: 108). Some Asians began to speak of 'inner city godfathers', and a 'colonial mode' of running inner cities fostered by local politicians who, by controlling the 'godfathers', could control the community (Asian councillor quoted in Bradford Commission 1995: 198). The political battle to represent 'Asian' wards became intense, and some saw the transfer of clan battles and religious differences from the Asian sub-continent to inner-city Bradford having a very negative impact on democracy and representation in the city.

The police, like other sectors of the Bradford's public services, were drawn into relationships with these self-appointed spokespersons of the Asian communities. Much hard and productive work was invested in this. The police also made sincere efforts to find a 'correct' way to engage with black and minority ethnic communities, including the youth of the District, particularly after the 1995 riots. A minority ethnic community relations officer was appointed at Inspector level. A Minorities Police Liaison Committee was set up. A Projects Officer was appointed to the Community Involvement Unit specifically set up to work with youth in the Oak Lane/Manningham area. They had to tackle some difficult cultural issues, such as forced marriages. These initiatives, successfully mounted, created new channels of communication through outwork in communities, but their impact was limited, particularly with regard to Muslim youth. Some officers built good relationships with inner city Bradford and the council estates which ringed it, but youth and community policing tended not to be valued within the service as 'real' police work.

From rally to riot: 7 July 2001

It was in this context that the riot erupted. Saturday 7 July should have been the last day of the Bradford Festival, an annual event which brought the District's cultural communities together. However, the British National Party (BNP) announced a march through the city and in response the Bradford Anti-Nazi League (ANL) and Trades Council Anti-fascist group called for a counter demonstration. The police cancelled the last day of the Festival and the Home Secretary banned the BNP march. The anti-fascist demonstration was not covered by the Home Secretary's remit, and hundreds of people poured into Centenary Square in the centre of the city to protest against the Far Right. The crowd included people of all ethnic origins, men, women and children, though a large crowd of Asian male youth was immediately visible. Although there were sightings of Far Right activists in nearby pubs and provocatively in the Square and surrounding streets, the police consistently argued that, as the BNP march had been banned, there was nothing to justify the disorder which broke out towards the end of the day.

As the rally crowd was dispersing mid-afternoon, to different parts of the city, police were already on the Square with horses, dogs, vans and dressed ready for disorder. Two incidents brought the Asian youth streaming back – one was a confrontation between an Asian lad and known Far Right activists, while the other was the stabbing of a white youth by Asians. Mayhem broke out, with the police later accused of driving the angry crowd towards the largely Asian area of Manningham. It is not clear that they had such control. They aimed to get people away from the city centre, and after pushing them back, police formed a battalion at the bottom of White Abbey Road and tried to hold the line. The riot that ensued lasted from around 7.00 pm on 7 July to the early hours of the next morning, with criminal acts of looting characterising the final hours. More than 320 police officers were injured as they battled rioters who hurled missiles and petrol bombs, and pushed burning cars towards them. The total cost of the riot was £27 million (see Hussain and Bagguley, this volume), of which the policing operation accounted for £3.4 million (West Yorkshire Police 2002: 3).

Policing the riot

Although police training, in Bradford as elsewhere, was rethought in consequence of urban unrest, only one of those we interviewed spoke of any training in cultural diversity or race issues. A frontline officer, he described how his induction included being 'made aware of differences in society ... we were taken to mosques, spoke to community leaders'. He had also served with an Asian officer on the beat for some years and he reflected that this had made him more aware that he was seeing things 'through a white man's binoculars'. Unusually he had then made the effort to learn Urdu: 'I'm trying to reflect the community I serve'. He nevertheless spoke stereotypically of the riot, believing that it reflected a 'crowd mentality' inherent to the Asian community.

Other officers seem to have learnt on the job, visiting Asian homes and trying to make sense of cultural differences in family relationships and the socialisation of young people. This struggle to understand had impacted on their views of the riot – a senior officer assumed that pubs were looted and burned down because 'They don't want a pub on their street corner, cos we're not supposed to drink', while another insisted that among the rioters there was 'a lot of drinking' which had made their behaviour more unruly. Some of them had also learnt from experience that there were generational differences within this 'community', but they also perceived elderly Asians to be on their side – there was, he ventured, 'respect for law and order within the elders'.

The tendency to stereotype meant that officers were surprised by some of the events of the riot. At one point the battleground engulfed a Labour Club in which members were still drinking, unaware of the mayhem around them. Rioters set the club alight, though fortunately those who were trapped inside were rescued. Describing these events one officer told us: 'An Asian guy came up to us … and said, there's people in there, you need to get them out … what struck me was that it was an Asian that said [this]'. The same officer was amazed to see some Asians trying to intervene to stop the rioting. Reflecting on facing a continuous barrage of bricks and stones from rioters, another officer wondered about the culture of aggression: 'I don't think that's an Asian thing … I think whites are just as bad at that'.

Accepting and working with cultural difference creates many confusions within a service which sees itself as 'disciplined' and under orders to 'hold the line'. In the riot the 'line' referred to the battle lines in which police and rioters confronted each other for several hours, but it can also refer metaphorically to the regime of police understanding and delivery. And here, 'the line' is not so clear at all. If the 'cultures' designated within multicultural policy were 'a fixed array of customs, values and traditions' (Brah 1993: 443), at least there could be formula for dealing with those who are 'different'. But 'culture' is a moving and fractured object, with very fuzzy boundaries; there are no stable certainties, as Brah points out and as local police sometimes recognised.

There is the constant collapse of 'difference' into 'inequality', with police enduring accusations of racism when they distinguish between one 'culture' or 'community' and another. There is a thin line between acknowledging difference, and discriminating in a way which amounts to unequal treatment. This dilemma is now pervasive in police work and the police brought to the riot certain ways of dealing with it. There was the ultra-cautious approach, driven by fear of unfounded accusations. There was also anger at the seeming injustice of such allegations. It is not surprising that accusations of racism resurfaced in the context of the riot. Many rioters – and some other witnesses – allege that the riot was in part a response to police racism and brutality. Instead of protecting those who claimed to be protesting against the threat (and indeed the seeming reality to the rioters) of an NF/BNP (the labels were used interchangeably) march into Bradford, the police were seen as turning on the protestors and sparking off reactive violence. In the melée that ensued, the police are accused of 'kicking people like animals' and using racist language, and hence the claim that 'the police are racist'.

The police understood that they became a proxy for the Far Right groups ('We were Aunt Sallies'), but they were angry that this translated into accusations of racism against them, and they were dismissive of the rioters' claim that this was a riot against racism (even of the NF/BNP). They could not conceive of a spontaneous burst of outrage by Muslim youth against a Far Right group which appeared to question their very existence. Many of our police interviewees regarded this as simply an 'excuse to go on a rampage'. From their perspective the white skinheads that were seen as 'NF' were probably 'just football supporters not racists', from a grouping called 'The Ointment'; and consequently, for one frontline officer, 'There didn't appear to be a cause … to warrant a riot of that scale'.

If police took the 'racist' argument seriously, it was as a mirror image of the one used by rioters. 'The rioters are racist', said one woman officer who had been severely injured in the course of the battle. 'They're racist against the police because … they're predominantly white the police.' Given the ferocity of the encounter, it is not surprising that the fearful example of PC Keith Blakelock, who was killed in the Broadwater Farm riot, becomes a potent one and is mentioned by more than one interviewee. From the frontline, one officer reported seeing how a colleague 'ran into a restaurant, stumbled, fell … and then this mob just rushed in, threw bricks at him … PC Blakelock, in London, that's probably what happened to him.' Another expressed her fears thus: 'If they'd have got one of us on our own they'd have killed us. I'm perfectly sure of that.' The 'them' and 'us' in this view is clearly racially framed.

Police perceptions of the rioters as the racists is also backed up by arguments that they 'targeted white businesses' in the course of the mayhem. Most businesses – three garages, several pubs and the Labour Club – which were torched and/or looted, did have white owners, though not all of them. One of the third parties, an Asian businessman of considerable wealth, was called to the riot scene as one of his own garages was attacked. For most of the police, however, the 'facts' spoke for themselves: 'I think that the reason some of the white businesses were attacked is because they were perceived to be in their territory. We own this, you've no right to be here, and I think racism did play a part in the sense that I think that was manifested in some of the targeting that went on.'

Multicultural 'awareness' vies here with a racialised discourse of 'territory'. It is notable that this is expressed by both rioters and police. The rioters were often fiercely committed to Bradford: 'I'm proud of Bradford; I was born in Bradford, brought up in Bradford, all I know is Bradford ... racist parties shouldn't be allowed to come into a multicultural city'. This sense of belonging was threatened both by the police who made them feel as if they 'didn't belong' and the NF who were 'coming into Bradford and causing trouble ... we've got to defend our territory'.

The police were also mainly local and they had a similar loyalty to the city, but as they saw it, the threat to Bradford was from the rioters. A senior officer expressed his fury: 'The bottom line is, I was born here, I've lived here all my life'. Another said how 'gutted' he had felt and he concluded: 'It's fine for people to have different perceptions and concepts of what their Bradfordianness is. But the trouble is, if there isn't some convergence, we've got a problem.'

The police had another more palatable explanation for the violence displayed in the riot, preferring to see it simply as 'criminality', and to put its severity down to a 'universal hatred' of the police. The young men rioted because 'they were criminals and they hated the police anyway'. This enabled the police to explain the riot in 'normal policing' terms.

Many of the rioters we interviewed had a history of run-ins with the police, mostly around the petty criminality of drugs, street fighting, small-scale theft and driving offences. A proportion (around a quarter) had no criminal records whatsoever. In the course of the riot many criminal offences were committed – looting, violence, arson and extensive destruction of property – all subsumed under the charge of 'riot'. Many rioters acknowledged that they had histories with the police and that a desire to get even played a part for some of them. Ironically their experience with the police had also led them to a view of 'normal' policing. The use of excessive force was in their opinion 'not normal policing', whereas it was 'the police's job' to keep the Far Right out of the city. It was accepted that the police 'have got a job to do ... to protect people and to keep the peace'. It was even said that police 'have to do everything by order and by law' and that 'they don't hate us...they are humans'. In the heat of battle, however, the humanity on both sides was disguised, with one woman police officer saying bitterly that 'You were just a mass of blue and if a brick hit one of you, then that were fine' – a perception echoed in rioters' accounts.

The dehumanising of the police force was heightened by their donning of 'riot gear' and by the deployment of other military equipment. Police reported that, even before the actual riot began, at a point when 'the mood shifted and ... there were sort of like pushing and shoving ... we were ordered to get kitted up'. The police were now dressed in uniforms that looked more military than civilian in order to cordon off the main square, accompanied by horses, dogs and police vans. As the riot took off they donned helmets, visors, body armour and flameproof overalls, and carried shields and batons. A woman officer described how long it took to get all this on – or off (ten minutes). Video camera crews were heavily used and surveillance helicopters hovered overhead. At one point the police even considered using rubber bullets but ultimately refrained.

Despite this technical escalation, police ranks were critical of its effectiveness. Against the barrage of stones, bricks, barrels, petrol bombs and cars set alight, police radios did not work effectively, visors misted up and deadened the sound of shouted orders, shields were too short to protect ankles. Equipment was 'sub-standard' said one. Even more significantly, the police acknowledged that they were unable to gain control because of the superior technical and organisational capacity of the rioters. The lads' use of mobile phones was a powerful tool in mobilisation. A police constable was precise: 'Whatever techniques that we may have employed in the past were effectively being used against us … but with greater effect'. The rioters were 'inventive': cars were used as barricades, house walls were knocked down for missiles, bottles and petrol got together to make bombs, masks and bandannas used to hide faces. 'It was almost a battle of wills and it was a battle of techniques.' Reflecting afterwards, a senior officer compared the 1970s, when the burning of a police vehicle would have been inconceivable, with the riot of 2001 – 'unbelievable' – when burning vehicles were propelled towards police lines and police horses were injured.

The capacity of the rioters was not directly linked to their culture or race – one senses rather the serious respect of fighting men and (a very few) women for a credible enemy. But when this is put together with the ethnic geography of Bradford and the appearance of 'Asian youth' massed in conflict against white police, it takes on a racialised aspect. In the initial phase, in Centenary Square where the rally took place, a senior officer conceded with the benefit of hindsight, 'encircling a crowd creates confrontation' – and in this case it also antagonised people who 'genuinely want to protest'. One of the ANL rally organisers insisted that 'people who go to protest against Fascism, as far as I am concerned are protesting for … a peaceful city, against racists, against divisions, and I don't think it's a good signal that the police were there in their riot gear'. While the police denied that the donning of 'protective gear' was a provocative move, the military response heightened the rioters' sense of being treated in a very different way – a racist way as they saw it – to others who demonstrate, as well as dehumanising the police themselves.

In addition the local knowledge of rioters as the battle set in on a long road leading to a predominantly Asian area prevented the police getting a grip. Many were critical of their own performance or the orders they were given: 'The [rioters] had better tactics and better plans than us. They took the high ground, they left us to run up a hill.' Police were effectively immobilised on this hill for several hours so that even rioters asked why they had not cut round and split them up.

Despite considerable effort having gone into 'community relations' work by the police, when it came to the riot they found themselves without effective allies on the ground. They had created a grouping of 'elders' (males, usually people of some repute, wealth and/or social standing within the Asian Muslim community), while their other key linkage was with the Youth Service, many of whom were themselves of Pakistani Muslim origin, and young males like the rioters. During the peaceful rally the police log records advice to contact Asian elders and there are several later entries recording (tersely and without detail) the attempts by 'mediators' to intervene. None of these efforts was successful.

Youth workers in particular found themselves caught in the middle. The Youth Service 'ended up actually in between ... a lot of people were angry with us because they thought we'd colluded with the police ... we were saying to the young people don't bite and we were saying to the police ... move back, right, you know you're provoking it'. These appeals fell on deaf ears all round. In addition, the police and others 'tried to bring in ... the same old community leaders, the stereotypes ... that actually don't have the control that they argue that they have'.

Rioters spoke with contempt for such 'leaders' – MPs, councillors and religious elders: 'I will not listen to someone I've no respect for'; 'What did they ever do for us?' In short and despite their best efforts, the police had been insufficiently aware of the social dynamics of the Asian Muslim 'community' in Bradford, including its internal contradictions and generational conflicts, its social class and other divisions. They were thus unable to effectively mount a response which drew on local networks of support. The 'peacemakers' had ambivalent views of the police, and despite their despair at the behaviour of the rioters (which threatened their own property and standing) they also hated the Far Right. The police had also assumed that youth would be compliant, indeed culturally respectful, towards elders and leaders of repute. And in the end the militarised response took over from any more culturally aware attempts at dialogue.

Conclusion: the contradictions of policing a multicultural society

At issue here is the problem of policing a multicultural society where inequalities coincide with racial distinctions and a racialised social geography. The police see themselves as a 'professional' force, serving the *whole* of the 'community'. 'We did it the British way', said one of the frontline officers. The 'British way' entails a model of policing that is impartial and rule-governed. Some police officers recognised the contradictions between 'policing for all' and pluralised policing which responds sensitively to a culturally diverse population. A supervisory officer expressed a pessimistic view: 'There's such a gap between the two societies'. A frontline officer thought that more community policing was crucial to preventing future disturbances, but that it was necessary to clarify which 'community' was being served in the end – 'the local one or the city community?' A more senior officer expressed support for the view that the police 'should be building bridges with communities and we should become one big community', but 'England's … not a melting pot, it's a *smorgasbord*'.

In the absence of a single 'big community', police are also forced to rethink their role in society. Are they an arm of the state? To what extent can policing allow safe space for political dissent as one aspect of responding to diversity? What are the boundaries which make promotion of some views unacceptable? A senior officer stated the case: 'Part of our role is to protect those people [demonstrators] and enable them to have protests – and yet we become that face of authority that ends up getting attacked on that night'. For some police here, struggling with these dilemmas, the riot brought them to contentious conclusions. One senior officer insisted that both the BNP and the Anti-Nazi League 'have a right to express their views; the problem is they are extreme views'. Both 'have got to take as much responsibility' for sparking off the riot, 'cos they do kick off and there's not a great deal of difference between them'. This may be so, but again the police have failed to read the extent of alienation of ethnic minority young men, to recognise the implications of low educational achievement among Asian Muslim youth in Bradford and the lack of meaningful opportunity for them to express frustrations of numerous kinds.

We have tried to bring out the paralysing contradictions between policing 'for all' and policing which responds institutionally as well as individually to social and cultural diversity. While the former emphasises universal concepts of public order and public safety, the latter opens a lens to the particular experiences of the disadvantaged and discriminated. It was the poor quality of this lens which led the police to misrecognise the mood of young Asian men gathered in Centenary Square on 7 July. The presence of a few Far Right activists was sufficient to provoke the shared sense of denigration which the Far Right deliberately nurtures. Peaceful and legitimate protest did not, in our view, inevitably have to turn into riot. Recognition of the right to protest and the strong and, in this case, bitter feelings that protestors may have, requires an active policy of reassurance and understanding towards the plurality of social and cultural identities and beliefs among our publics.

Chapter 6

The Bradford 'riot' of 2001: the diversity of action

Yasmin Hussain and Paul Bagguley

Introduction

In this chapter we examine the idea that riots are composed of a crowd with a singular collective identity. This typically entails the claim that they are acting with some kind of common purpose. In contrast to this claim, we want to show that there is considerable diversity of action even in an apparently homogenous crowd with a supposed common goal. Following previous violent events in Oldham and Burnley earlier that year, the Anti-Nazi League organised a demonstration in Bradford city centre on 7 July 2001 to oppose a rumoured march of the neo-fascist National Front (NF). Attacks on young Asian men and women in the city centre after the demonstration had ended constituted the context of the violence in Bradford. The police reported at least 300 crimes were committed ranging from robbery and looting to arson and assault. In addition, there were arson attacks on six pubs, a Labour club and a Conservative club; 300 police were injured, including two stabbings; £27 million in damage was incurred; 256 people were charged (178 with riot); and over 100 adults sentenced to an average of four years' imprisonment (West Yorkshire Police 2004).

We begin the chapter with a critical review of some recent attempts to explain violent crowd behaviour or riots. These share a common preoccupation to seek out a collective identity in the crowd, and aim to explain crowd behaviour through this putative mechanism of collective identity. We then go on to present some of the evidence from our research on the Bradford riot reported in more detail elsewhere (Bagguley and Hussain 2008). Here our main concern is with the diversity of actions within the crowd. Although superficially homogenous, being largely composed of British-Pakistani men, there was considerable diversity in their actions. Unlike previous commentators who have tried to link the category of crowd action – looting, watching, attacking the police, etc. – to a category of person such as age or gender, we show that any one individual's actions during the event may vary and that both young and old were involved in the same type of action. We suggest that future analysis should focus upon the types of action rather than types of person and attempts to impute a collective identity to the crowd.

Contemporary approaches to understanding and explaining 'riots'

The work of Reicher and his colleagues (e.g. Drury and Reicher 2000; Reicher 1984) is the most sustained programme of empirical work on crowd behaviour in the UK and encompasses not just urban riots, but also various kinds of political demonstrations as well as football hooliganism. ESIM (the Extended Social Identity Model), which builds upon the early work of Reicher (1984), entails four principal claims. First, members of a crowd act in relation their social identities. These are understood in terms of their position in relation to other social groups and what kinds of actions they see as possible and desirable given their social positioning. Secondly, crowds are seen as involved in intergroup interactions. While the members of their crowd, the 'in-group', may understand themselves and their actions in terms of their own social identity, the members of the 'out-group' (typically the police) may interpret the actions of the crowd quite differently. Thirdly, when there is an asymmetry of perceptions and judgements of the crowd between the crowd members and the police, so that the police see the crowd as being illegitimate and act on this perception, then the social position of the crowd will change. Typically, this involves the police trying to disperse the crowd or prevent the crowd from carrying out its preferred course of action. This change in the social location of the crowd results in a change in the crowd's social identity. There follows a transformation of the behaviour of the crowd in line with its new social identity (Drury and Reicher 2000: 597). One consequence is for the crowd to take up a more 'extreme' or 'radical' social identity against the police (Drury and Reicher 2000: 598). This formulation shares many characteristics of what McPhail (1991: 13–20) criticised as the 'transformation hypothesis'. It also assumes that there are 'extremists' there in the first place. Reicher (2001) has argued that normally members of the crowd see themselves as moderates who react against the illegitimate actions of the police. The overall effect is to create a singular collective social identity within the crowd that leads to a sense of empowerment. This is understood as a feeling of confidence in the ability to act to change circumstances (Drury *et. al*. 2005; Drury and Reicher 2005). However, the focus of this sense of empowerment is very much a subjective one, and there is little analysis of what may sustain it over time. This work gives the notion of social identity a remarkable degree of both superficiality and fluidity: 'superficial' as it seems that they label how individuals have an apparently common interpretation of police actions, for instance, as being an expression of some shared social identity or other. These common perceptions are formed in a matter of moments and shift quite quickly, hence their *fluidity*. This tends to rule out the wider social context and the broader stronger identities that members of the crowd bring with them to the situation. It tends to rule out of the analysis the wider structural context and important past events. Crowds are presented as over-creative in both the actions they engage in and the social identities that they supposedly construct in their conflict with the police. This is not to dismiss entirely the importance of changes in behaviour that occur within crowds, but merely to note how Reicher and his colleagues have exaggerated the power of the crowd to transform identity and how it rests on a crude dichotomy between 'moderates' and 'extremists'.

The flashpoints model of public disorder (Waddington 2007: 49) explicitly attempts to develop a multi-causal account of public disorder. The framework identifies interdependent levels of analysis from the macro social context to the micro social interactions between crowd members and police officers. The flashpoints model attempts to create an explanation of disorder that is produced through a procedure of generalisation. As Keith (1993: 80) has argued, this produces an analysis that conflates events such as urban riots, picket line violence and football violence that have quite different origins and histories. Furthermore, PAJ Waddington has argued that there is an explanatory deficit in these accounts which fail to specify why that particular incident caused the riot to ensue, when many other apparently similar incidents failed to do so (Waddington 1991: 230). He goes on to point out that some flashpoints occurred hours or even days before violence began. Temporal proximity of a flashpoint is of little help in helping us decide why the riot took place. In addition he argues that the significance of a flashpoint depends upon how people interpret an event or action, but he sees this as undercutting the ability of the analyst to identify with certainty any particular flashpoint (Waddington 1991: 232). Finally, he suggests that the flashpoint is always a police action to which the crowd reacts.

Researching the 2001 Bradford riot

The research sought to develop an understanding of the 2001 riots and the impact the riot has had on the British-Pakistani community in Bradford (Bagguley and Hussain 2008). This involved exploring in interviews what the riots meant for ordinary people, and the impact they had on other aspects of their lives. In the interviews there was a focus on respondents' views about how the police and the authorities responded to the riots, how the media represented them, and the extent to which the Far Right had an influence on the riots. This also entailed attempting to provide an understanding of identity in the Pakistani community, and to locate their experiences and perceptions in an appropriate cultural context. These aims provided the themes for the interviews, and respondents also completed a short self-completion questionnaire providing basic demographic details about themselves. The semi-structured interviews allowed respondents to integrate aspects which they themselves thought were important. In total, 34 interviews and one focus group were conducted. Comprising 19 male and 21 female participants, interviewees' ages ranged from 16 to over 60, with slightly more young women and older men. The riot took place in the postal districts BD8 and BD9, and interviewees were largely drawn from these two areas.

Ensuring that all the respondents were Pakistani and Muslim was important, as those involved in the riots were predominantly from a Pakistani background. Religion was important because when considered in conjunction with a person's 'ethnic' background, it provides a sense of cultural identity. This is an important mediator of a person's experience and understanding of the events in Bradford in 2001, especially in the light of subsequent media and political focus on Muslims. All of those interviewed have been given pseudonyms.

Bradford 2001: background and overview

In this section we provide a brief account of event based largely upon newspaper sources, as this provides a summary of 'public knowledge' about the riot. Around noon on Saturday 7 July 2001 several hundred people of a variety of ethnic backgrounds gathered in the centre of Bradford to attend a demonstration organised by the Anti-Nazi League and their allies against a threatened march in the city by the National Front. The police had successfully requested the Home Office to ban the march and a counter-march planned by the Anti-Nazi League (Bagguley and Hussain 2008: 55).

By 3:00 pm the Anti-Nazi League rally was by all accounts winding down, although some of those attending were still present in Centenary Square and the police were requesting them to disperse having been herded into a corner of the square (*Daily Express* 9 July 2001). Around 2:45 pm the police turned back five NF supporters who had arrived at Bradford Interchange railway station, and it was reported that they had complied with the police and left Bradford (*Bradford Telegraph and Argus* 9 July 2001; *Daily Express* 9 July 2001). However, at around 4:00 pm news of a racist attack on an Asian man in Ivegate outside Addison's bar reached some in the crowd in Centenary Square a matter of yards away (*Bradford Telegraph and Argus* 9 July 2001).

From this point on press reports suggest that conflict then developed between South Asian men in the city centre and the police. The police were busy arresting South Asian men, while some of the crowd were reported to be smashing windows, looting shops and throwing missiles at the police. Around 5:00 pm, two white men were stabbed by a group of South Asian men around Thornton Road (*Bradford Telegraph and Argus* 9 July 2001; *Daily Express* 9 July 2001; *Yorkshire Post* 9 July 2001). The only way out of the city centre at this stage was through Westgate and up White Abbey Road, as the police had blocked other exits from the city centre. In addition, they were pushing the crowd in that direction. As more police arrived the violence escalated from throwing stones and other missiles at police on Westgate at about 5:45 pm to a group of around 60–70 South Asian men throwing petrol bombs at the police from 6:20 pm onwards on White Abbey Road. By this time the city centre had been cleared and was quiet (*Bradford Telegraph and Argus* 9 July 2001; *Daily Express* 9 July 2001). This is the symbolic boundary between the city centre and the South Asian neighbourhood broadly known as Manningham. From this point onwards burning barricades had been erected by some of those in the crowd. The police had dog handlers, helicopter surveillance of the crowd, and about a dozen mounted police on the scene. Several attempts by community leaders to negotiate between the police and the crowd failed (Bagguley and

Hussain 2008: 59–60). The police repeatedly charged the crowd with officers on horseback, and gradually over several hours the crowd retreated up White Abbey Road and Whetley Hill (*Bradford Telegraph and Argus* 9 July 2001; *Daily Express* 9 July 2001; *Yorkshire Post* 9 July 2001).

The diversity of crowd action

In many respects the crowd in Bradford was strikingly homogenous in terms of ethnic and religious background and gender. They were overwhelmingly Pakistani men. According to figures from the West Yorkshire police, of the 305 people arrested, 88 per cent were South Asian, 10 per cent were white and 2 per cent were African Caribbean (West Yorkshire Police 2004). It has also been reported that 60 per cent of those arrested for the most serious public order offences were unemployed (Carling *et al.* 2004). The 2001 Census shows that 44.8 per cent of Pakistani males aged 16–24 in Bradford were economically inactive and of the economically active 27.2 per cent were unemployed, giving a probable unemployed rate of 72 per cent. The equivalent figures for those over 25 years old are 32.1 per cent 17.5 per cent and 49.6 per cent (source: Office for National Statistics 2001 Census). In terms of labour market status the rioters who were arrested do not seem to have been unrepresentative of Pakistani men from Bradford.

It is important to recognise that some of those in the crowd were seeking to prevent further violence; others were actively helping those caught in the arson attacks on pubs, while others still were spectators. Oberschall (1993) made a useful set of distinctions between different levels of participation based upon his analysis of the Los Angeles riot of 1965. These range from activists who directly engage the police, looters who take advantage of the premises previously broken into by activists, others who encourage the activists and the looters through to those who simply observe the events (Oberschall 1993: 243). Keith's (1993) analysis of arrest statistics of riots in London during the 1980s attempts a similar exercise in disaggregating the image of the rioter. He highlights how different actions are related to different categories of person within the crowd (Keith 1993: 98). The nature of any individual's involvement and actions changes during the riot so that raw arrest data can only be a representation of the illegal acts of which they have been accused of committing. As McPhail (1971) has noted, this is a major problem for measuring participation in a riot.

First of all we need to extend Oberschall's typology of actions. Once we question the assumption that the crowd had a common goal or collective identity, we can see that other possibilities of types of action emerge. To Oberschall's activism, looters, jeerers and observers we can add restrainers and helpers. Restraining action refers to those try and prevent activists or others from their actions. This is distinct from helping as helping action typically did not aim to stop the riot. The restrainers had a distinct role in trying to act as intermediaries negotiating between the rioters and the police. Helping actions are those that help the police with information, phoning the fire service or providing sustenance. Intervening to help individuals threatened by the actions of the rioters or to prevent attacks on property were, as we shall see below, carried out in some cases by those who at other points had been involved as active participants. One of our critical findings is that some individuals performed different actions at different times. For instance, both restrainers and helpers at various points became activists. The problem as we see it is that too much analytical attention has been given to the activists and implicitly equating types of action with particular categories of actor. This may be a reasonable assumption to make most of the time, but it is one that is not sustainable if we take seriously arguments that people's behaviour in these circumstances is both situationally specific, and the processes through which they become involved casual and unpredictable (Abudu Stark *et al.* 1974; McPhail 1971; Oberschall 1993: 256–8).

The watchers or observers of the riot were apparently quite numerous, with some of our informants suggesting that they significantly outnumbered the active participants. As Alisah Khaleeq told us, although she saw some 'lads' throwing stones at the police, as she remembered the event many more were just watching:

> There were a lot of bystanders just watching. There were about a hundred lads throwing stones but the rest were just there watching. I don't even think a hundred were throwing stones, I think it was less than that, but there were a lot more just watching what was going on. (Alisah Khaleeq, 38, Community Development Officer)

The following instances illustrate the ways in which some in the crowd attempted to persuade active participants to not carry out certain acts. In one case this was to dissuade them from breaking into cars, setting them on fire and rolling them down the hill towards police lines. The reason for this was that the vehicles were seen as local South Asian people's property. Furthermore, it also illustrates that it was not just 'elders' acting in this way but younger people present who at other points may have been active participants:

> There were a few of them saying 'no that's it' when they got to the point when they were burning the cars and rolling them down. There were people saying 'look you are going too far now'. The elderly, mostly the elderly but there were a few young ones saying 'look why are breaking these cars, setting them on fire and rolling them down, these are our cars'. Because you know then they realised that we were damaging our own property ... (Kamran Ahmad, 19, student and Omar Akhbar, 20, fast food restaurant manager)

Some from the local South Asian community were helpers, being rather more active in their support of the police, for instance serving the officers with tea and biscuits on the streets where the violence was taking place. As Zahida Ali recalled:

> Yeah there were people talking to the police or offering them Rich Tea biscuits or a cup of tea, I saw some of that going on yeah. But that was like a lot of the older generation of Asians what did not probably have an understanding or probably did not know what was going on. (Zahida Ali, 31, support worker)

One important episode during the riots was the setting on fire of local pubs and the Labour club. At this point some bystanders acted to help those inside the building escape, despite the fact that the police and the Fire Brigade were seemingly unable to assist. Zara Hussain, who herself tried several times to contact the fire service, recounted the following:

> A man had come to the pub about five minutes before and he was knocking on the door because people were barricading themselves in you see as they were afraid of being attacked and he was telling them to get out because he had seen what they had done to the other pubs down the road, the Labour Club and the Upper Globe. And I think he realised that people could get hurt ... he was an Asian, Pakistani man ... I rang the fire brigade a few times. I rang them three or four times but obviously they could not come until the police had made that place safe. (Zara Hussain, 29, student)

In another illustration of how individual rioters were not always engaged in violent actions against the police, property or other people, one of our interviewees recalled how a journalist was helped by some of them. Instead of stealing her camera, they removed the film, returned it to her and then escorted her to the police lines. He suggested that the reason for this was to prevent any photographs she had taken being used as evidence in any future prosecutions against them:

There was a reporter kind of behind or amongst the rioters and she had her camera taken off her by the rioters. They were thinking you are taking our photos what do you think you are doing. So they didn't actually take the camera but they took the film out of it and they returned the camera and says 'Get out of it before we jump you'. But ... they had the sense to take the film out of the camera, return the camera to her, take her back to the police line, it was like an escort before she got jumped by all the others. About seven guys around her, escorting her to the police line. (Imran Ismail, 28, welfare adviser)

A number of newspaper reports of three of the trials illustrate quite graphically how in different contexts the same individuals acted in quite different ways. In the first case, Mudasar Khan, who was imprisoned for riot, was protecting a white owned property in the city centre early on in the events (*Bradford Telegraph and Argus* 23 January 2002). In the second case, Mohammed Bashir served drinks to the police, but was jailed for four years for his later activities during the riot (*Bradford Telegraph and Argus* 8 October 2002). Finally, Mohammed Ali Zaman was jailed for two and a half years for throwing three stones, but had also tried to protect a garage and persuade others to stop the violence and leave the area (*Bradford Telegraph and Argus* 29 June 2002).

It would be too easy to dismiss these as just a few exceptional examples. However, these kinds of helping and restraining actions are not the ones that tend to be picked up on by police, bystanders or the media. The more spectacular violent acts capture people's attention and stick in their memories. The important point that they illustrate is the diversity of action within the crowd, and the significance of the point made by McPhail (1971) long ago that individuals engage in a variety of behaviours with quite different meanings and motivations at different points during such episodes of collective violence.

Conclusions

In this chapter we hope that we have been able to show that the idea of a cohesive crowd with a common purpose and shared collective identity is both theoretically unwarranted and really lacks sufficient empirical foundation. On the contrary what this really directs our attention towards is the phenomenon of diversity of the types of actions among the crowd and the diversity of any one person's actions over the duration of the event. We have cited instances of the different types of action that individuals engaged in at different points during the Bradford riot. Quite what people did at what point in the riot is evidently contextual, rather than springing from some putative collective identity. While not all individuals involved would fit this pattern, this is sufficiently widespread to seriously question previous models based upon assumptions of collective identity and common purpose.

Chapter 7

From petrol bombs to performance indicators: the 2001 riots and the emergence of 'community cohesion'

Paul Thomas

Introduction

The violent urban disturbances occurring in several industrial towns and cities in the north of England during the summer of 2001 are accepted as being a watershed for 'race relations' policies (Solomos 2003). A new concept, 'Community Cohesion', was introduced to explain these disturbances (Cantle 2001), and was rapidly operationalised as a policy priority. Since 2001, Community Cohesion has become the guiding principle of *all* policy approaches to ethnicity and 'race relations' (Department for Communities and Local Government 2007b; Home Office 2005; Local Government Association 2002). The central concern of this new approach is *ethnic segregation*, the belief that different ethnic groups have developed 'parallel lives' (Ritchie 2001), with little connection or contact between them, and that consequent damage has been done to common values, identities and unity. This suggests that the previous policy model of 'multiculturalism' has been unsuccessful, and that a fundamental rethink of political assumptions and priorities is underway – something apparently confirmed by overt attacks on 'multiculturalism' by prominent figures (Phillips 2005). For some anti-racist critics, this has been supported by a governmental discourse around the problematic 'otherness' of ethnic minority, especially Muslim, communities, such as failure to learn and use English, the negative impacts of continued trans-continental marriage links, and a growth in extremist Islamist political activity (Alexander 2004; Cantle 2001; Department for Communities and Local Government 2007a; Kundnani 2002; Travis 2001).

This chapter draws on field research around the impact of Community Cohesion on work with young people in Oldham (Thomas 2006, 2007) to discuss how and why the 2001 urban disturbances have proved to be a policy watershed in Britain, and what the key themes and concerns are of this new policy agenda – how we have moved from petrol bombs on the streets of Oldham, Bradford and Burnley to public bodies being required to show progress on 'performance indicators' around Community Cohesion (LGA 2002). In doing so, the chapter discusses whether Community Cohesion does indeed represent the 'death of multiculturalism' (Kundnani 2002) and a return to assimilationist approaches more familiar to the republican citizenship approach of France (Bertossi 2007), or whether it is actually a much-needed adjustment *within* Britain's multiculturalist model.

The 2001 riots as a political watershed

The violent urban disturbances in Oldham, Burnley and Bradford in 2001 were the most serious outbreaks of disorder in Britain since the widespread inner-city disturbances of the early 1980s. The governmental response was to swiftly establish an independent Inquiry Panel, reporting in December 2001 (Cantle 2001), alongside an official governmental endorsement (Denham 2002), with these documents proposing Community Cohesion as a concept to both understand the disturbances and to map future policy directions. While not actually using the term Community Cohesion, local inquiry reports mirrored these concerns in focusing on parallel lives (Clarke 2001; Ritchie 2001). In all cases, these reports focused in only a very limited way on the actual events of the disturbances, seeing them as symptomatic of wider and deeper problems within the state of national ethnic relations. This was in stark contrast to the forensic examination of the events of the previous watershed 1981 urban disturbances in Brixton, South London (Scarman 1981), and suggests that the 2001 riots provided an opportunity to advance a new policy dialogue around 'race relations' that was already under way (Commission on the Future of Multi-Ethnic Britain 2000). This analysis indicated that the 2001 disturbances could have happened in numerous British towns and cities. However, this perspective arguably downplayed specific and important causal factors for the disturbances, such as far-right racist political agitation (Bagguley and Hussain 2003), local policing, the misrepresentation of crime data around racial harassment and racist violent attacks (Ray and Smith

2004), and media amplification of local racist fears of such crimes (Kalra 2002). All of these are significant factors in previous, race-related urban disturbances in Britain (Gilroy 2002; Solomos 2003).

Ignoring any suggestion of local specificities, Community Cohesion was rapidly deployed as the new policy priority for British 'race relations', with specific guidance given to all local authorities to 'promote' cohesion, and to measure it through regular qualitative surveys against performance indicators, with a steady growth in positive attitudes towards diversity and national identity expected over time (DCLG 2007b; LGA 2002). Experimental activity to generate 'evidence-based practice' was funded in a number of locations (Home Office 2003), and Community Cohesion confirmed as a central priority for national Race Equality strategies (Home Office 2005), with the implication that all types of public funding to community organisations should demand the 'promotion of cohesion'. All British schools now have a duty to promote cohesion, despite wider governmental policies of 'parental choice' and an expansion of the religious school sector that arguably work against this (Cantle 2005). The 7/7 London tube bombings in July 2005, and subsequent terrorist plots, have added further urgency to this focus on cohesion and 'integration' (DCLG 2007b), with many of the measures originally proposed in 2001 (Cantle 2001), such as English language tests for all new migrants to Britain, more focus on 'Britishness', and greater policy engagement with young people and women within Muslim communities, activated in the wake of 7/7. This policy direction, persistent attempts by politicians to discuss 'Britishness', and the claim by the Head of the Government's dedicated racial equality agency, the Commission for Racial Equality (CRE), that Britain was 'sleepwalking towards segregation' and that multiculturalism was to blame (Phillips 2005), just as that body was disbanded to create the new Commission on Equality and Human Rights, all suggest that the previously dominant model of multiculturalism is indeed dying, or already dead (Kundnani 2002). This claim is investigated further through discussion of the key themes and concerns of Community Cohesion.

Community Cohesion: key themes and concerns

'Community Cohesion' had no pedigree as a term prior to its deployment in 2001 (Robinson 2005). Definitions of the term itself were surprisingly brief in the governmental reports (Cantle 2001; Denham

2002), leading to considerable academic analysis and argument over its true meaning (Alexander 2004; Amin 2003; Kalra 2002; Kundnani 2001; McGhee 2005; Thomas 2007). Much of this debate has failed to draw on any empirical evidence as to how Community Cohesion is *actually* understood and put into practice, something that this chapter, and the more detailed research that it draws upon (Thomas 2006, 2007), aims to compensate for. A number of key themes can be detected within the Community Cohesion discourse and policy deployment. They can be summarised as:

1 Ethnic segregation is real and growing, and is causal to tension and mutual fear.
2 Community and individual 'agency' and 'responsibility' play a significant role in accepting and deepening this segregation.
3 The problematic nature of over-developed 'bonding' social capital in the absence of forms of 'bridging' contact.
4 The negative, unintended, consequences of past 'race relations' policy approaches.

The latter three themes are based on the core premise that ethnic physical and cultural segregation is real and growing , a situation of 'parallel lives', where little social interaction takes place, and leading to a clear lack of 'shared values', or concern with commonality (Cantle 2001). While individual and institutionalised racism, such as Oldham Local Authority's past policy of allocating Asian and white tenants to different housing areas, clearly helped to create segregation (Kundnani 2001), the suggestion here is that the 'agency' of individuals within all communities has played a role in accepting and so deepening this segregation (Greener 2002); the belief that individuals and communities have *chosen* to live separate, parallel lives, shown by their housing and schooling decisions.

This is highlighted by the focus on both 'white flight' (Cantle 2001) and ethnic minority 'congregation' (CRE 2001). This is arguably part of wider and consistent focus on agency across New Labour social policy (Greener 2002), part of the 'third way' belief that government alone cannot guarantee social change in an era of rapid global economic and social change, and that individuals must share responsibility for improving the community and their own individual situation (Giddens 1998). Here, there is a clear communitarian suggestion that past policy approaches have focused on the rights of different ethnic groups without stressing the necessary and balancing shared responsibilities we all have to build a cohesive community

(Cantle 2005; Etzioni 1995). Allied to this is what can be described as the problematisation of bonding social capital (McGhee 2003; Putnam 2000), the belief that the disturbances have exposed a reality of insular monocultural communities with little interest in, or empathy for, other ethnic communities in a situation of minimal contact.

From this perspective, there is an urgent need to develop avenues for meaningful bridging social capital which will enable dialogue across ethnic divides, so facilitating the development of shared values and priorities. In the case of the northern towns and cities experiencing violent disturbances in 2001, the once-dominant textile industries, and their trade unions, partially provided forms of bridging social capital in the past (Kundnani 2001). The disappearance of these industries, and the failure to develop viable, post-industrial economies in such areas (Byrne 1999) is clearly relevant to the lack of bridging social capital, as is the suggestion that within many of the communities experiencing post-industrial social exclusion as 'losers' in a rapidly globalising economy, inward-looking and defensive forms of 'neighbourhood nationalism' (Back 1996) are developing. Here, monocultural community identity is strongest among those who have been most damaged by economic change (May 1999).

Underpinning all these themes is the belief that multiculturalist governmental policy approaches over the past 25 years have, while achieving notable progress in tackling racial inequality (Solomos 2003), had unintended, negative consequences (Cantle 2001). In particular, these policies have allegedly deepened and solidified the divides between different ethnic communities. This analysis sees policies flowing from the previous watershed moment of the 1981 urban disturbances as having privileged essentialised, separate ethnic communities, and their 'community leaders', through funding for ethnic-specific facilities and organisations. Alongside this came a focus on 'ethnic data', with the inclusion of an ethnicity question in the 1991 Census, and the use of such data to identify areas of the economy and society where non-white ethnic minorities were underrepresented, or doing less well than average, with the clear implication that this 'ethnic penalty' is due to individual and institutional white racism (Solomos 2003).

Arguably, ensuring equality in terms of educational and employment outcomes, and in community facilities for each *separate* ethnic group took priority in Britain over common needs and identities, including taking priority over multiracial movements against racism (Sivanadan 2005). While this policy approach of political multiculturalism (or 'anti-racism' as it was popularly labelled) became increasingly dominant in Britain following the urban disturbances of 1981, which were understood to be about structural racial disadvantage and blatant everyday racism, the seeds of this approach could be seen from the late 1960s onwards, when the then-Labour government accepted that policies of assimilation had not worked in a period of rapidly increasing racial tension (Solomos 2003). This led to the gradual development of pluralist political structures of consultation that accepted ethnic difference, and which attempted to accommodate differences around religion, custom and dress within the public domain of schools, welfare services and the workplace. It was particularly recognised in the establishment of the CRE in 1976. While representing a long-overdue strengthening of weak anti-discriminatory measures, this saw the downplaying of what had originally been a parallel policy track, the importance of 'promoting good relations between different racial groups' (Cantle 2005; Solomos 2003). This suggests that while trying to remedy profound ethnic inequalities, and accommodate ethnic differences, policy approaches since 1981 have actually accepted and deepened ethnic segregation through focusing on the separate 'needs' of each, essentialised ethnic group while neglecting common forms of identity and the inter-ethnic contact and dialogue which can develop it. Here, Community Cohesion can be seen as a necessary and overdue correction to the successes and associated problems of past policy approaches, with a focus on common needs and identities, rather than on difference (Cantle 2001, 2005).

The 'death of multiculturalism'?

This explicit criticism of 'multiculturalism' for perpetuating, or even partially *causing*, ethnic segregation, and its juxtaposition with integration (Cantle 2005; Phillips 2005) seem to suggest that multiculturalism is indeed dying, and that it has been killed by Community Cohesion (Alexander 2004; Kundnani 2002). This position is understandable, given that pronouncements by politicians in 2001 seemed to very partially focus on the agency of ethnic minority communities in creating segregation (Travis 2001). These comments, made soon after the attacks of 11 September 2001, helped to set a tone for long-running public debate focused on the apparent 'refusal' of some ethnic minority communities to 'become British' (Goodhart 2004) with the suggestion here being that the 2001 disturbances represented a refusal by Muslim communities to integrate, encouraged by multiculturalist policies. For others, rather than symbolising a lack of interest in British citizenship, these riots represented frustration by South Asian young people at their inability to access 'mainstream' British citizenship because of racism and social exclusion (Amin 2003).

Here, the Community Cohesion discourse might be seen as a racialised narrative that blames the victims of racism for their own situation, so conveniently avoiding focus on the real, structural causes of this segregation and alienation (Alexander 2004; Burnett 2004). Indeed, the very existence of segregation, a central tenet of the Community Cohesion analysis, is questioned in a situation where all British young people experience the same educational curriculum and, increasingly, the same mass-media-based youth culture (Kalra 2002). Community Cohesion, these critics suggest, has turned the symptom of ethnic segregation into the cause of inequality and alienation among Britain's non-white ethnic minorities. The subsequent questioning of the continued use of South Asian community languages, the linking of this with Muslim community educational underachievement (Ritchie 2001), the questioning of future minority language translation of public documents, and a move towards ending public funding for community groups serving specific ethnic communities unless they clearly promote cross-community contact (DCLG 2007b), all suggest a move away from multiculturalism and back to the discredited policy of assimilationism for some (Alexander 2004; Kundnani 2002).

A parallel policy concern with 'Preventing Violent Extremism' (DCLG 2007a) that focuses solely on 'extremism' with Muslim communities, with no interest in the growth of support in some white communities for violent, Far Right groups (Solomos 2003), arguably confirms this. Is Community Cohesion really a rejection of previous multiculturalist policy approaches? Although there is clear agreement that Community Cohesion represents a policy shift, there is little empirical data on how it is actually understood and operationalised at ground level. The discussion below aims to counter this deficit.

Research evidence

Field research was carried out in Oldham, site of one of the 2001 disturbances. It focused on one key group of welfare professionals, youth workers, and on how they have understood and operationalised Community Cohesion within their work with young people since 2001. Individual youth workers at all levels of responsibility from both statutory and voluntary/community sectors were interviewed, using semi-structured, qualitative approaches. Youth work is a relatively marginal part of the British welfare state, but it has a proven record of working with the most marginalised young people (Davies 1999), something recognised in the various Community Cohesion reports, which called for increased state funding for youth work (Cantle 2001; Denham 2002; Ritchie 2001). While recognising that shifts in approaches and priorities of welfare professionals are always situated and contingent, the research focus outlined above has hopefully generated evidence around the meaning and implications of this new policy approach.

Detailed findings are discussed elsewhere (Thomas 2006, 2007), but may be summarised as follows: Community Cohesion had clear understanding and support from youth workers in Oldham, who highlighted significant changes to the assumptions, priorities and methods of their professional practice with young people. This new post-2001 policy of Community Cohesion was understood as distinctly different, and better, than previous policy approaches. There was a clear consensus that Community Cohesion means the promotion and facilitation by youth workers of 'meaningful direct contact' among young people of different ethnic backgrounds:

Building relationships, friendships, and knowing what other cultures, other religions are doing and why, and understanding each other. (Asad, male, Bangladeshi origin)

Bringing young people together across ethnic divides has become the fundamental policy priority for youth work agencies in Oldham following the trauma of the 2001 disturbances, and this has been done in a number of ways. Youth clubs and projects serving different communities have been linked up (including areas of the same ethnic background with conflicts over 'territory') and given the responsibility of devising a number of shared events, trips and festivals during each year, so that the young people of different backgrounds have the chance to build dialogue and relationships. Town-wide events, such as parties for Christmas and the Muslim Eid festival, are held, at which delegations of young people from every youth project come together for shared activities and discussions. This may seem very normal, routine work with young people, but in the context of an ethnically segregated, tense town like Oldham, such work is risky and innovative. The risk is illustrated by this account of a joint holiday trip involving white and South Asian youth groups:

We went for an Indian meal on the first night we took them to Whitby ... and one of the white lads said, 'God, if people on Thorndale knew what we're doing now, we'd get leathered' [beaten up], and that was just going to a restaurant. (Johnson, male, white origin)

Given this reality of racialised 'neighbourhood nationalism' (Back 1996), a key principle of the new work is that the activities bringing young people together are about fun, using sports, art and drama, and outdoor activities, rather than discussions and conferences about racism. This is a deliberate attempt to portray ethnic diversity as normal and positive, with everyone having common identities of being young people from the same town who have the same interests and the same desire for fun and new experiences. The aim here is that, rather than make young people talk about diversity and racial tension formally, dialogue develops informally through friendship, talking at a time when they feel comfortable. This is illustrated by an account from a large residential trip where delegations from every high school in Oldham take part in activities organised by the youth workers with the aim of encouraging mixing:

One of the Muslim young women was praying at night, so the other girls watched her pray and asked her really interesting questions about it. The fact was that it was done at one o'clock in the morning, and they really should have been in bed, but I didn't stop it because it was a really interesting dialogue going on. (Mary, female, white origin)

These new approaches are seen by youth workers as in clear contrast to the past when different areas and communities had no contact or joint activities at all and each kept to their own area, with insularity and separation the result. This past policy approach included the 'norm' that young people were served by youth workers from the same ethnic background, with it being 'inappropriate' to have workers of a different background working with ethnic minority young people. Community Cohesion in Oldham has meant a total reversal of this, with youth workers being deliberately encouraged to work with young people of a different background, in order to encourage dialogue and questioning, and to have a diversity of positive role models. This has included a Pakistani-origin youth worker moving to an all-white social housing area seen as a stronghold for the far-right British National Party:

I've never had a problem here working as a Black worker ... yes, people have taken me very well. (Qummar, male, Pakistani origin)

Working with a different community in a situation of segregation and racism (Ritchie 2001) has obviously been challenging for youth workers, with some facing racist abuse, but all supported this new policy direction, believing that it is vital to provide young people with what may be their first-ever chance to get to know and debate with an adult from a different ethnic background. This new approach has involved prioritising direct contact among young people of different ethnic backgrounds in an informal and fun atmosphere, with a clear focus on common identities and experiences, supported by a more diverse group of youth worker role models. This is all seen as in clear contrast to the pre-2001 policy direction, which youth workers in Oldham understood as 'anti-racism'. Youth workers understood anti-racism as meaning that they should only work with young people of the same ethnic background, that there was nothing to be gained from bringing young people together, and that youth work projects on racism should involve quite formal, lesson-type approaches telling young people that racism is wrong, and punishing any behaviour or comments seen as 'racist'. This, and the especially negative reaction youth workers reported receiving from white young people in response to these approaches, echoes studies on the downside of 'anti-racism', as it has often been understood and practised (CRE 1999; Hewitt 2005):

It's (anti-racism) not respectful, it's not effective, and I actually think it is damaging as well. (Alex, female, dual-heritage background)

Multiculturalism – alive and well?

This empirical evidence sheds light on the meaning and importance of the key Community Cohesion themes and concerns discussed above. The analysis of deep and problematic ethnic segregation, and of considerable 'agency' in perpetuating that division, is accepted by the respondents. Does that mean, in its focus on commonality, that Community Cohesion represents the 'death of multiculturalism' (Kundnani 2002)? This data suggests that, as it is being actually understood and practised, Community Cohesion represents a new and re-focused *form* of multiculturalism (Watson 2000), rather than a rejection of it. The key issue here is Community Cohesion's acceptance of the reality of ethnic diversity, with youth work in Oldham focusing on negotiation, accommodation and dialogue *between* those differences, rather than attempting to deny or undermine it (Thomas 2006, 2007). Not only does the Community Cohesion activity with young people focus on negotiation of their different experiences and understandings, but it works with and accepts their continued need for separate facilities and identity. This need for locally based youth provision representing specific ethnic backgrounds and identities here runs alongside, and is a vital component of, the activities that bring young people together with others of a different ethnic background, as shown by this example from a young women's drama project:

> It had to be both, it had to be work with their own community and the opportunity to integrate and mix with others. (Deborah, female, white origin)

In working in this way, and so ensuring that the 'meaningful direct contact' between young people only occurs after preparation work with, and agreement from, young people of each ethnic background, youth workers in Oldham are practising what could be termed 'transversal politics' (Yuval-Davis 1997). Here, a 'rooting and shifting' of attitudes can take place, whereby attitudes to 'others' can be re-considered and amended because one's own identity is *not* being threatened or put under unwanted scrutiny, with the informal, fun element of the youth work activities, often delivered on 'neutral territory', crucial to the progress. These approaches support 'Contact Theory' (Hewstone *et al.* 2007), the belief that, in a reality of stark ethnic segregation and conflict, contact must take place in groups, be chosen voluntarily and be sustained over time to have a meaningful impact on mutual prejudices and fears. Critics of Community Cohesion suggest that 'voluntary' activities like these youth work examples, and parallel 'twinning' activities between schools with different ethnic populations, are prioritised because government lacks the political will to tackle the fundamental segregation issues of housing and schools (Kalra 2002), but the evidence from attempts to force the creation of 'socially (i.e. class) mixed' housing areas is negative, with much more positive evidence from initiatives promoting *voluntary* contact and co-operation between social (rented, low income) and owner-occupied (middle income) housing areas (Robinson 2005). This all stresses the importance of continued, ethnic-specific community agencies that can work with and prepare specific ethnic (co-terminus with geographic in Oldham) communities for Community Cohesion approaches, and the acceptance of the reality of diversity within those approaches. For that reason, the clumsy understanding of Community Cohesion currently resulting in the withdrawal of funding in some areas for organisations serving single ethnic/religious groups is badly misguided (Bourne 2007).

More importantly, this acceptance of diversity while focusing on the need for commonality rather than being contradictory to the government's wider Race Equality measures (Back *et al.* 2002) is actually quite consistent. Here, an over-arching 'human rights' framework is being developed that recognises diversity of *all* kinds, but which also insists on universal adherence to 'core' values whereby religious/ethnic 'identity' cannot be allowed to supersede fundamental individual rights. In an increasingly complex and 'hybrid' (Hall 2000) Britain, Community Cohesion is part of attempts to create 'cooler', de-centred and intersectional forms of identity, rather than (inevitably conflictual) 'hot' forms of identity (McGhee 2005, 2006).

Conclusion

The 2001 disturbances have been a turning point in British policy approaches to 'race relations'. For some, the renewed focus on commonality, rather than the continued prioritisation of essentialised ethnic difference, inevitably represents the 'death of multiculturalism' (Kundnani 2002), but this chapter suggests that the allegation of a move back to assimilationism is misplaced. Empirical evidence from Oldham suggests that these fears are not borne out by the way Community Cohesion has actually been understood and operationalised. Rather than denying or opposing ethnic difference, Community Cohesion youth work in Oldham accepts difference and is engaged in negotiating dialogue and contact between that difference through enjoyable and informal forms of youth activity which enable relationship building and prejudice/fear reduction without existing community identities or assumptions being overtly challenged. This represents a 'transversal politics' (Yuval-Davis 1997) that fulfils the necessary conditions for 'contact theory'-based work (Hewstone *et al.* 2007).

The fact that this Community Cohesion actively accepts both diversity itself, and the need for specific ethnic groups to have distinct identities and facilities within the process, suggests that this represents continuity with previous forms of 'multiculturalism' (Solomos 2003). Additionally, this Community Cohesion-based youth work has also been concerned with 'difference' on the basis of class, territory, dis/ability, and sexuality, suggesting that a more 'critical' multiculturalism (May 1999) is being accepted and worked with here which considers the variety of influences on individual identity, rather than privileging essentialised forms of ethnic identity (McGhee 2006). In this way, Community Cohesion, and the way it is practised by youth workers in Oldham, represents not the 'death of multiculturalism', but a rejection of one form of it, 'anti-racism', in favour of a more complex and 'critical' multiculturalism.

Chapter 8

From rumour to riot: the 2005 Lozells disorders

Mike King

Introduction

The riots that occurred in the Lozells area of Birmingham, Central England, towards the end of 2005 were somewhat unique in character. Unlike previous inner-city riots in England and Wales during the 1980s (and indeed in Lozells and the neighbouring district of Handsworth in 1981 and 1985), they did not involve direct conflict between the (primarily) African-Caribbean population and the police. Nor, like the disorders in the rest of the country during 1991–2, was it a case of white working-class youths living on housing estates on the periphery of cities set against the police. Similarly, they differed from the 2001 riots examined above, involving South Asian youths and the police, in addition to antagonism between white neo-Fascists and South Asians. Rather, they entailed members from the African-Caribbean and South Asian communities in conflict with each other and, in turn, against the police. This chapter will outline the unfolding events of the Lozells disorders, superficially caused by a rumour concerning the rape of an African girl by South Asians, as well as the policing operation.[1] It then moves on to consider the wider contextual factors and arguments put forward as to the underlying causes of the riots, as well as the present realities. It concludes by comparing in more detail these events with the 1980s Handsworth/Lozells riots.

Rumour

Apparently a rumour had been circulating for some time that a girl had been 'gang raped' in a 'beauty parlour' located in Wellington Road, Perry Barr, Birmingham (Appleton 2005; Dosanjh 2006). The police became aware of the rumour on 12 October 2005 when they received an anonymous call that two Eastern European males had raped a girl at the rear of the shop (interview with West Midlands Police) and this rapidly escalated to 'critical incident' status (*Guardian* 4 May 2006). The police followed up this allegation with a scene of crime investigation and, by 17 October, the rumour had become that the victim was a young black girl. By Tuesday 18 October it had taken shape into being that a 14-year-old African girl had been detained in the rear of the shop premises and gang-raped by 35 South Asian males (interview with West Midlands Police). The alleged incident was reported on two local 'pirate' radio stations, and then rumour asserted that the victim was an 'illegal immigrant'. One of the pirate radio station DJs organised a protest outside the beauty parlour. In turn the West Midlands Police engaged the consultancy firm of West Midlands Mediation and Transformation Service (WMMTS), a publicly funded non-profit organisation that has a history of work in the area concerning gangs and guns, in an attempt to de-escalate the situation (*Guardian* 29 November 2005). Subsequently, a 30-year-old woman lodged a formal complaint with the police of sexual assault at a different beauty parlour shop owned by the same franchise.[2]

Protest

On Tuesday 18 October, about 200 people gathered outside the beauty parlour in a 'stop traffic protest'. Over the following two days, police strategy meetings discussed the merits or otherwise of allowing a proposed rally to go ahead outside the shop on Saturday 22 October. It was decided that this should be allowed to take place on the grounds that it could potentially constitute an important release valve of tension felt especially in the African-Caribbean community. Accordingly, it was decided to make it a formally approved rally, even to the extent of the local authority providing and erecting barriers (police interview). On Friday 21 October, five men from the shop (including the shop owner) were held for police questioning, and at midday on Saturday the planned protest (200–400 strong) went ahead. This protest coincided with a 'Campaign for Silent Victims protest in Birmingham and London' which had been organised some time before these events.

As part of a decided rally dispersal process, a public meeting was arranged by the police to take place that evening. A local bishop (also a member of the Police Authority) offered his church as a venue and members of both communities were informally and formally informed in advance. About 300–400 people assembled at the church, being principally drawn from the African-Caribbean community, but key South Asian community members (including from the local mosque and the local MP) were also present (West Midlands Police interview). The meeting was addressed not only by the bishop and the MP, but also by two senior police officers. At this, the police announced that there had been five arrests on suspicion in connection with the alleged rape and that another woman had lodged a formal complaint with them about sexual harassment at a different shop within the same franchise.

Riot: 22–23 October 2005

Accounts of what happened immediately after the above meeting differ: for some commentators, South Asian youths gathered outside church shouting abuse, whereas others suggest that armed/masked African-Caribbean youths emerged from the church and side streets and headed towards the mosque (*Guardian* 29 November 2005). We were informed by a senior West Midlands police officer that disorder actually broke out while the meeting was going on, so a public order response was made to 'sterilise the area before the meeting was safe to disperse; the balcony was filled with gang members who left 15–20 minutes earlier'. Two days of rioting followed, initially by 30–100 youths rampaging along Lozells Road (*Guardian* 24 October 2005; UK Indymedia 2005; BBC News online 2005b) and later it had increased to 400–500 rioters (police interview) involving petrol bombs, cars being burned, South Asian shops looted and the South Asian Resource Centre being attacked. Further, four African-Caribbean youths were attacked (one of whom was fatally stabbed) by South Asian youths. There were also 'credible' sightings of groups of youths carrying petrol bombs, machetes and firearms (Independent Police Complaints Commission 2006). Indeed 23 firearm (mainly handgun) incidents occurred in three days: 13 on Saturday night/Sunday morning and 10 on Sunday night/Monday morning. On Saturday one shot from a shotgun was fired towards a line of public order police officers, resulting in one police officer receiving shotgun wounds to his leg (interview with police). In an incident apparently unconnected with the disorder, one African-Caribbean youth died from a shooting which occurred in the early hours of Monday 24 October (Independent Police Complaints Commission 2006). Over this period the police recorded 347 crimes including 5 attempted murders (Black Radley Report 2007: 5).

Policing the events

The policing of the events took two main forms. First, as well as involving WMMTS in an attempt to de-escalate the situation at a grassroots level, the police through their Gold strategy operations[3] engaged in multi-agency consultation in addition to daily communication with representatives from the two main communities, and especially so with the African-Caribbean community that felt particularly aggrieved (police interview). Secondly, the police mounted an operation (code-named *Operation Javari*) to deal with the 'escalation of violence and disorder' in Lozells and Handsworth area (IPCC 2005). This latter form involved saturation policing (including the deployment of helicopters, dogs and armed police officers) entailing more than 7,000 policing hours, with 600 police officers being deployed each day. The operation commenced on Thursday 20 October, with patrols in neighbouring Perry Barr. Police patrols then increased on Friday and throughout the weekend. Heavy rain may also have contributed to further crowd dispersal. One week after riots, 600 police officers were still patrolling the Handsworth and Lozells area (UK Indymedia 2005; BN Village 2005).

Root causes – wider contextual factors

While rumour would seem to have been the immediate cause of the escalation of conflict in Lozells, a number of deeper underlying determining factors need to be taken into account. In order to understand these, it is necessary to consider the wider historical, socio-economic and environmental contexts of the area, which may be summarised as follows.

Economic and political marginalisation

The Black Radley Report (2007), commissioned by Birmingham City Council, provides a rather bleak picture of social reality in the Lozells area:

97

The Lozells and East Handsworth ward is the most populous and the most overcrowded of all the Birmingham wards. It has the highest ethnic minority population ... It has high levels of unemployment; high levels of teenage pregnancy; high levels of crime, youth crime, hate crime and drug crime; high levels of gang violence and anti-social behaviour; the third highest asylum and refugee population in Birmingham; and significant health inequalities. (Black Radley Report 2007: 5)

According to the 2001 Census of Population the same ward contained 28,806 residents, 29.6 per cent of whom were under 16 years of age; 57.2 per cent were between 16–59, and 13.3 per cent were 60 and over. Ethnic minorities constituted 82.6 per cent of the population in the ward (excluding those with a White Irish background), compared with 29.6 per cent for the whole of Birmingham and 11.8 per cent for the country as a whole. Over 50 per cent of these were of South Asian (mainly Pakistani) origin, and 20 per cent African-Caribbean, compared with 3.6 per cent and 1.8 per cent respectively for the whole country. Also, 55.0 per cent of households lived in rented accommodation (Birmingham City Council 2006a; Office for National Statistics 2007). Further 19.7 per cent of residents in the Lozells and neighbouring Aston and Newtown areas were unemployed in 2001, compared with 4.2 per cent for the whole country (Birmingham City 2006b: 22; Office for National Statistics 2002).

Some commentators have argued that within such socio-economic conditions found in Lozells though, there is relative economic and political marginalisation of the African-Caribbean community compared with that of the South Asian community. In this respect the area has changed over time from being primarily African-Caribbean to the African-Caribbean community seeing 'their' area increasingly taken over by South Asians (*Guardian* 24 October 2005). This would seem to be especially visible simply in terms of the number of shops that are now South Asian-owned on Lozells Road, which Vulliamy, writing in the *Guardian* (29 November 2005), estimates to be approximately 90 per cent. In this respect Appleton (2005) describes the apparent 'economic disparity' between the communities as being visible from a 'glance down the Lozells Road'. She suggests that South Asian run shops include:

a substantial supermarket, a smart restaurant and two Asian clothes shops. A large new mosque is nearly finished ... . By contrast, there are only a handful of British-African-Caribbean-run shops – two takeaways, a hairdresser, and a run-down grocery store.

Further, not only do the South Asian shops cater for the African-Caribbean market, but suggestions are that they have increasingly also been intruding into a traditional African-Caribbean preserve, namely that of hair and beauty products. Vulliamy (*Guardian* 29 November 2005) quotes a 'militant black view' on these developments put by one of his interviewees:

We have a South African situation here … White on top, coloured Asian in the middle and African at the bottom. If you want a taxi – Asian. If you want petrol – Asian. Off-licence – Asian. Access to banks – Asian. Even Afro-Caribbean food – Asian.

A South Asian interviewee, in contrast, argues that:

We arrived on Lozells Road just after the high-street stores were closing … . Property was cheap and we put everything we had into the area. Now, it is revived, there are no vacant lots. I refuse to say that it has anything to do with racism; it is about business competition, and certain individuals wanting to create trouble because of competition for public funding – that is all.

The latter point is also raised by Appleton (2005), who stresses that given the contemporary nature and structure of local authority politics and regeneration funding 'different groups are encouraged to play up their victimhood and unique cultural identities, in a bid for public funds and social authority'. This problem would seem to be exacerbated by two further factors. First, there seems to be an apparent political marginalisation of one community over another. In this respect, a West Midland police interviewee argued that 'the South Asian community is less fragmented and better represented, even in terms of local councillors'. Secondly, there is a lack of political representation of certain groups within both communities. To this end, the Black Radley Report (2007: 12) pointedly states:

There is a strong perception that political and community leadership in this area of the City is partisan, out of touch with the realities of specific groups (including ethnic groups, age groups, gender groups) and, as a result, unable to represent the views and needs of those groups.

Rival gangs

An additional contextual issue is a history of drug-related gang violence in the Lozells area and in this respect one cannot ignore the possibility of rival gang involvement in the disorders. Indeed, Appleton (2005) depicts the disturbances as resembling 'gangfights' rather than 'communities in revolt'. The two main African-Caribbean gangs, who are split geographically, are the Burger Bar Boys and the Johnson Crew, their names being derived from two cafés in Handsworth (Wilson 2005). Rivalry between these two gangs resulted in a drive-by shooting and deaths of two African-Caribbean female bystanders in 2003 (BBC News online 2005a). According to a senior West Midlands Police interviewee, these two gangs are especially involved with crack cocaine and cannabis, and differ from the South Asian drug criminality in the area which is more organised, more covert and entails heroin. The Black Radley Report (2007: 15) also mentions that:

> There is a view that the inhabitants of Lozells appear to have reached a point where crime and drugs are regarded as a normal way of life … . A significant number of boys are involved in local gangs and illegal activities.

In this respect, the senior West Midlands Police interviewee stressed that there is an inevitability of 'individuals with a high street profile' becoming involved when tension in the area reaches a certain stage, as it did during the Lozells disturbances. However, these may equally have acted to escalate as well as de-escalate the tensions through 'self-policing'.

Criticisms against the police

Concerning more immediate factors, some commentators levelled three main criticisms of the police's handling of the events. The first questioned the choice of the venue on Saturday evening following the shop protest, given that it was held at a church frequented primarily by African–Caribbean community members; also, its location and timing, given that the church was in geographical proximity to the local mosque and that the meeting was held in the early evening when, during the current Ramadan celebrations, there would be passing traffic to the mosque (Dosanjh 2006). In this respect, the Silver Commander of the police operation informed us in interview that he was well aware of criticism concerning the choice and timing of venue, but it 'was regarded as a sensible strategy at the time and in that context'. The second criticism comprised a 1,000-strong petition earlier that week urging the police to take more urgent action concerning the alleged rape, and thirdly that the police arrived late on the scene of the Lozells Road rioting (Dosanjh 2006; UK Indymedia 2005).

Present realities

The state of post-riot 'normality' still exists in Lozells and Handsworth today, which given the reality of the area means 'a situation of chronic tension' (police interview). Certainly, in the aftermath of the disturbances a 'committee of senior people from across the City' was formed into the Lozells Partnership Group which in turn led to the Black Radley Report (2007). However, the report concludes: 'Since the riots of the 1980s ... the health, employment, skills, regeneration and social problems remain' (Black Radley Report 2007: 31). As a West Midlands Police interviewee indicated, it is questionable to what extent the Black Radley Report was simply seen as an end in itself and whether there has been any significant increase in local funding since the disturbances.

Conclusion: comparing differences

Rioting being founded on rumour is somewhat unique in instances of disorder in Britain, although this is nothing new in the USA. In this respect Waddington (1992: 57–9) points to three early instances of rioting founded on rumour. The first occurred in Harlem in 1934 following a rumour that a black youth had been killed after being caught shoplifting. The second, in Detroit in 1943, concerned a rumour that a black woman and her baby had been murdered by a group of whites. The subsequent rioting resulted in 25 black and nine white deaths. Vulliamy (*Guardian* 29 November 2005) mentions a concurrent rumour at the time that a white woman had been raped and murdered by a group of black men. The third example, to which Waddington refers, was again in Harlem, in 1943 where it was rumoured that a black soldier had been shot and killed by a white police officer. In contrast to the Lozells events, however, none of these former examples resulted in black against black disorders.

To understand the Lozells disorder in a little more depth, this concluding section compares the 2005 events with earlier riots that occurred in the Lozells and neighbouring Handsworth area during the 1980s.

Handsworth riots 1981

Following the inner-city riots which occurred in Bristol in 1980 and Brixton 1981, a number of other riots took place around the country, including three nights of rioting in Handsworth. Although the Scarman Inquiry report did mention that Birmingham local councillors felt that factors such as a remote police organisation, unemployment and alienation (particularly on the part of African-Caribbean youth) played a part in the riots (Scarman 1982: 220–1), it pointed to the Handsworth riots as likely to have substantially consisted of a 'copy-cat element' and the police-community relations to have been 'generally, though not universally' sound (Scarman 1982: 33). Waddington (1992: 90) questions this finding, pointing to a significant factor in all of the riots at that time being that they 'were set against a background of intense and arbitrary stop-and-search operations' by the police, primarily against African-Caribbean youths.

Handswort/Lozells riots 1985

While not an issue concerning the 2005 riots, one factor in the Handsworth/Lozells riots of 1985 would also seem to be overly repressive policing policy and practice, in that a harsher regime against drug and minor traffic offences was instituted following a change of Police Superintendent (Benyon and Solomos 1987: 6; Rex 1987: 109; Waddington 1992: 91). Indeed, the Silverman Inquiry report, instituted by Birmingham City Council, specifically points to the 'trigger' being the arrest of an African-Caribbean male concerning a suspected traffic laws offence and an apparent physical assault of an African-Caribbean woman by police officers during the scuffle. Interestingly for our comparison with the 2005 riots, it is questioned whether or not the assault actually occurred as no woman came forward later (Silverman 1986: 53–5). In any event, there followed two days of rioting, mainly on the part of African-Caribbean youth, during which two South Asian men died when their post office was set alight (Benyon and Solomos 1987: 5).

Another potential factor considered by the Silverman Inquiry was racism directed by the African-Caribbean community against the

South Asian community in that again, like the 1981 and the 2005 disorders, South Asian shops were attacked. However, although accepting 'a certain amount of friction' had existed between both communities (Silverman 1986: 78), the report found that:

The fact that Asian shops were attacked is simply because the shops were there, and the great majority of shops in this area, in Lozells Road and other parts of Handsworth, are mostly Asian owned shops. In fact, the rioters themselves included a few Asian youths and the shops damaged or destroyed included Afro-Caribbean shops, and shops belonging to White: Polish and Greek. (Silverman 1986: 79)

The report does, however, point to continuing problems of housing and unemployment. Concerning the latter, it states that unemployment in Birmingham as a whole in January 1986 amounted to 21 per cent, and 26 per cent for males. This compared with a rate of 38 per cent in January 1985 for Handsworth alone (being almost three times higher than the national average at that time), 46 per cent for males and 54 per cent of those aged between 16–18 being unemployed (Silverman 1986: 37–8). In this respect, the report especially highlights unemployment as a major underlying factor in the disturbances:

The Tribunal has investigated many contributory causes to the recent riots. The total of these causes in a complex and difficult matter, but there is one central theme from which many problems flow, and which stands out above all others: and that is the problem of mass unemployment. ... Unemployment in Handsworth/Lozells is one of the worst, perhaps the worst, in the whole country. ... It is surely no accident that the riot happened in Handsworth. (ibid.: 38)

To conclude, it is worth reiterating that in 2001, the unemployment rate in Lozells and neighbouring Aston and Newtown areas of Birmingham amounted to not merely three times higher than the nation as a whole as in 1985, but almost five times higher than the national rate. However, as has been stressed, unemployment can only account for one factor contributing to the riots. While we have indicated significant differences here in the immediate superficial determining factors giving rise to the riots in the Handworth/Lozells area between those of the 1980s and 2005, the underlying wider contextual factors in common would seem not only *not* to have improved in the intervening period as indicated in the Black Radley Report, but perhaps even intensified.

Notes

1 To this end, it draws from a number of interviews undertaken by the author with current and former senior West Midlands Police officers, one of whom was a member of the Lozells policing strategy team.
2 This case was later dropped for lack of evidence following a failed identity parade.
3 Police forces in the UK designate a hierarchy of 'Gold', 'Silver' and 'Bronze' categories to command officers in public order situations, with the 'Gold' commander maintaining overall control.

Part III

The French Riots, 2001–2008

Chapter 9

The French riots and urban segregation

Hugues Lagrange

Introduction

The three weeks of rioting in October and November 2005 were exceptional, even by French standards where protests are a living tradition. The very magnitude, intensity and spectacular nature of these riots drew the attention of the international press. But what made France the scene of these riots? Conditions of anger and frustration, a propensity for bravado and craving for media exposure are all permanent features in the lives of youths from poor neighbourhoods. So why in 2005 did it all blow up into short but repeated clashes, the burning of cars, spilling over its confines and expanding the epicentre of the riots? Why did the fires burn so brightly in the autumn of 2005 in particular, though not previously and certainly not to this degree? As often happens, local players and observers all claimed: 'We saw it coming'. Many a time, we also heard the argument that media coverage of the initial clashes is sufficient to explain their spread among youth groups through a copycat effect. But why, then, did these dynamics not persist in 2007 and, moreover, why did they not occur to this degree between the years 1980–2004?[1]

This chapter tries to shed some light on the underlying causes of the riots by analysing relevant social and structural dimensions, notably the demographic, housing, employment and segregation patterns of the towns involved. At the outset of the riots, I hypothesised that such behaviour was a spectacular extension of the type of ordinary misconduct – petty thefts for 'fun', insulting policemen, causing damage, joy-riding, travelling without tickets on public transport – regularly engaged in by the youth of these housing estates.

Several of my earlier or ongoing studies (Lagrange 2007) on the socialisation of adolescents in poor neighbourhoods had suggested that misbehaviour of this nature actually stems from the relative deprivation and frustration caused by youths negatively comparing their circumstances with those of other, more affluent sections of society. There seems a distinct possibility, though, that the frustration arising in this case may also have a fundamentally symbolic underpinning, related to feelings of rejection and humiliation. It is difficult to explore directly the sense of hurt pride, injustice and resentment that we take to be underlying the riots. However, what we *are* able to do with relative ease is explore any links between, on the one hand, the characteristics of particular locations – for example, whether they are highly segregated or a designated ZUS, ZRU (tax free zone) or ANRU – and the people who inhabit them (whether young, old, migrant, poorly educated or unemployed) and, on the other hand, their propensity to riot.

Locations of the November riots

So what were the typical contexts in which the rioting occurred? Which towns and neighbourhoods were most notably affected and why? In a bid to answer such questions, we took as our global point of reference towns of more than 65,000 inhabitants outside Île-de-France (Paris and its region) and towns with more than 25,000 inhabitants in Île-de-France – a total of 210 towns overall. To begin with, we then codified the *intensity* of the rioting occurring in the towns of this size, which we measured according to the simple index of the number of days on which such violence actually occurred. This index was then correlated against a broad spectrum of possible characteristics of the 210 towns included in the sample (see Table 9.1, below).

Contextual aspects of their development

Based on our evidence, it is possible to make a number of generalisations about the context in which the rioting developed and spread.

First, it is observable how the riots primarily originated from, and then spread across, those public housing estates known in France as Sensitive Urban Zones (ZUSs). Only a small fraction (some 15 per cent) of the neighbourhoods involved are not classified as ZUSs

Table 9.1 French towns with more than 65,000 inhabitants (more than 25,000 in Île-de-France): Correlation between intensity of the November riots and characteristics of the population of the towns.

	% less than 20 years	% of illiteracy	% of house-holds with 6 and more members	Existence of a ZUS	Jobs created in ZRUs	Renewal agreement signed (ANRU)
Number of riot days	0.49***	0.40***	0.57***	0.31***	0.27***	0.28***

Number of towns constituting the sample: 210.
Percentage of population less than 20 years of age: in the town or in the ZUS if the town has one.
Percentage of illiteracy: in the town or in the ZUS if the town has one.
Percentage of households of 6 and more members: in the town or in the ZUS if there is one.
Number of riot days: 0 = no riots, 1 = one day of riots, 2 = 2 or more days of riots.
Existence of a ZUS: 1 if the town has a ZUS, 0 if not.
Jobs created in the enterprise zone (see below): log (net jobs created in the enterprise zone between 2000 and 2004)
ANRU renewal agreement (see below): 1 if the town has signed one of the first 60 demolition/reconstruction agreements, 0 if not yet signed.
***: significant at 1/1000

(see Appendix). In terms of gauging the relative impact of these riots, we should caution that the simple index of the absolute number of cars burnt could actually be misleading. Based on this index alone, the most urbanised spaces – Paris, Lyon, Marseille, Bordeaux, Toulouse, the North and the north-east border of France – are those that stand out as the worst affected. However, a simple calculation of the number of riot days in each *département* (administrative subdivision), weighted according to the population of the towns,[2] shows that the relatively worst affected are those areas adjoining Seine-Saint-Denis *département* in the north of Paris – *départements* that are not so urbanised. We would therefore be mistaken to regard these riots as having been the monopoly of large cities.

That said, we are not aware of any riots having occurred where the actors involved came from middle-class or affluent neighbourhoods.

Among the 25 ZUSs where the median income was the highest in relation to the larger town which they form part of, three experienced riots, while among the 25 ZUSs with the lowest income (on an average approximately one third of the towns) about ten experienced riots. It therefore seems fair to say that riots are more likely to occur in towns where income levels within public housing neighbourhoods are much smaller than average than those existing elsewhere in the town as a whole. This situation prevailed, for example, on the 'La Source' housing estate (*cité*), which is embedded in the town of Orléans.

Second, it is imperative for us to reiterate the point that the age structure of the inhabitants in relevant housing estates appears to have been another important factor in the rioting. Those neighbourhoods tending to be involved in the November riots were those where the percentage of the under 20s age group was very high (at least 35 per cent). However, it should also be pointed out that, even in Seine-Saint-Denis, the *département* most affected by the riots, there are towns with large housing estates whose residents are disproportionately represented in the under-20s age range, which nonetheless remained calm. Having a relatively youthful age structure is, therefore, insufficient in itself to qualify a town to have riots.

Third, one might well speculate that unemployment, especially among the youth, is likely to have affected their propensity to riot. In addition to the demoralising effect of their own jobless status, young adults may consider the unemployed condition of older people of working age as a further disincentive and source of despair. Improvements in national employment levels between 1997 and 2001 failed to benefit those individuals under 25 years old lacking qualifications. Indeed, there is a correlation between the consistently high levels of unemployment among this group (35–40 per cent) and correspondingly high levels of delinquency among adolescents living nearby. The main mechanism through which unemployment levels influence adolescent delinquent behaviour is the difficulties their elder siblings have in finding employment (Lagrange 2003). If, on the one hand, unemployment of the less qualified has declined slightly since 2002, on the other, that of youth from the neighbourhoods who are the most qualified – i.e. college educated – has increased, making them the principal victims of discrimination on the labour market. At the same time, the abolition of *emplois jeunes* (jobs subsidised by the state, created in 1997 by Prime Minister Lionel Jospin) in 2003 (after Jacques Chirac's election as President in 2002) and their tardy restoration under other appellations sent contradictory and demobilising signals to these youths. A number of youths who had in the past benefited from state-subsidised jobs – provided for a period of several years but unlikely to be transformed into permanent positions – managed to find employment in the commercial sector; however, their younger siblings feared that this transfer from subsidised to private sector jobs would no longer be available after 2004.

We have used an unemployment index of 15–25 years of age in 2005, only available for *départements* outside Île-de-France. We have also calculated an index of the differential unemployment rates between metropolitan areas, encompassed towns and their ZUSs. Unfortunately, though, we have had to depend on data from the 1999 census. We can, however, ascertain from this that a higher level of unemployment in a town,[3] in comparison with its metropolitan area, is directly correlated with the spread of riots in 2005.

Fourth, the urban locations where the riots tended mostly to occur were those residential areas which had benefited from the government's *politique de la ville*, i.e. they had been given political priority, not only because of the 'deprivation' that characterised them, but also because of the social tension that had been a feature of their existence over the past couple of decades (in the ZUSs, in particular). Indeed, those neighbourhoods where the riots occurred were invariably those accorded the 'maximum priority' even among those already singled out for special attention. Such locations were given the label *Zones Franches Urbaines* (ZFUs[4]). Today there are about one hundred ZFUs in France, each of which attempts to facilitate the establishment of enterprises via tax reduction programmes. Have jobs been created in these zones? Have these jobs benefited the residents of underprivileged neighbourhoods to the degree intended by the law? We have taken as an indicator of activity in the ZFU, the net jobs created between 2000 and 2004. Surprisingly, our analysis shows that there is a greater likelihood of riots occurring in locations where the ZFU has produced a relatively *high* number of jobs. This paradoxical link could be explained by the fact that precisely those ZFUs where the maximum jobs have been created were generally those most deprived (with an unemployment level much higher than parts of the town outside the ZFU).

Fifth, one frequently cited argument[5] maintained that a nationwide housing demolition and reconstruction programme, implemented by the government's *Agence Nationale de Rénovation Urbaine* (ANRU – National Urban Renewal Agency) may have played a significant, albeit inadvertent, role in promoting the riots. This programme, established under a law passed in August 2003, was designed to enhance processes of social integration and economic sustainability in neighbourhoods classified as sensitive urban zones. In practical terms, the law initially resulted in the eviction of families living in the most rundown buildings. This practice subsequently gave rise to an argument, most prevalent in the Paris area, that parents had found it more difficult during the time of the riots to prevent their children from going out at night. The basis of the argument was that parental authority had somehow been undermined, either by the insecurity created by the threat of eviction or the actual re-housing of families in hotels awaiting permanent reallocation of homes in some far-off area. Though only anecdotal in nature, this argument was so heavily promulgated in the Paris area that I felt obliged to investigate it more systematically.

It struck me that a more recent legal development may have been significant in this respect. Established by the *Agence Nationale de Rénovation Urbaine* (National Urban Renewal Agency), a renewal programme for the period 2004–2013 was authorised by new legislation, dated January 2005. Under this law 250,000 apartments were to be demolished, 400,000 rental-housing units rehabilitated, and 250,000 others upgraded into residential quarters. The sensitive urban zones covered by the agreements represent about 300,000 apartments, which is undoubtedly huge in number. The zones targeted are characterised by a large public housing stock (approximately 70 per cent) and by a vacancy rate of nearly 10 per cent. The National Observatory for Sensitive Urban Zones report (ONZUS Report) stated that 2005 should represent a year of peak activity in the fields of 'construction, demolition, rehabilitation and upgrading'.[6] The authors maintained that such demolitions 'can necessitate the mobilisation of vacant apartments in the existing stock on site or from any other public housing in order to re-house the families whose homes have been demolished...'. It is perfectly understandable to us why families who had suddenly been told that they would have to move to other apartments while waiting for accommodation, or stay in hotels requisitioned for this purpose, would have grown perturbed at the prospect – especially in the case of illegal immigrants. When we examine the location of the first 62 agreements signed in July 2005, with 67 other projects signed later, we see that most of the towns covered by these agreements were affected by the urban violence in November (see Appendix).

The towns that had signed an agreement with ANRU and those where the riots took place were mostly one and the same. The correlation is significant and seems to confirm the hypothesis that the initial measures taken by ANRU added to the apprehensiveness of the people living in the public housing neighbourhoods and fuelled resentment against the authorities. As usual, in the face of statistical evidence, one may object that some of the towns formally selected had not yet implemented this programme while others not selected had begun. It remains, however, that on average, as with the ZFU, those towns that were involved in the programme were the areas most in need of renovation.

Sixth, the non-French reader of this chapter may be surprised by the absence of systematic discussion of the ethnic characteristics of the neighbourhoods participating in the riots. This is due to the fact that, while census data provides information on the nationality of the residents of the towns, such information is not accessible at the neighbourhood level.[7]

It is notable that in the second week of the wave of rioting, especially in the west of the country, a number of towns where large families of black African origin are settled were apparently the scene of fights.[8] We have tried to ascertain whether this impression gained from anecdotal and media evidence is actually verifiable. Studies carried out on misconduct and learning difficulties in several towns in Île-de-France show that today there is clearly a marked tendency towards delinquency and school under-achievement among French-African children from large families. In the absence of precise statistics related to ethnic origin, we have been forced to operate on the basis of two approximations: first, the percentage of foreigners from outside the European Union in the town as a whole; and second, the percentage of large families (of six or more members in the ZUS when there is one, and in the town as a whole when there is no ZUS).

It can be seen on the basis of this analysis that the riots tended to occur more frequently in those sensitive urban zones (ZUSs) with relatively higher instances of large families comprising six or more members. The concentration of large families correlates very significantly with the geography of the riots.[9] The intensity of the riots is somewhat less closely related to the proportion of foreigners from outside the European Union in the town. The riots are not, however, linked simply to the percentage of youth of African ancestry in a town, which was the stereotype most commonly present in the media. They are much more precisely correlated with the level of segregation of these people. The degree of segregation of these groups within each town is a measure *independent* from the proportion of foreigners from African ancestry in the towns being considered.

We have thus constructed a dissimilarity index (i.e. spatial segregation) based on the ratio of nationals to foreigners,[10] both in the ZUS and, correspondingly, outside the ZUS (Figure 9.1). To provide a clearer picture, let us take as an example two towns, A and B, in which the percentage of foreign families (in dark grey) is absolutely identical, both in the sensitive zone (SA) and outside the sensitive zone (CA) but where the relative size of these groups differs. As we can see when comparing the dark grey and light grey areas in both towns, the percentage of segregation (or dissimilarity) is clearly higher in A, because the size of the sensitive zone is relatively larger. The coefficient of segregation simultaneously takes into account dissimilarity in the percentages of the different populations between the zones but also the relative weight of the zones within a whole (the town in this case).

Thus, we can apply this type of comparison to Paris and the three *départements* in its inner suburbs (Seine-Saint-Denis, Val de Marne, Hauts-de-Seine) by simplifying the spatial distribution as represented in Figure 9.2.

The only systematic spatial segregation index that we can construct on the basis of official census data in France merely distinguishes between French nationals and foreigners and this is what we have calculated in the absence of a more specific index. The percentage of foreign families in the ZUS can be interpreted as an approximate index (what economists refer to as a 'proxy') of the percentage of

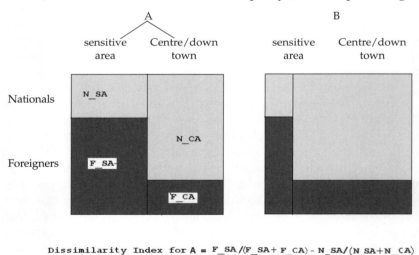

Dissimilarity Index for $A = F\_SA / (F\_SA + F\_CA) - N\_SA / (N\_SA + N\_CA)$

Figure 9.1 Coefficient of segregation or dissimilarity in two hypothetical towns A and B.

Paris and its suburbs

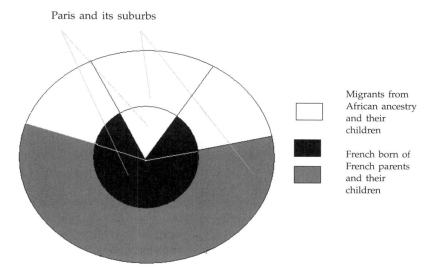

Migrants from
African ancestry
and their
children

French born of
French parents
and their
children

Figure 9.2 Dissimilarity in the Paris metropolis. Simplified distribution of
the population of Paris and the first *banlieue* circle.

families of African origin – considering that the large majority of
foreigners living in the ZUS are from Africa (mainly the Maghreb and
black Africa). This raw index is correlated, but rather inadequately,
with the geography of the riots. However, a simple tabulation of
the percentage of towns where riots took place as a function of the
segregation index of the foreign population between towns and their
ZUS, suggests that above a certain value of the dissimilarity index
(about 0.2),[11] the probability of occurrence of riots decreases (see
Figure 9.3 below).

The probability of the occurrence of riots is 45 per cent in towns
with little segregation (index 0.01). It is nearly twice as high (80
per cent) in towns where the segregation coefficient of the foreign
population between the ZUS and the rest of the town is 0.2, smaller
(60 per cent) in towns which have a higher segregation coefficient
of the foreign population (0.3 or 0.4). As a result it is necessary to
take this curvilinear effect into account. The probability of riots is a
little smaller in the more segregated zones – i.e. where confrontation
between the French and the foreign population is negligible – than it
is in areas with medium level segregation. The probability of riots is
the smallest in towns in which there is no segregation of the foreign
population (or no ZUS).

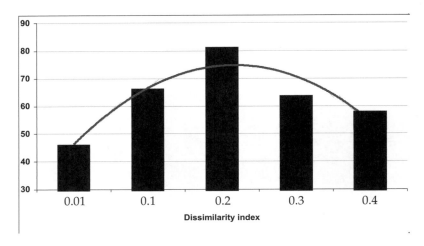

Figure 9.3 Percentage of towns that experienced riots according to the foreigners segregation index between the town and its ZUS(s).
Source: Computation by the author. French/foreigners dissimilarity index calculated for the population within the ZUS and outside the ZUS for each town.

Aside from those factors just mentioned, we also set about exploring the possible influence of a host of other characteristics of the towns studied. Thus, we have also taken into account the percentages of non-graduates and foreign families in the ZUS, or in the town as a whole where there is no ZUS. The number of variables tested is obviously limited to easily accessible information: those that are tested only provide a rough description of what characterises the 'time bomb' on the one hand, and the immediate reasons for concern on the other.

We have tested several probability models of the occurrence of riots by simultaneously synthesising the various contextual elements – the percentage of large families in the ZUS and the share of under-25s among the unemployed – and variables coding (1) the activity of ZFU, and (2) the location of demolition and re-housing programmes. In the models (1) and (2) we have classified towns correctly in 75–77 per cent of the cases and thus have made erroneous retrospective diagnoses in 23–25 per cent (see Table 9.2 below). The model (3) reproduces the analysis by taking as riot activity index the logarithm of the number of cars burnt. It is remarkable that despite the differences in construction between the two indices indicating the intensity of the riots, the explanatory variables and their contributions are very similar – in other words, the nature of the interpretation proposed is not greatly dependent on the index used to characterise urban riots.

Model (4) tests the hypothesis that the Far Right vote (for *Front National* and the much smaller party MNR) for the 2002 presidential election has a link with the same socio-demographical factors as the riots. This is partially true: this vote is correlated to the percentage of the illiterate population and the percentage of foreigners in the town. However, this vote is not related to the high prevalence of the large families in the town, and is inversely related to the unemployment differential between the town and the urban area where it is located. That is to say that the votes cast in favour of the Far Right parties are all the more numerous in those towns appearing to be 'doing better' economically than the metropolitan area to which the town belongs (cf. infra), but with a significant foreign population and a high level of illiteracy.

The retrospective prediction that the logistical model gives are not symmetrical: thus according to model (1), in 33 per cent of the cases there were no riots whereas 'conditions' were rife; against this, in 17 per cent of the cases there were riots whereas all the 'conditions' were not present. Every formal model has its limitations and this is certainly no different. However, at the very least, it does give us a basis to reflect on and generate further questions to address in our research.

The graph in Figure 9.4 illustrates the results of this analysis. The grey columns represent the number of days of rioting experienced in November 2005 by towns, the adjoining white columns shows the predicted number of days of rioting according to the logistic regression model (1) of Table 9.2.

Interpretation of the results

We can interpret the role of 'large families' in a simple and classical way, which goes something like the following: in these families, supervision of adolescents is difficult to administer; the fact that they are therefore not subjected to proximate discipline facilitates accounts for their involvement in the riots. However, even if this is true, it surely represents only part of the story. It is impossible to overlook the fact that, in these ZUSs, families with a large number of siblings tend to belong to one ethnic group in particular. Recent studies show that involvement in delinquency and assault by adolescents raised

Table 9.2 Ordered logistic regressions#. Variables explained: number of riot days in the *commune*; log of the number of cars burnt in the *commune*; % of dissenting votes.

Dependent variables	(1) No. of riot days in the town	(2) No. of riot days in the town	(3) Log no. of cars burnt	(4) Dissenting votes (votes for extreme right parties)
% of families of 6 or more members in the town	6.6***		2.9**	
% of non-graduates in the town		3.1***		7.1***
% of foreigners in the town		3.0**		4.8***
Variance unemployment rate in *commune* urban unity	2.94**	2.17*	–	–3.0**
Intervention by ANRU (yes/no)	2.4*	3.1**	2.3*	
Town with a ZFU (yes/no)		–	2.8**	
French/foreigners segregation between ZUS and Municipality	2.7**	2.6**	5.2***	
No. of towns	210	210	210	210
Pseudo_ R2	0.20	0.15	0.08	.12
Wald Chi2	80.5	83.3	66.7	59.0

#*Ordered logistic regression with Stata software. For the sake of simplification we have removed the thresholds separating the different modalities of dependent variables, but the tested models are not 'riots vs. no riots' but 'no riots vs. 1, 2 to 7, plus days of riots or discrete measures of number of cars burnt'.*
Dependent variables: No. of riot days: 0 = no riots, 1 = 1 day, 2 = 2 to 7 days, 3 = 1 week or more; log of no. cars burnt recoded in 6 positions; % of votes cast in 2002 for the FN* and the MNR (FN's scissionist party): dichotomised variable.
The segregation variable is the dissimilarity index between French nationals and foreigners within the ZUS and outside the ZUS for each town. We have linearised the index by taking differences to the modal value. The asterisks have the usual meaning: *significant to 5%, **to 1%,***to 1/1000.

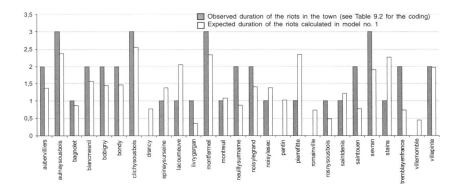

Figure 9.4 Towns of Seine-Saint-Denis; intensity of riots in November 2005 (in grey) and probability of the estimation of their intensity based on the explanatory variables used (in white)

in black Sahelian African families is considerably higher than the involvement of adolescents raised in families from the Maghreb and even more in comparison with those raised in indigenous French families.[12] Part of this over-involvement of adolescents from Sahelian Africa is linked to the number of siblings[13] – typically more in these families than in corresponding Maghrebian units – and to the poor educational qualifications of the parents. It is also associated with the academic failure occurring at the primary school level.[14] If we were to overlook the involvement of these youth from African immigration and in particular from Sahel, we would not be able to fully understand the specific nature of these riots, be they in the Paris area or in a chain of towns running through the West of France. These towns where families from Sahel (whose children are now grown up) settled do not figure among the riot zones during the previous decades (1980–1990s).[15] Although we cannot include it explicitly in the quantitative analysis of the riots, this suggests that the specific conditions of the socialisation of adolescents from black African families can explain the depth of their involvement in the autumn 2005 riots.

The fact that the dissimilarity index is a direct determination of the occurrence of riots, whose effect combines with the frequency of large families (model 1), suggests the possible significance of social segregation from the host society as a possible explanation of disorder.[16] It can easily be imagined how ethnic minority youth might perceive such segregation as the result of deliberate exclusionary policy, driven by racism, rather than the product of self-segregation practices at different levels of the social spectrum.

All things being equal, the salience of rioting is positively linked to higher unemployment levels in towns in comparison with the metropolitan areas in which such towns are located.[17] When we take into account the rate of youth unemployment in the ZUS, we find that it is negatively associated with the riots – i.e. the rate of unemployment among the 15–25 year olds does not appear empirically as a factor fuelling riots.[18] Monographic studies undertaken by the author in the Paris region show that risk of unemployment (measured by its rate among elder siblings) has disastrous consequences when it comes to socialisation or the feeling of injustice, independently of the concrete job prospects for the youths themselves. This indicates that the job outlook that counts is really one which affects families at large (see argument on page 110, and Lagrange 2003).

We can posit at least two possible interpretations of the association between the existence of an Enterprise Zone (ZFU) (and its implications for government job-creation investment in the area) and the occurrence of riots. First, the very act of ploughing in investment is a symbolic acknowledgement of the severe lack of local employment already existing in these zones. It is equally possible, however, that – as suggested by observers in the towns of Seine-Saint-Denis – the ZFUs have created expectations that they have not been able to fulfill. Certainly, they seem to be constantly consumed by a condition of relative deprivation/frustration, exemplified by the comments of one youth from Saint-Denis who complained: 'The jobs created around the *Stade de France* [the vast stadium built for the World Football Cup in 1998] are not for us'.[19] The same observation can be made regarding towns in Seine-Saint-Denis that have seen a reduction in the jobs for youths from poor neighbourhoods during years 2002–2004, in comparison with what it was several years ago, despite the expectation of jobs from the *Paris Aéroport* (a huge company) in that area.[20]

The statistical analysis also shows that the sites of the riots, especially during the first ten days, had no correlation with the geography of urban violence in France during the 1980s and 1990s. This absence of correlation indicates that the contribution of a culture of protest is likely to be small or non-existent. This absence of transmission of a culture of protest between the seniors and the participants in this riot episode explains the isolation of the 2005 rioters. Therefore, the inability of the political parties, specifically the Socialist party, whose average membership is over 45 years of age, found it difficult to play a role, leaving aside their political hesitations concerning the riots.

Conclusion

What really gave these riots their specific character is, first, the manner in which the incapacity of these youths to access social positions was combined with the new effects of ethnic segregation in poor neighbourhoods in France. The economic arguments have proven to be less effective in designing the geography of the riots than segregation, the percentage of large families of African ancestry and housing decay. The segregation of people of African origin is greater than that of immigrants from Europe.

According to the above analysis, the riots were not linked to the mere presence of youth raised in Muslim families. When taking into account relative proportions, Maghrebian youth have been less involved than Sahelian youth – also Muslims but living in wider and poorer families, in more segregated suburbs. A huge price has to be paid for the segregation of these districts – less effective schooling, stigmatisation of the people and thus the risk of greater unemployment, delinquency, larger subsistence budget for households. It also has cumulative effects, such as the unattractiveness of these neighbourhoods dissuades enterprises from establishing themselves there and drives out the more mobile inhabitants. This, we argue, is the underlying foundation of this riot episode. It is in line with the geography of public policies of the town and emphasises its obvious limits; it can very likely fuel the demand for recognition by youths from immigrant backgrounds in the form of revolt against institutions that in their eyes represent the state, in other words the police.

Like the revolts in earlier times and the videogenic strategies of contemporary pressure groups, the riots of November 2005 must be understood within the specificity of characteristics of the dialectics of structure and accident.

Notes

1 For a detailed analysis of the sociopolitical conditions of the breakdown of social cohesion, see Lagrange (1989).
2 Towns in these *départements* with a population exceeding 65,000 inhabitants.
3 In France, municipalities, if embedded in a larger urban area, keep their autonomy and distinct economic and financial characteristics; for example Lyon's metropolitan area, on average wealthy, encompasses poor municipalities like Villeurbane, Vénissieux, Vaulx-en-Velin. To simplify matters, we will use both terms 'municipality' and 'town' as synonyms.

4 These are zones where enterprises are exempt from the social security costs pertaining to the employer for new recruits for one or several years on condition that they reserve at least 25% of the jobs created for ZFU residents.

5 During November and December 2005, the *Conseil Général*, elected local authority of Seine-Saint-Denis, the *département* most affected by the riots, launched a number of public meetings between inhabitants and social services executives where this idea was raised several times (I was an invited expert at these meetings).

6 *Rapport de l'Observatoire National des ZUS* (2005). Paris: DIV, 57.

7 Dealing with the ZUS, we can only apply the distinction 'French/ foreigners', which thus disregards the importance of French citizens of foreign origin (mainly second-generation youth) and amalgamates foreigners of all origins.

8 The riots were able to recruit among the large families from Sahel because they were the latest arrivals and the large number of siblings made the task of socialisation very difficult as compared with other groups of poor immigrants.

9 The two variables – the high percentages of under-20s and also of large families – are closely linked.

10 It was impossible with public data to distinguish the nationality of foreigners when one considers subdivisions of the town or municipality (ZUS/non-ZUS areas).

11 This ratio varies between 0, no segregation, and 1, absolute segregation. The ratio of 0.4, in the French context expresses a relatively great dissimilarity or segregation.

12 Cf. Lagrange (2007). By 'indigenous French families' we mean families whose members are born in France at least since the parents' generation.

13 See Lagrange (2007).

14 If school success, given the same social background, of children of migrants from Europe and the Maghreb is somewhat better than that of adolescents from indigenous French families, that of sub-Saharan children is globally worse. In addition, for second-generation youths from North Africa holding the same qualifications, access to jobs is definitely more difficult than for youths of European origin.

15 The correlation coefficient with the distribution of riots in 2005 is small.

16 It cannot be substituted by other variables like the percentage of non-EU migrants in the town.

17 Level of unemployment measured by the 1999 census – there is to a certain extent some stability in the geographical distribution of unemployment.

18 This argument supports the idea that these riots were not motivated by direct economic incentives, but by a feeling of segregation and unfairness not linked to the actual rate of unemployment of youngsters.
19 Discussions with social activists working in liaison with the *Conseil Général* de Seine-Saint-Denis in December 2005.
20 These towns do not have ZFUs.

Appendix

Table 9.3 French towns with more than 65,000 inhabitants (more than 25,000 in Île-de-France): Number of riots and ZUS

	ZUS		
riots	no	yes	
no	69.1	33.6	100%
yes	30.9	66.4	100%

Table 9.4 French towns with more than 65,000 inhabitants (more than 25,000 in Île-de-France): Number of riots and Renewal agreements signed

National renewal agency agreement

riots	no	yes
no	48.8	14.7
yes	51.2	85.3
Total	100%	100%

Table 9.5 French towns with more than 65,000 inhabitants (more than 25,000 in Île-de- France): Number of riots and large households

Households 6 and more	Riots no	yes	
0–3%	75.0	25.0	100%
4–7%	45.3	54.7	100%
8–12%	18.5	81.5	100%
more than 12%	17.4	82.6	100%

Chapter 10

Urban renewal = riot revival? The role of urban renewal policy in the French riots

Renaud Epstein

Introduction

Following the passing of the Law for the City and Urban Renovation on 1 August 2003, hundreds of French towns undertook demolition and reconstruction work designed to radically remodel the mega-housing complexes in their neighbourhoods. Two years later, a wave of riots swept inexorably through these neighbourhoods. One is therefore entitled to wonder whether the National Urban Renewal Programme, and its plan to invest close to 40 billion Euros in 530 neighbourhoods, played a causal role in the autumn 2005 riots?

The question may appear paradoxical, as urban renewal aims specifically at resolving the structural problems of these neighbourhoods – problems that have been suggested as the underlying cause of the riots in the first place (i.e. mass unemployment, poverty, stigmatisation and discrimination). Nevertheless the question still deserves to be asked, if only because several foreign commentators on these riots, looking for points of comparison, have found similarities with North American towns in the second half of the 1960s. In fact the latter also had some connection with urban renewal operations that took place in the black ghettos (Castells 1977; Fullilove 1994), whose logic was denounced by civil rights activists in a powerful slogan, borrowed from Malcolm X: 'urban renewal = Negro removal'. It is not necessary to cross the Atlantic to establish a link between urban renewal and past riots. A simple perusal of French history will suffice: the first urban renewal operation conducted in Paris between 1853 and 1870 resulted in a popular uprising, the 'Paris Commune'.

This modernisation drive in the capital, undertaken by Napoleon III and his Prefect, Georges-Eugène Haussmann, was in response to the great fear felt by the bourgeoisie after the three-day revolt in 1848, which resulted in the overthrow of the July Monarchy (Faure 2004). Plans had been drawn up for a radical transformation of Paris's urban setting, which included the resettlement of workers in the northern and eastern suburbs. These changes had given rise to social conflicts and economic problems that, in equal measure with the 1870 defeat by Germany, had triggered the 1871 revolt, ending with the installation of a short-lived proletarian government (Harvey 2003, and for a discussion of this neo-Marxist reading of Haussmann's Paris, see Faure 2008). The possibility that contemporary urban renewal may have had a similar inducing effect is explored in this chapter. Following a brief review of the history of the *politique de la ville*[1] implemented from the early 1980s onwards (ironically, as a civic reaction to earlier riots), we shall examine statistical and empirical data which enables us to address the possible link between the national programme for urban renewal and the 2005 riots.

Politique de la ville: a policy prompted by the riots

Very few French people remember the sporadic riots that occurred in the Lyon suburbs at the end of the 1970s. Yet the disorders that set ablaze the mega-housing complex of the Minguettes in the same Lyon suburb in 1981, two months after the election of François Mitterrand, have left a deep scar not only on collective memory, but also on French public policy; indeed, the Minguettes events gave birth to a policy specifically directed at the social mega-housing complexes, the *politique de la ville* (see also Jobard and Hamidi in this volume). This policy increased in importance during the last quarter of the century, as other riots took place in the areas it targeted (Bachmann and Le Guennec 1996).

In the aftermath of the Minguettes riots, the government decided to set up three consultative groups that were meant to tackle problems relating to the integration of youth, prevention of crime and social development of deprived neighbourhoods. Reports by these bodies put forward similar diagnoses and recommendations – namely, that prior and existing policies in the relevant areas were altogether too rigid and over-centralised and that it was therefore necessary to replace them with more flexible and bottom-up initiatives.

Several schemes recommended by these reports were implemented and actually served as the framework of the *politique de la ville*: for example, social development of neighbourhoods, local taskforces for the integration of youth, and municipal councils for the prevention of delinquency. At the same time, the Ministry of Education introduced a policy of 'priority educational zones' (ZEP) which targeted these very localities. Within the framework of these schemes, the state allocated additional funds to local governments that were willing to try out the new programmes. These programmes presented novel characteristics, not previously known in French public policy, including: comprehensive approach (articulation of urban and social initiatives), transversality (involvement of several ministries), targeting (based on identified areas and not on social categories), and citizenship (through support to associations which unified the dynamic forces existing in their neighbourhoods, and which posed a constructive challenge to the lack of social and urban services).

The *politique de la ville* emerged as a consequence of the 1981 riots and spread to an increasing number of neighbourhoods during the 1980s (from 148 in 1984 to nearly 500 in 1988), in the context of industrial restructuring, mass unemployment and consequential problems of community life. It evolved radically after the 1990 Vaulx-en-Velin riots, which re-occurred in the Lyon suburbs, after the death of a disabled rider on a motorbike during a police chase. Two months later, François Mitterrand placed the *politique de la ville* at the top of his second mandate's political agenda. Thereafter, several laws were passed for a more equitable distribution of public housing and financial resources among the rich and poor districts in the agglomerations. The first urban regeneration operations were initiated in 13 *cités*. Each ministry was ordered to participate in the *politique de la ville* exercise, which they did by setting up several schemes involving an increasing number of neighbourhoods (751 in 1995, 1,300 in 1999).

The experimental policy implemented in some neighbourhoods in the early 1980s alongside the administrative system thus made way for a national umbrella policy applicable to all French cities (Donzelot and Estèbe 1994). But this policy followed a bottom-up logic as its content was determined on the basis of diagnosis and projects put together in each town by government services, elected representatives and heads of various institutions (low-income housing companies, employment agencies, social security agencies, etc.). These actors had a diversified inventory of strategic options at their disposal, corresponding to a heterogeneous understanding of the problems. They could consider these neighbourhoods from the angle of resources, handicaps or symptoms (Béhar 1995; Kirszbaum 2004). Thus,

- The initial approach took the form of support to associative initiatives in working-class neighbourhoods. The *politique de la ville* endeavoured to empower their inhabitants by obtaining the means to develop their individual and collective resources.

- The second approach involved reinforcing existing public utilities, and the resources at their disposal, to compensate for the disadvantages of the neighbourhoods and their residents. That is to say, based on the logic of affirmative action focused on certain districts on a socio-economic basis rather than by special measures for certain ethnic minorities.

- In addition to these two neighbourhood-centric approaches, a third one considered them as symptoms of a crisis whose causes were to be found in the malfunctioning of agglomerations and framework policies of the central and local governments. Thus the problems observed in neighbourhoods could only be dealt with on a broader scale (town or metropolitan). At best, neighbourhoods acted as a testing ground for new modes of town management.

From 1981 to 2002, the priority given by successive governments to one or the other of these approaches was never mutually exclusive. It was always left to local players to adapt and combine them on the basis of locally defined diagnoses and priorities. Despite this diversity, various evaluations have enabled the preparation of a general balance sheet of 20 years of *politique de la ville*. What emerges from these evaluations is that it appears to have had a considerable effect on public action. The *politique de la ville* has served as a model – in the dual sense of prototype (experimentation) and ideal (exemplarity) – for numerous policies in an institutional context disrupted by the decentralisation laws of 1982–1983. The measures conceived in a compartmentalised and top-down manner, and applied equally in all French towns, made way for more bottom-up and transversal policies, ensuring that town mayors were in control of local public action. However, there is no doubt that the initiative has generally failed to achieve its intended impact. While the *politique de la ville* and its actions may have improved the social and career prospects of some residents of the targeted neighbourhoods, it did not succeed in encouraging them to stay. Therefore, as revealed in the 1990 and 1999 censuses, the concentration of poor, insecure and isolated people actually increased. The results have not improved since then. On the contrary, the recent improvement in the statistical sources has confirmed the magnitude and the widening of the gap separating the neighbourhoods targeted by the *politique de la ville* from their environment on a multitude of inputs: unemployment, academic failure, poverty, feeling of insecurity, well-being, etc. (Observatoire national des ZUS 2007).

This failure of the *politique de la ville* is not really surprising, as additional financial resources granted by the government to this policy after each local riot in the 1990s were never enough to compensate for the discriminatory effect of other public policies. Whether it is school, social or employment policies, French authorities always distribute fewer resources per inhabitant to the poor housing estates than to other neighbourhoods. In some cases, the implementation of the *politique de la ville* in targeted *cités* or neighbourhoods was in fact accompanied by a withdrawal of regular facilities, reinforcing the feeling among residents of being abandoned and ostracised.

The result was not very positive. Consequently, Jean-Louis Borloo, appointed *politique de la ville* Minister after the 2002 general elections, received full support to implement a radical reform. His Law for the City and Urban Renovation of 1 August 2003 focuses state urban policy action on a single issue: urban renovation through a national programme aimed at 'destroying urban ghettos'. The objective is to restructure the most deprived neighbourhoods and attract new populations through major work on housing: the demolition of 250,000 dwellings in tower blocks replaced by as much in detached houses or small buildings, rehabilitation of another 400,000 by 2013. Five hundred and thirty neighbourhoods are currently involved in the programme.[2] The 10 billion euro national subsidy for local operations stems from credits from various sources, combined to form a one-step funding centre: state, social partners, and *Caisse des Dépôts et Consignations* (public bank). The objective of this pooling of credits into a single agency, the *Agence Nationale pour la Rénovation Urbaine* (ANRU) (National Agency for Urban Renewal), is to simplify the usual financial channels, and thus improve their effectiveness while shortening allocation times.

Thus, the former transversal and local *politique de la ville* was replaced by a town planning policy monitored from Paris (Epstein 2005). The evolution is not merely institutional, as it is accompanied by a strategic shift: the *politique de la ville* is no longer a question of the endogenous development of working-class districts or the transformation of agglomeration governance, but exclusively the diversification of neighbourhood residents through massive demolition of social housing dwellings in high-rise estates and the implementation of situational prevention methods. That is to say, a policy based on the belief that urban planning and architecture can solve social and security problems.

Urban renewal = riot revival?

Until 2003, the evolution of the *politique de la ville* took place *in reaction* to riots. The situation changed with the national urban renewal programme that preceded the 2005 riots. It would be hazardous to say that the riots were a reaction to urban renovation operations. Nevertheless, possible links need to be explored.

First of all it should be emphasised that these links were never mentioned by scholars, political leaders, grassroots workers and other commentators who spoke out during the 2005 riots, or in discussions that followed. One must remember that urban renewal is among the few public policies that have escaped from any kind of critical scrutiny after the riots.

Why should it therefore be necessary to study a hypothetical link between urban renewal and the riots, especially as such a possibility was not even raised by the few groups of inhabitants who mobilised in opposition to the demolition operations? The answer to this question is that those neighbourhoods subjected to urban renovation operations were more prone to disturbances than others. As Hugues Lagrange (2006b) demonstrates, riots broke out in more than 85 per cent of the towns that had been the first signatories of urban renovation agreements, whereas the same was true of only 66 per cent of towns with a neighbourhood targeted by the *politique de la ville*.

These results match those established by the *Conseil national des villes* (National Council of Cities). A study conducted by this official body (which answers directly to the Prime Minister) emphasised how the areas where the most violent events took place in November 2005 were actually those in which investments in urban renewal were the greatest.

To explain the correlation he established between the location of the first urban renewal operations and the November 2005 riots, Lagrange formulated the hypothesis that these operations probably contributed towards increasing the vulnerability of the most insecure groups in these targeted areas. Threatened by expulsion or re-housed in hotels while waiting for the allocation of new lodgings, the families living in the damaged buildings scheduled for demolition found it very difficult to prevent their children from going out in the evenings during the riots.

This explanation is not really satisfactory for it can only be applied to a few neighbourhoods. In most of the sites targeted by the national urban renewal programme, riots took place while the urban renewal projects were still in the study stage. Demolition operations had thus not yet begun. This chronological review takes us back to the connection between urban renewal and riots. The administrative data on which Lagrange based his work do not enable us to make a distinction between the towns signing up for urban renewal agreements, those that had started implementing the programme in autumn 2005, and those for which the operation existed only on paper. This point was raised by the president of ANRU and its director during a hearing conducted by a Senate investigative commission in May 2006. However, the argument used to challenge any questioning of their actions does not exhaust the question. It forces us to envision other hypotheses in order to explain why towns that signed to urban renewal agreements were more affected than others by the riots, including areas where demolition and re-housing operations provided for by the agreements had not yet been implemented. The answer may lie in other areas of enquiry.

A survey conducted in the weeks preceding the 2005 riots in four neighbourhoods covered by urban renewal allows us to advance supplementary hypothesis.[4] Data collected during this survey is all the more interesting as the town of Montfermeil, which includes a part of Les Bosquets, is one of the *cités* studied. This neighbourhood played a very special role in the autumn 2005 incidents:[5] disturbances started on 27 October in the adjoining Chêne Pointu *cité*, and from there immediately spread sideways. After three nights of fighting, police officials estimated that the violence had subsided. The explosion of a tear gas grenade in front of one of the mosques in Les Bosquets on the night of 30–31 October proved them wrong. This incident and its political handling palpably increased the tension. The violence then spread to several neighbourhoods in the Paris suburbs and, from November onwards, to the whole country.

Les Bosquets neighbourhood, which groups together dilapidated blocks of flats in co-ownership, and wherein newly-arrived immigrant families are concentrated,[6] has always been the focus of the government's *politique de la ville*. The Bosquets urban renewal agreement was one of the first signed in Île-de-France on 17 December 2004, during a highly publicised ceremony in the presence of the Minister, Jean-Louis Borloo. Under this agreement, 650 housing units (nearly two thirds of the total housing stock) were to be demolished and 520 units reconstructed. The total cost of this project was estimated at 350 million euros, making this urban renewal operation the costliest in France.

The exceptional resources thus mobilised for improving living conditions did not reduce tensions between residents and the authorities. On the contrary, the atmosphere of mutual distrust intensified as the project progressed. Convinced of the validity of their actions and the inability of the residents to grasp a complex project, public decision-makers did not try to involve them in its planning. As the project manager told us, 'Everyone thought that, considering the people affected by the operation and the state of the site, the project could only be a bonus for the residents. We never imagined that the people would disagree with us.'

On the eve of the riots, massive demolitions were planned but had not yet started. Residents were not given adequate information regarding the nature and scheduling of the project and the re-housing plans involved. True, some panels presenting the urban project had been displayed in public service centres in the neighbourhood, but they were far too vague and technical to satisfactorily answer the inhabitants' questions. The friction between decision-makers and inhabitants was, in fact, exacerbated during the course of the single public discussion forum devoted to the project. Worried about their future, uncertain about re-housing conditions, residents pelted the mayor of Montfermeil with questions: Were they going to be re-housed? If so, where, when and under what conditions? How much compensation would the owners of the demolished buildings be entitled to receive? These were all questions that the mayor steadfastly refused to answer. Known for his right-wing stand on immigration and elected by a white majority from residential areas which boasted individual houses (rather than high-rise apartments) around Les Bosquets, the mayor did not hide his intention to take advantage of urban renewal to induce some of neighbourhood residents to leave the commune. The meeting ended on a stormy note, leaving the residents in a state of anger (stones were thrown at the mayor's car) mixed with resignation, although it remained obvious that the dilapidated state of the neighbourhood made it fit for little other than demolition.

Far from removing public fears relating to the consequences of demolition, the rare attempts undertaken to inform the inhabitants about the project only served to reinforce them. At the same time, they gave credibility to a widespread feeling in the neighbourhood – and not without basis in the case of Montfermeil – that the urban renewal operation was aimed less at improving the living environment of the residents than at ensuring their expulsion from the area. In this conflict-ridden atmosphere, one spark was enough to set the whole neighbourhood ablaze – which is precisely what happened after the deaths of Zyed Benna and Bouna Traoré, trapped within an electric transformer where they had hidden in order to avoid a police check.

Not all urban renewal operations in France were undertaken with the same disregard for residents of the concerned neighbourhoods. In most towns, local representatives and social housing organisations have set up concerted procedures in conformity with the recommendations of the *Agence nationale pour la rénovation urbaine* (ANRU). Nevertheless, the official discourse of national and local officers in charge of urban renewal, which insists on the importance of residents' involvement in the operations to improve the living environment, hardly stands up to an empirical analysis. Collaborative procedures in three other sites, considered as models in the matter (Reims, Dijon and Nantes), indicate an overall lack of participation. Additional studies in half a dozen other sites corroborate this analysis: the inhabitants of targeted neighbourhoods are not even informed about the contents of urban renewal projects, just as long as these projects are not explicitly decided in agreements signed with ANRU. Neighbourhood residents were systematically left out of the definition of the urban renovation projects. Actions dubbed as concerted were developed, but they are really part of the communication and social support spheres, rather than participation. It is as if dialogue with the residents had only one objective: to obtain their consent to a policy which claimed to improve their living conditions, but which was defined without them and which they sometimes perceive – perhaps with reason – as being turned against them.

The correlation to be found between the signing of the urban renewal agreements and ensuing riots is therefore not that surprising. Seeking the consent of residents for urban renewal projects, more than their involvement in their development, was possibly accompanied by a reinforcement of distrust felt by the people towards public authorities who appeared to be refusing to listen to them. The urban renewal policy would have thus created a breeding ground for the riots, which can explain the speed with which they spread through sites hit by the ANRU to affect hundreds of localities.

When prophecy fails

This hypothesis, which focuses on the lack of recognition of inhabitants of disadvantaged neighbourhoods, may therefore throw some light on the underlying causes of the riots. It permits us licence to rephrase the slogan made popular by the leader of the Nation of Islam, by saying that, at least according to the evidence, *Urban renewal = riot revival*.

It would, however, be hazardous to attribute the 2005 riots entirely to the impact of the urban renewal programme, even if such an assertion seems more justified than the claim put forward by Jean-Louis Borloo that the programme reflected 'the expression of the inhabitants, that testifies to their rediscovered dignity' and made it possible to contain the spread of the autumn 2005 disturbances. Immediately after the riots, an efficient blame-avoidance strategy (Weaver 1986) was implemented by Borloo, who effectively reaffirmed that his policy had enabled the worst to be avoided:

> One has only to compare the sites that had benefited from ANRU funds and the trouble spots. You will observe that in neighbourhoods where urban renovation policy was underway, there was very little violence. Only a little tension by way of unconscious imitation could be seen.[7]

This false statement served thereafter as the basis for campaigns promoting urban renovation, which have continued unabated ever since. The success of the communication operation (the word *propaganda* would probably be more appropriate) is uncontestable. In the discussions that followed the riots, all public policy came under intense scrutiny. Notably the *politique de la ville* encountered severe criticism and no one defended it. Urban renovation has, on the other hand, completely escaped from being called into question. On the contrary, it was upheld by all political parties and a growing number of city mayors. This support was translated into acts through the extension of the programme in time and space. Towards this end, it was granted additional funds, which enabled the Minister to proudly affirm that his programme was more costly than that of the Channel Tunnel!

Notes

1 *Politique de la ville* does not mean, as a literal translation might suggest, urban policy for a city as a whole, but is rather the policy for 'disadvantaged neighbourhoods' with difficulties in the areas of housing and urban environment and in the socio-economic fields of employment, academic success, health, public order and security and urban services. The vast majority of these neighbourhoods are *cités* which provided homes after the Second World War for the population arising through demographic growth and the rural exodus, along with needs brought about by the country's industrialisation.

2 For a total investment budget of around 40 billion euros. A quarter of this amount corresponds to national subsidies managed by ANRU and three-quarters to local financing (local governments and social housing organisations) backed by subsidised credits.

3 It should be noted, however, that after having disputed its validity, they based themselves on the correlation established by Hugues Lagrange to defend their actions before the senators: the over-representation of the neighbourhoods listed in the urban renewal programme among the rioting neighbourhoods was thought to have proved the relevance of the targeting retained, which gave priority to the toughest neighbourhoods.

4 Surveys conducted in collaboration with Jacques Donzelot, commissioned by the Evaluation and Follow-up Committee of the ANRU (Donzelot and Epstein 2006).

5 For a detailed presentation of the events that took place in Clichy-sous-Bois and Montfermeil, see Kokoreff 2008.

6 We are talking about a multi-ethnic neighbourhood containing 39 per cent foreigners. More than 40 per cent of the population is less than 20 years old.

7 Forum de la presse quotidienne régionale, 17 November 2005.

Chapter 11

Riots and protest cycles: immigrant mobilisation in France, 1968–2008

Camille Hamidi

Introduction

The November 2005 French riots generated passionate interpretive discussions which were markedly in contrast to the silence of the rioters, and which highlighted the difficulty that the latter were experiencing in making themselves heard. Foremost among these discussants were advocates of a political – or proto-political – reading of the riots predicated on the theory of a 'generation gap'. This theory maintained that the young rioters had chosen to reject the supposedly more passive posture of their seniors, the 'big brothers',[1] who had aspired to join the mainstream via school and profession, especially in the public sector. The seniors had seen their hopes dashed by discrimination and unemployment, which was why the juniors harboured no illusions. Their revolt was thus both a mobilisation 'by proxy', on behalf of their seniors, but also a rejection of their perceived docility (Beaud and Masclet 2006; Kokoreff 2008).

Those students of political mobilisations by immigrants[2] will already have been familiar with the above explanation, due to its salience at the time of the 'March for equality and against racism' in 1983,[3] which symbolically marked the ascension of second-generation immigrants into the realms of political and media visibility. Participants and observers alike described the march as the first real immigrant mobilisation. Such action sought to put an end to decades of passivity during which the parents' generation had remained silent and submissive. As it happens, this perception was erroneous, since earlier generations had already mobilised on various previous occasions, particularly in the 1960s and 1970s. In the following section we revert to an historical overview of these migrant struggles and their failures, so as to try and understand the reasons for the recurrent amnesia affecting observers and concerned players, and to help to explain the persistence of urban riots in France.

Immigrant mobilisation: a subject still to be explored

For a long time immigration was considered an illegitimate field of research in France. Even though the situation has improved considerably in the last 15 years (Noiriel 1996; Sayad 2002), a sustained focus on collective action by French immigrant society has yet to be securely established.

This abiding lack of interest within the social sciences concerning immigration issues is a reflection of a wider indifference existing in French society. One reason for this has to do with the process of national construction, which (in contrast to, say, the United States of America) predated any great influx of migrants. Thus, while France has long incorporated a substantial 'foreign' presence, this section of its population has not been considered truly fundamental to its 'being' (Noiriel 1996). The second reason for this lasting invisibility is due to the way in which emigrating and immigrating societies, as well as the immigrant community, have allegedly conspired to maintain what Sayad (1999) refers to as a 'helpful illusion'. According to Sayad, this illusion actually comprises three separate components: first there is the illusion that immigration constitutes a temporary 'fix' which, in reality, always turns out to be permanent; the second illusion is that the immigrant presence continues to be justified according to its original *raison d'être* – i.e. as labour force brought up to France for conjectural labour market needs; and last there is the related illusion specifying the political neutrality, if not apathy, of the immigrants. To maintain this third illusion, immigration has to be conceived as the temporary export/import of people, and not as the long-term relocation of citizens. Such analysis enables us to appreciate the manner in which immigrants have traditionally been conceived from a solely economic perspective, as a temporary 'workforce', and *not* as political players.

To these explanatory factors we might add reasons related to the constitution of the different social sciences in France (Schnapper 1998). For example, French Marxism long gave precedence to the study of class over race in the study of processes of socio-political domination.

Methodological reasons also played their part: for instance, the belated introduction of field investigation as a recognised mode of enquiry was instrumental in holding back the study of French ethnic minorities.

Once French sociologists and political scientists finally did get round to showing an interest in the nation's immigrant population, they initially regarded them as objects and categories of public policy, and not as political subjects. This was partly due to the reasons outlined above, but it was also related to the fact that basic political entitlements, such as the right to create voluntary associations (finally passed in 1983) or the right to vote (promised by François Mitterrand during the 1981 presidential race), was denied to aliens. The study of the immigrant peoples' mobilisation was therefore slow to arrive, emerging timidly as it did towards the late 1980s.

Such as it is, the literature contains three major analytical strands. A common practice among some authors advocating *indifferentiation* is to apply to the specific field of immigrant mobilisation a general sociological interrogation, drawing on the sociology of social movements. Approaches in this vein tend to study *conscience constituents* (i.e. 'traditional' French political activists typically coming from Left organisations or parties, or from Christian organisations), rather than militant leaders from the immigrant milieu, in order to explain these 'improbable mobilizations' (Mathieu 2006; Siméant 1998; Péchu 2006); and whenever they show an interest in the latter, they tend to exclude from the analysis all that pertains to the specificity of these peoples resulting from their migratory trajectory or their ethnic origin (Hmed 2007).

Inversely, those we can qualify as advocates of *distinctiveness* tend to apply more focused problematics to the study of immigrant mobilisations, namely the problematics of integration and the dialectics of community/assimilation. These authors who generally view things from a Tourainian perspective (associated with the renowned sociologist, Alain Touraine), try to determine whether or not collective mobilisations may be indicators or instruments of the integration of these peoples; or on the contrary, symptomatic of the failure of this integration. But it sometimes happens that these very macro-sociological questions are not firmly supported *empirically* and are based on a particularly vague, polysemic concept – integration (Dubet and Lapeyronnie 1992; Jazouli 1986; Lapeyronnie 1987, 1992).

Lastly, we can identify a third, rather heterogeneous analytical trend, conceived of by scholars who are also, in different capacities, activists involved in the migrant struggle (Abdallah 2000; Bouamama

1994; Boubeker and Hajjat 2008; Hajjat 2006). This position induces them to be attentive to specific issues – such as the collective memory of mobilisations and its transmission from one generation to the next, or the question of the autonomy of these movements – and sometimes to neglect other issues, such as the study of motivations and the determinants of commitment. Keeping these specificities in mind, these studies prove to be rich and often innovative.

The history of immigrant struggles[4]

With the help of these different analytical traditions, we shall now traverse the history of immigrant mobilisations. Withtol de Wenden and Leveau (2001) propose a three-phased sequence to this history, which is often applied in the literature.

First sequence: from the late 1960s to the late 1970s: the primo-migrant mobilisations

In the 1950s and 1960s, immigrant mobilisation was chiefly directed towards the country of origin, around the struggle for independence, and after that, the relationship with the authoritarian regimes that were established south of the Mediterranean. As the prospect of returning became increasingly remote, due to tighter anti-immigration policy and the growing rigidity of French borders, the struggle shifted, such that major mobilisations were organised in the late 1960s around living and working conditions in France.

The immigrants mobilised themselves first in the factories where they worked, displaying a massive presence in the strikes of the early 1970s. The hegemonic figure that dominated the struggles at that time (Geisser *et al.* 2006)[5] was that of the 'migrant labourer'. Since the structural organisation of work in the factories was often carried out according to national origin (Pitti 2005; Sayad 1999), the immigrants sometimes conducted *de facto* independent struggles, but the 'worker' reference remained central to their mobilisation. With a few notable exceptions, such as the strike in the largest Renault car factory near Paris in 1973, which included demands pertaining to the rights of aliens and the fight against discrimination, their demands were not specifically related to immigration (Pitti 2001).

Running parallel to these factory-based mobilisations were instances of collective action connected with housing and living conditions. Two such examples are the mobilisations in the Pennaroya factories in 1971–1972[6] and the 'rent strikes' organised in the Sonacotra[7] hostels for workers. The latter were notable for their duration and scale, to the extent that they lasted from 1973 to 1981, and affected approximately 30,000 strikers in more than 130 hostels (Hmed 2007). In both cases, non-migrant conscience constituents played important supportive roles by suggesting tried-and-tested repertoires of collective action, media access and legal expertise, etc. In the main these constituents stemmed from two political traditions: the Maoist extreme left, and left-wing Catholics and/or the anti-colonialists. But one of the special features of these mobilisations was that they created independent forums or committees so as not to be too dependent on the non-migrant conscience constituents for determining chosen courses of action and the nature of particular demands.

One institution in particular played a highly significant role during this period. This was the *Mouvement des Travailleurs Arabes* (MTA – Movement of Arab Workers) (Hajjat 2006), which was founded in 1972 in Paris by Arab and French activists affiliated to the *Gauche Prolétarienne*[8] and derived from the Palestinian committees.[9] Their ideology was simultaneously Marxist and pan-Arab, while at the same time they were the first to show an interest in the living conditions of migrant workers living on French soil. The MTA was thus founded as a reaction to the racist crimes committed in the early 1970s,[10] and it played an important role in the hostel strikes, as well as in the mobilisation of the 'paper delinquents' (i.e. illegal aliens) who appeared at this time. The leaders of the MTA wanted a highly independent movement, based on political and organisational autonomy, in order to further a range of demands that had previously been neglected by their partner organisations (the labour confederation in particular). Moreover, their commitment to cultural autonomy was reflected in the fact that they were among the first to level such specific cultural demands as the right to celebrate Eid or learn Arabic in France. The MTA was eventually dissolved in 1976 in the face of a collusive alliance by most of the trade unions, the Home Ministry, the national associations of the home countries and the Muslim religious authorities, all anxious to preserve their share of influence over the immigrant population.

The second half of the 1970s – marked by the discontinuation of the labour immigration in 1974, the weakening of extreme left organisations and the repression of migrant activists, many of whom were deported from the country – brought this phase to a close. A section of the militants turned to various forms of 'cultural action'. For example, some former MTA leaders created a street theatre group, *El Assifa*, while others founded the magazine *Sans Frontière*, in 1979. This was conceived as the first independent immigrant weekly written by and for immigrants and it was a testimony to their desire to be free of the stewardship of the Christian and Left conscience constituents.

Second sequence – the 1980s: the failure of attempts to impose a hegemonic mobilisation

In the late 1970s, urban riots erupted in several towns located in the suburbs of Paris and Lyon. In this context, the election of François Mitterrand in May 1981 raised high hopes, some of which were subsequently satisfied. The new socialist government introduced new rights for aliens and authorised the formation of foreign voluntary organisations. However, this state of grace was disappointingly short lived. The summer of 1981 saw a proliferation of urban disorders within the *banlieues* and corresponding police reaction. Again, a series of hate crimes against young Arabs living in the *cités* took place in 1982, at the same time as the *Front National*, the extreme right wing political party, won its first, highly publicised, local electoral battle in 1983. This period is often depicted as a key turning point marking the emergence of new generations of immigrants and the presentation of a novel range of demands in the public sphere. However, it is fair to say that, while some mobilisations represented a break from earlier forms of political protest, others continued to follow the precedents set in former protest eras.

The early 1980s saw the emergence of less formal movements which chose to denounce police and judicial discrimination and the social causes of urban violence via various forms of cultural action. One such movement, Rock Against Police, was created by a group of young boys from the Paris region in April 1980. This initiative was modelled on the British Rock against Racism movement, from which they borrowed the ideas of concerts in the housing estates and the production of films which focused on the banlieues. *Zaama d'Banlieue*, a group of young women founded in 1981 in Lyon, was one of the leading organisations of this kind. Following the occurrence of a fresh series of hate crimes and police violence, young immigrants living on deprived estates also adopted more traditional methods of action, such as organising demonstrations and setting up a legal cell for the families of the victims. An independent press agency, *Im'media*, was formed in 1983 with a view to overcoming lack of access to the media. In 1985, other young people joined *Zaama d'Banlieue* activists to found JALB (*Jeunes Arabes de Lyon et de la Banlieue* – Young Arabs from Lyon and the Suburbs). The latter would play an important role in the political mobilisation of immigrants in the 1980s, in particular, organising a long hunger strike in 1986 against the so-called 'double sentence'.[11] Inspired by the Black movement in the United States and in the UK, all these groups sought to construct an independent immigrant movement and to break free of the stereotype of the 'Beur',[12] which was ceaselessly propagated by the media of the day.

In fact, the early 1980s are best remembered for the 'March for Equality and against Racism', better known as the *Marche des Beurs* (Bouamama 1994). The idea of staging such a march was first conceived of in the summer of 1983 by youths from the Minguettes neighbourhood in Vénissieux, in the Lyon suburbs. Having formed a voluntary association some months earlier, they had undertaken a hunger strike designed to force the authorities to enter into negotiations so that increasingly bad relations with the police would not be allowed to degenerate any further. The precise inspiration for the march was the wounding by police officers of Toumi Djaïda, one of the leaders of the association and an emblematic figure in the locality. Young people in the area appealed for help to Father Delorme, a local Catholic priest, who had often participated in immigrant mobilisations. They also solicited the support of CIMADE, a largely Protestant organisation, sympathetic to immigrant affairs, for help. With the help of such individuals and institutions, a group of 12 marchers (youths of Maghrebian origin and also conscience constituents) started from Marseille on 15 October, their numbers swelling as they crossed France on their way to Paris. Each time they halted they were greeted by local forums that organised debates around the key issues of segregation at school, police brutality, and employment discrimination. The political impact of the march increased ten-fold when another racially motivated murder was committed that November. Spurred on by this development, the marchers made a triumphant entry into Paris. One hundred thousand people joined the demonstration and President Mitterrand was on hand to receive a delegation from the marchers at the Élysée Palace.

However, both the organisation and objectives of the march were contested at the outset by several voluntary organisations, who objected to the presence of non-migrant 'conscience constituents', whose paternalism and ideological position they condemned. The mobilisation of the conscience constituents was essentially a reaction to the success of the *Front National*, whereas militants from migrant backgrounds were demanding *equality of rights*. In addition, an association known as *SOS Racisme* was created, due to the initiative of certain sections of the ruling *Parti Socialiste* who wanted to use the opportunity of the immigrant mobilisations for partisan advantage. *SOS Racisme* managed to attract considerable media attention, with the help of the networks and contacts set up by the *Parti Socialiste* in the media, the entertainment industry, etc. More than trying to politicise the *banlieues* youths or to take their local problems in hand on the basis of an on-the-spot political or social work, *SOS Racisme* focused its energy on the organisation of a series of festive events,[13] during which the social conditions of youth immigrants rapidly gave way to a more overall protest against the *Front National* (Juhem 1998, 2004). Inevitably, tensions came to the fore during the first national 'Convention of the youth immigrant associations' organised during the summer of 1984, and became even more widespread in 1985 after two rival marches were organised, one by the associations in favour of autonomy, which was not given as much space by the media as that organised by *SOS Racisme*. The hope of creating a united front gradually died amidst disagreements over priorities, with some associations being fixated on cultural issues and others more preoccupied with matters of policing and criminal justice.

Lastly, issues focusing on the nature of the relationship between new and older generations of activists also served to divide the movement. In one well known example, the authorities and media deliberately orchestrated a schism between different generations of migrant workers during a strike by the immigrant workers of the Talbot car factories at Poissy (greater Paris area) in February 1984. The younger *Beurs* were portrayed at this time as secular and firmly on the path to integration, whereas the older migrants, who were asking for a decent place of worship in the factory, were said by the then Prime Minister (Pierre Mauroy) not to form 'part of French reality', as leading an 'ayatollah's strike'. This process of divide and rule reaped dividends: some young militants organised a demonstration in support of the strikers to set up a bridge to the 1970s mobilisations, but went largely unsupported by their peers (Polac 1994).

Third sequence: mobilisation since the 1990s

The analyses by Leveau and Withol de Wenden, mentioned earlier, define the period that commenced in the 1990s as a phase of decline in the tendency for political mobilisation when the main option left was to focus primarily on sociological and cultural actions at the local level. The close links now forged between the government and certain migrant associations thus made them dependent on public funding and grants, and weakened their fighting potential. It is also in this period that Muslim cultural associations emerged in France, embodying a new 'centrality of protest'.

Here too, the reality is more complex than these authors seem ready to indicate. Alongside local associations with a social or cultural vocation, organisations that had a more political and rebellious discourse also emerged, whose militants subscribed to the line adopted by earlier mobilisations. Some were created in the wake of urban riots, which again shook France in the 1990s (Jobard, this volume): *Agora* in Vaulx-en-Velin,[14] *Association des Jeunes de Sartrouville*[15] (Association of Sartrouville Youths), and later, *Bouge-qui-Bouge* in Dammarie-les-Lys.[16] Others joined hands on the issue of 'double sentence'.[17] All these organisations in the mid-1990s joined together to form the *Mouvement des Immigrants de Banlieue* (MIB). Today, the MIB comprises only a very small group of active militants, and functions mainly as a reserve network, ready to intervene in support of a mobilisation against police brutality or the 'double sentence' by networking between the generations and different networks of activists.

Alongside such organisations, Muslim associations emerged in the 1990s to push forward existing demands relating to Islam. Such associations are divided between the major national federations, often linked to the country of origin, and local associations incorporated into the *Collectif des Musulmans de France* (Forum of French Muslims), anxious to develop an Islam accessible to the non-Arabic-speaking second generations and to broaden the scope of activities and discussion around the *banlieues* and immigration issues (Morin 2003). The Gulf War, the Islamic attacks perpetrated in Paris in 1995, the repercussions of the Algerian civil war from 1991 onwards, and the war against terrorism that was getting underway led these associations to establish close links with the MIB in Paris or similar organisations in Lyon.

The current political landscape is therefore scarcely unified (see also Kokoreff, this volume). Small local organisations are numerically dominant, but they exist with the help of scarce resources and try to focus some attention in the shadow of much more visible national organisations. On the one hand, the movements close to the *Parti Socialiste*, the latest being *Ni Putes Ni Soumises* (Neither Whores Nor Submissive). NPNS was created in 2003 with the aim of promoting gender equality and secularism in the *banlieues*. Very much in the media eye and with a weak grassroots base in the suburbs, the NPNS is blamed by immigrant associations for contributing to the stigmatisation of the *banlieues* and Islam.[18]

On the other hand, a new autonomous structure, the *Mouvement des Indigènes de la République* (the Republic's Natives Movement), was born in the wake of polemics around the ban on wearing the veil in school and a bill passed in March 2005 which directed that the school curriculum recognise the positive role of the French presence overseas, and in particular in North Africa. The MIR, which was also created in reaction to NPNS, holds a very radical discourse, considering that the treatment of peoples from former colonies prolongs the colonial period in new ways. They refuse to entertain an alliance with the Left parties and the conscience constituents and they mainly focus on social representations in order to throw light on the post-colonial reality in France, notably through the social sciences and the media. This priority given to the post-colonial issue and to social representations over the concrete social and urban issues finally set them apart from the largest part of the *banlieues* associations and from other autonomous organisations like MIB.

Conclusion

This history of immigrant mobilisations demonstrates the frailty and poor institutionalisation of the movements. Such frailty is partly common to all 'poor peoples' movements' (Piven and Cloward 1977) and is partially explicable in terms of their limited social resources. However, there are more specific reasons for this condition. One is related to the repression that the leaders of these movements underwent during the mobilisation in the factories in the late 1960s, as within the MTA, and during the riots in the early 1980s and 1990s the more active of the foreign militants were expelled while others were threatened, and some organisations entirely dissolved. Other leaders were integrated (co-opted), either into public structures, often set up after urban riots, or in organisations responsible for community building and social work among immigrants, or in political parties with influence at the municipal level, which had the effect of discrediting them in the eyes of their constituencies and of depriving the movements of some of their leaders.

Another explanation is linked to the confrontational relationship of these movements with the organisations supporting them. Lastly, a final hypothesis pertains to the ethnic segmentation of the mobilisations that can be observed in the 1970s and 1980s. Without resorting to essentialist views of ethnicity, it can be explained by the role of networks in mobilisations. The initial collective actions in favour of independence were structured on a national basis; these networks were reactivated during later mobilisations. The abeyance organisations helped in linking up two phases of the mobilisation when the political context was less favourable: they facilitated the survival of activist networks, maintained a repertoire of aims and tactics, and promoted a collective identity (Taylor 1989). This can explain the ties between mobilisations, even though new militants had arrived, but also the discrepancies and difficulties of transmission that arose with the arrival of new waves of immigrants, who could not identify with the existing organisations.

Anyway, the November 2005 rioters did not burst onto a virgin political space unoccupied by mobilisations: if there was a split between the generations, it resided in the fact that the younger generations either ignored or could not identify with earlier mobilisations. When we examine the link between the riots and collective action, we realise that disorders generally led to the more traditional mobilisations and organisations: this proved to be the case in the early 1980s, in the 1990s and again in 2005. Furthermore, well established local associations generally served as a safeguard, preventing the development of fresh riots in the locality. If we look at the 2005 riots, it seems that they mostly affected neighbourhoods in towns where there was a large percentage of recent immigrants, mainly from Sub-Saharan Africa (Lagrange 2006a). Even if it is risky to switch from this aggregate data to an individual interpretation of the profile of the rioters, one can envisage that the difficulties that organisations experience when trying to last and attract new generations, who also correspond to the new waves of immigrants, can help to explain the location of the last major riot that occurred in France. It is as if we were witnessing a cycle of protests, typified by the riots, followed by the emergence of new organisations which provide outlets for the articulation of protests. Given time, these organisations begin to lose their influence and legitimacy with the arrival of new generations, who see no alternative way of expressing their disaffection other than to engage in rioting.

Notes

1 Girls and young women were markedly absent from this episode.
2 In this chapter, 'immigrant' will be taken in the broad sense, which includes the primo-migrants and subsequent generations.
3 This march, organised across France, ended with a massive demonstration in Paris and a reception by President Mitterrand.

4 The following analysis has benefited from discussions taking place in a research seminar called *Immigrés en lutte*, that I have co-organised since 2005, along with Sophie Beroud and Nancy Venel, in our research centre, Triangle-CNRS.

5 To speak of 'hegemony' and the 'centrality' of protest, rather than militant generations, makes it possible to avoid overly unifying the various historical sequences.

6 The Pennaroya group principally produced lead and aluminum. The predominantly North African workers were housed in insalubrious hostels adjoining the factory where they had to constantly breathe toxic fumes, which caused many occupational diseases. In 1971, the workers made a list of union demands common to the various factories. Thereafter, they organised a strike, at the end of which most of their demands were met.

7 The SONACOTRA (National Organisation for the Construction of Housing for Workers) managed a number of the hostels for migrant workers. It was created during the Algerian war to house French Algerian Muslims. The staff that looked after these hostels often came from army backgrounds and the hostels reproduced certain forms of colonial management in metropolises (Hmed 2006). Triggered by the hike in rents, the mobilisations started at the end of the 1960s, and became widespread and unified from 1973.

8 The *Gauche prolétarienne* is a spontaneous Maoist organisation, one of the leading extreme-left groups appearing in the aftermath of May 1968 revolutionary disorders.

9 These committees were created in 1970 in reaction to the Black September events in Jordan and clearly followed an anti-Zionist line.

10 In particular, a series of racially motivated murders and attacks were committed in the summer of 1973, especially in the South of France.

11 Idiom used to designate a deportation sentence against aliens, including those who have legal status, which is added to an imprisonment sentence, both for an offence other than illegal stay.

12 *'Beur'* is slang for Arab.

13 SOS organised a series of big free concerts that attracted huge crowds, for instance (Juhem 2004).

14 A town in the Lyon suburbs where massive riots took place in 1990.

15 A town in the nearby outskirts of Paris where riots took place in 1991.

16 A town in the distant suburbs of Paris, hit by riots in 1997 (Jobard and Linhardt 2008).

17 'Double sentence' (*double peine*) is the infamous designation for two overlapping measures liable to hit legal and illegal aliens in France. Such 'aliens' may first receive a custodial sentence and then they may also be deported back to their country of origin, on the basis of a judicial decision, on the grounds that they constitute a perceived 'threat' to French society.

18 Ironically enough, the founder of NPNS, Fadela Amara, is now a member of the government – as Minister for the *politique de la ville*.

Chapter 12

The political dimension of the 2005 riots

Michel Kokoreff

Introduction

To what extent may the 2005 French riots be regarded as a 'political protest'? What sort of meaning is it possible to attach to these disruptive events which consisted of property destruction, arson and hit-and-run fights with the police but that, in contrary to (say) the legendary May 1968 disorders, did not represent any clear and obvious political message or demand, and did not produce any emerging leadership or aspiring political movement? Many public and political discourses of the day portrayed the rioters as 'criminal delinquents' or in the best case as the victims of *'crise des banlieues**', resulting in both cases in the *de-politicisation* of their actions.

This chapter is predicated on the hypothesis that the 2005 riots represented the stark crystallisation of a vast diversity of political ideas and processes operating not only within the riot-affected *cités* (as already stated by case studies like Amrani and Beaud 2004; Bachmann and Le Guennec 1997; Jobard 2005, 2006; Masclet 2003), but also, more generally, in a society fixated on the possibility of an internal threat to its security (Beck 1992; Castel 2003; Kokoreff and Rodriguez 2004).

In order to defend this hypothesis, we will first establish the idea that the eruption of these riots was meaningful to those involved – that they represented profound feelings of injustice and a collective demand for respect. Such interpretations of the riots will then be tested out on the basis of field surveys undertaken over a span of approximately 15 years (Duprez and Kokoreff 2001; Kokoreff 2003) and observations made *a posteriori* on the 2005 riots on the basis of a study conducted in several cities of the Paris outskirts (Kokoreff 2008).

The rioters of injustice

It is in the vested interest of the state to depoliticise the collective emotion and anger of those who take to the streets, primarily by striving to discredit it. In the present case, the government's handling of the crisis gave the riots a distinct political hue. Right from the outset, the Interior Minister Nicolas Sarkozy's position, as represented in the media, was designed to criminalise the initial outburst that was consequent on the death of the two young boys. Thus, the 'official version' broadcast by the media insisted that the police had not 'given chase' to the group of adolescents returning from a football game in Clichy-sous-Bois, but that these youths had simply taken flight after an attempted 'burglary'. This public 'dishonouring of the dead' had a profound symbolic effect (Fassin 2006). The same may also be said of the praise proffered by the Interior Minister to riot police forces the day after two tear gas shells were thrown on the mosque in Clichy. These events and the official reaction that followed were widely interpreted as a slur against Muslims and strongly affirmed the anti-police and anti-authority sentiments harboured by migrant youths and their families. Finally, Prime Minister Dominique de Villepin's decision to invoke emergency constitutional provision, dating back to 1955 and the time of the Algerian war, just as we appeared to be witnessing an abatement of riotous activity, clearly seemed to betray a *post-colonial* approach towards the suburbs.

The personal dimension to this crisis undoubtedly helped to crystallise underlying political sentiments. It is unquestionable that Nicolas Sarkozy was the principal player in this drama, the epilogue of which was his subsequent victory in the presidential elections. It was to his direct and macho-like challenge to their sense of dignity and self-respect that the youths from *banlieues* responded with such desire for confrontation. Although socially marginalised, morally scorned and politically inaudible, the participants found through the medium of such spectacular collective violence a means of acquiring public visibility. But this could also be regarded as a trap which they fell into as a result of a lack of internal organisation and external support. In addition, the discrediting of the troublemakers, referred to by such epithets as the *cités'* gangland bosses', was given impetus by the long-term conflict occurring in the higher echelons of the State, involving de Villepin and Sarkozy. Each of these major government personalities was at this time constantly 'daggers drawn' in competition for the future leadership of the conservative party, and each was attempting to outdo his rival in capturing the support of the law-and-order faction within its midst (Jobard 2008). Within opposition ranks, the de-politicisation of the riots had been carried out with gusto by the *Parti Socialiste*, which aligned itself with the Government's position and voted for Emergency, while the left-leaning *Parti Communiste* and Green Party each voted against.

It is difficult to escape the impression that the primary motivation for rioting was a deep-seated feeling of rejection and injustice. This sentiment constituted a common experience, especially among French youth immigrants from North and sub-Saharan Africa, who were not only overrepresented in the relevant *cités*, but also involved in strained relations with everyday institutions, such as school, welfare and housing agencies, employers, police and justice officials, whose discriminatory attitudes have been evidenced by numerous scientific studies of the last decade (for an overview, see Kokoreff and Rodriguez 2004: 169–219; and on police and justice profiling, Jobard and Névanen 2009). The events alluded to above – the death of two adolescents, the mosque incident, etc. – crystallised this urban experience, fuelling not only the rage of the rioters, but also that of their friends, families and neighbours. In this sense, we can safely say that, if there was a revolt, it was particularly directed against those institutions of a Republic that did not keep their promises.

The sentiments of the rioters are illustrated in the following conversation, involving the author and two participants of secondary school age:

Question So why exactly did things explode in November?
Juvenile 1 There was a kind of tension. It had been in the air for a long time, it needed to explode and it will explode again.
Question Did you really sense that back in October–November?
Juvenile 1 Of course! Things accumulated. The two youths who died in Clichy, many of us knew them. And Sarkozy who showed up and insulted them like that on TV, added to it. Then there were all those daily provocations by the cops, here in the town. As soon as we get out, they talk badly, they insult us for nothing and suddenly it breaks down.

Question   How did you react when you heard about ... ?

Juvenile 1   Well, it hurt! We all said to ourselves, how it could easily happen to any one of us.

Question   So, what happened then? Did you gather to talk about it?

Juvenile 1   Yes, it was intensively discussed. We couldn't just do nothing and wait.

Question   So what did you do?

Juvenile 2   There were riots because people were not listened to by the state. Riot was their only means of speech expression. Had we engaged in peaceful demonstrations, it would have achieved nothing. The only means for us to be heard was to torch cars while on TV. I would say it worked.

Juvenile 1   What triggers rage is the hate that comes from being scorned. After the conflict, people talked about 'marginalisation versus integration', but what is all that about? People who talk to us about it don't even make a proper attempt to listen to us, to help us, so what is all the so-called integration for?

It was often claimed that the November 2005 rioters had 'nothing to say' and that the riots were like a silent movie upon which commentators were obliged to superimpose their own soundtrack. However, this notion must necessarily be called into question. It was not so much the *absence* of a political message that was apparent in the riots, but rather the fact that it was *inaudible in character*. As a matter of fact, the rioters' repertoire of protest made their voice inaudible: conventional demonstrations, not riots, are accepted ways of protest in France. Any other form, especially handled by people constantly put under suspicion of being routine offenders, is simply beyond the political pale.

Nonetheless, this hypothesis merits a more in-depth consideration. For, although we were indeed witnessing a national phenomenon, the action was not geographically uniform. In reality the riots we saw were *fragmentary*. Hence we should take stock of the diversity of situations and the contextual effects, and also take into account the various political, institutional and social players – whether elected representatives, the police or urban activists. By loosely referring to surveys conducted in 2006–2007 in the three communes of the Seine-Saint-Denis *département* (Saint-Denis, Clichy-sous-Bois, Montfermeil) and a working-class district situated in intra-city Paris, we shall set out to describe the rioters on the basis of the political circle and local political context to which they belong.[1]

Participating in the riots: actors and contexts

We begin by asking what sort of life the rioters were liable to have been experiencing prior their involvement in the 2005 disorders. What, for example, were the different types of social or political networks they formed part of? For simplicity's sake, I would draw here a series of concentric circles around the central actor (the rioter), such that the first circle would encompass local people – chiefly local activists who endeavoured to act as intermediaries between the rioters and the local public – while a second circle would contain such actors as social workers, teachers, and elected representatives who, while exerting local influence during the riots, had no wish to set themselves up as political spokespersons for the rioters, either during the disorders or in their aftermath.

We can confidently state on the basis of our field studies undertaken after the riots in Seine-Saint-Denis that the disorders were essentially *male-dominated*. It is therefore legitimate to ask where all the girls had disappeared to while the rioting was in progress. One thing distinguishing them from the 'lads' was that, despite the fact that young women were generally enduring patriarchal domination both within the family and in the neighbourhood, their degree of success at school was relatively greater than that of male peers, making them more attractive propositions in the job market. However, it remains apparent that they were still exposed to the same day-to-day injustice, violence and discrimination as that experienced by their male counterparts; and just because they did not burn cars or throw Molotov cocktails at schools or buses, it does not mean that they were not tacitly supportive of the rioters.

It has been consistently emphasised that it was primarily the youths of the *cités* who participated in the 2005 riots. What has not been made sufficiently apparent is the extent of the divisions that became obvious – in particular, between those subsections of youth known colloquially as the 'juniors' and the 'seniors' (the first ones being the pupils still at school and the second ones being the youths around 20 years old). It was certainly the case that the relative involvement of these subsections tended to vary from one neighbourhood to the next and at different stages of specific riots. Thus, during the first few nights of the riots at Clichy-sous-Bois, it was primarily the 'seniors' who instigated the conflict and set about fighting the police. In the *cité* situated in the 19th precinct of Paris, where a part of our survey was conducted, it was also the seniors who took to the streets every night. When provoked by the police, they reacted by showing their generational and territorial solidarity. As one young rioter proclaimed,

> This is war, and it is because of the youngsters who died and because of Sarko, for he said things that did not please the young. He called them all sorts of names, any old how! The housing estates are united and, on top of that, the police threw tear gas shells on the mosque.

In Saint-Denis, the largest town of Seine-Saint-Denis, where the riots were less severe, the behaviour of the 'juniors' and 'seniors' was markedly different. By and large, the latter remained detached from the incidents. Most had quit school very young, had no degree and, to top it all, were registered on the most underrated courses. The majority continued to live with their parents and did not work regularly, preferring to live off shady 'business deals'. They were not optimistic about their future and their attitude was one of resignation with regard to their situation. They were fatalistic when trying to objectify their circumstances: 'Blokes of 20–22 years, they don't give a damn about burning cars', said one. 'Burning cars, all of us have done it, we are past the age', explained another. The 14–18 year olds from Saint-Denis showed much more enthusiasm for the 2005 riots. Most of them were still in school, or had just left school – as such, they did not have anything like the same attitude of resignation as their seniors.

Simply to acknowledge that age was an important variable is not quite the same as offering an explanation for the overriding involvement of young men in the riots. To begin to understand the reason for their centrality we must first appreciate that clashes with the police are fundamental to the accounts of their daily lives. In this sense, it was easy for them to identify with the plight of the electrocuted boys from Clichy-sous-Bois. Indeed, the profile of the rioting youths we met in several Saint-Denis neighbourhoods was strikingly similar to that of the Clichy-sous-Bois victims. This intimacy with Zyed and Bouna was tangible, in the sense that some of the *cités* boys knew one of them through the football club he was registered with. The territorial logic of their actions is just as important to understand: youths who burnt cars, set the rubbish bins on fire or damaged public buildings tended to be brought together on the basis of prior network structures or were, in some cases, amalgamations of several pre-existing groups. Broadly speaking, such participants had 'nothing to lose' in terms of employment status or ownership of a small business, nor had they become as resigned or apathetic as their elders, for whom 'success' was no longer evaluated in terms of school or employment attainment but according to criminal prowess (Beaud 2002; Kokoreff 2003).

The role of mediators or 'go-betweens'

Numerous groups and individuals occupied the roles of political go-betweens during the riots. Often, such people were local working men and women of at least 30 years of age who were already well known for their community work. Such people would invariably appeal to the arsonists that violence and destruction of this nature was liable to lead them nowhere and that it would be more sensible for them to register themselves on the electoral lists. Some of mediatory groups involved acquired a high profile during the riots. However, the only go-between group that was able to reach a nationwide audience was the AC-LeFeu (*Association Collectif Liberté Egalité Fraternité Ensemble Unis*) of Clichy which incorporated members of the two dead boys' families. This movement played an important intermediary role during the riots, in cooling down the will for confrontations with the police, in seeking (and gaining) an access to the mayor, and in setting up conventional demonstrations and marches in Clichy. As a matter of fact, for all its affective ties to the two boys, rioting in Clichy was not as violent as in other places where there was an absence of go-betweens linking the rioters to the authorities.

Soon after the riots, AC-LeFeu launched a nationwide campaign aimed at collecting, distilling and representing the various grievances and complaints that were frothing within the *cités*. In so doing, they were reactivating two earlier forms of political protest: the 1789 grievance registers gathered by the Tiers-Etat (for presentation to the King) in the prelude to the French Revolution; and the 1983 March of the *banlieues* and immigrant youths, who converged to Paris by way of numerous French *cités*. The AC-LeFeu is now actively involved in the protracted fight for justice concerning the electrocution of the youths. It also operates as a support group for other victims of 'police brutality' and functions as a 'mouthpiece' in media discussions of issues relating to the *banlieues.*

Two potentially intervening movements or organisations – *Ni Putes Ni Soumises* (NPNS – 'Neither whores nor submissive') and *Mouvement des Indigènes de la République* ('Natives of the Republic') – were surprisingly absent from the riots. The former had been instigated in response to an atrocious crime in which young males set on fire and killed a local Arab woman accused of being 'a whore'. The latter, meanwhile, had arisen in response to the persistent racial discrimination perpetrated against 'coloured' French nationals and foreigners. Neither of these movements proved capable of representing the rioters, despite the fact that both enjoyed prior public prominence. This was probably because, in the *cités*, politics seem always to be connected to local charismatic go-betweens and to grassroots activism. Any attempt to set up bridges to political parties is invariably regarded with the highest degree of suspicion.

Citizens' mobilisation

We now come on to the third category of people involved in the rioting, who basically consist of on-the-spot peacekeepers who show a certain degree of political involvement on a daily basis, but who could not or did not wanted to take a leadership role equivalent to that exercised by the go-betweens. This group is best exemplified in Saint-Denis, bastion of the Communist Party since 1935. Here, where the area has since been remodelled according to a social mix of nationalities and cultures, rioting was characterised partly by the limited number of cars burnt out in the process (a relatively small total of 44 vehicles), but largely by the mobilisation of civilian groups driven by the desire to have their political demands satisfied. In this respect, the local grassroots' capacity to orchestrate such mobilisation demonstrates the enduring strength of the local political fabric, despite the weakening effects of a crumbling militant communist network, a growing propensity to refrain from voting, and the undermining activities of the Far Right.

The 40–60 individuals in this category took to demonstrating (sometimes in smaller groups) in the city centre, late at night. Several different membership tiers were involved. The first of these were trade unionists firmly cast in the area's communist tradition. The second was of more recent origin insofar as it comprised town council employees who saw their commitment as an extension of their professional activity. In the main, these were locally born men aged 35 to 45 years old, sometimes of Maghrebian heritage. A third stratum was generally recruited from the ranks of middle-class intellectuals. This incorporated extreme left and feminist activists chiefly concerned, among other things, with issues of local security. Lastly, it is important to include the various 'resident groups', which emerged from the *cités*. Comprising people of various national origins, this final tier was mostly female and brought together in an especially emblematic fashion the 'mothers' and single fathers of the area.

The kind of actions undertaken by these groups of people is exemplified by the following comment by Nacer, the 28-year-old head of the town's youth centre and life-long resident of Saint-Denis:

> As the riots started, we were, like, really blasé. We know pretty much how it goes. At the very moment where some burning cars were showed up on TV, or some youths were seen throwing stones at cops, we all said to ourselves: 'This is the very last thing to do!' It is undisputable that some youths use turmoil as a kind of a display cabinet. You can find every kind of people among rioters. Many young people participated simply to have their neighbourhood show up on TV. In Saint-Denis, as soon as we became aware of preliminary movements by the youth, we were convinced it could severely burn around, like during the 80s and 90s, so we decided to set up a series of discussions and debates in youth clubs. And within two or three days, we had succeeded in having small-scale debates on the riots all around the *cités*. We saw how many of the youths involved in the debates were thinking just like the rioters we were seeing on TV. The only difference was that we succeeded in getting them to think that the only, well, the *best* ways to solve a problem is a) to speak out, or b) politically engage in order to get things moving.

This highly singular example of Saint-Denis highlights the intriguing possibility that citizen mobilisation may have had a moderating effect on the riots. As in a handful of other examples, the fact that such mobilisation was sympathetic to the plight of local youth and was representative of the ethnic pluralism of the area seems to have shortened the duration of the riot – perhaps by offering a credible grassroots alternative to violence. 'Where it existed', remarks Hugues Lagrange, 'recognition was able to quite rapidly check the riots, but where on the contrary the local powers were reticent about granting this recognition, they had to mobilise much more energy to "douse the fire", and often the riots persisted' (Lagrange 2006b: 126).

Conclusion

The 2005 riots highlighted a host of political problems within French society and expressed both a profound need for justice and equality and a strident demand for recognition and respect. However, in order for such action to have any political impact, it requires the presence of appropriate mediators and/or the formation of effective alliances. This is precisely what was lacking among the youth who participated in the riots. As shown in our contribution, urban riots are generally marked in France (and the nationwide episode does not differ in this respect) by their close bonds to very local, if not parochial factors. The ages of the participants, choices of eventual targets, choices of modes of disruption, etc. are all linked to very local characteristics which rarely, if at all, give rise to a collective action of rioters from the different localities (the 1983 March being perhaps the sole exception, see Hamidi, this volume). As we have exemplified with the town of Saint-Denis, circles of supporters and go-betweens stand between the core rioters and the political authorities. But the main interests of these legitimate third parties lie first in pacifying the situation *on the spot* – and once they have succeeded in it, or once the situation significantly cools down, rioters show a high reluctance in collectively shifting to a more conventional mode of action and to an eventual integration into established political or interests groups. Everything stays in place, as if untouched by the violence that just occurred – and ready for the next wave of riots, which is certain to be led by the younger generation and/or newer French migrants.

Note

1 Ideally, we should include the police role as part of this analysis. However, there is insufficient space here to carry out such a task. Interested readers are directed to Kokoreff (2008: 183–240).

Chapter 13

Youth gangs, riots and the politicisation process

Marwan Mohammed

Introduction

Ever since urban riots began to occur in France in the late 1970s, the collective violence involved has been consistently attributed to 'youth gangs', thus ensuring a police hegemony over the way that the rioting is both perceived and responded to. Thanks to the negative connotations attached to the concept of the 'gang', it was possible for such riots to be conveniently interpreted via establishment discourse as the aggregated activities of individual rioters with definitions of criminality obscuring any underlying protest, and any possible scrutiny of relevant social issues giving way to a fixation on penal issues (Le Goaziou and Mucchielli 2006). This image of the gang evokes a classic image of a hostile and disorganised mob and excludes any acknowledgement of collective rationality. Indeed, it profiles the typical rioter as a nihilistic individual, characterised by violence, youth and alienation. However, the discipline of sociology has consistently shown that gang life should not be typified as universally transgressive and/or deviant. In the United States of America, for example, Martin Sanchez-Jankowski (1991) employed a study of several dozen gangs to highlight the political aspects of their collective life and the various forms of exchange and social brokerage engaged in with different types of public institutions.

Youth gangs observed in France are stable, enduring formations, with their own dynamics: their cohesion and peculiar sense of social identity do not vanish during a riotous event. In this chapter, we examine their specific role, especially in the autumn of 2005, on the basis of an ethnographic survey conducted in a housing project of the Paris region – namely, the Hautes-Noues[1] *cité* in the town of Villiers-sur-Marne. Through these youth gangs, we will examine the links between riots, delinquency and politics. The central point of the following discussion is that the younger youth gang members are the key players in the riots, not only because of their routine involvement in delinquent or criminal activities, but also because of their high level of politicisation.

In setting out this argument, we will first point out that the young gang members were seldom arrested by the police, although they *were* fully involved in the collective violence that occurred in the Hautes-Noues and its surroundings. We will then study the forms and targets of the offences committed during the riots, and try to decrypt the motivation behind these acts. Lastly, we will examine the relationship between these youth gangs and locally elected political leaders.

Methodological orientation

The analysis presented here derives from a doctoral thesis, conducted between 2001 and 2007, on the role of families in the forming of youth gangs. This ethnographic study, undertaken in a ZUS in the Paris area, is based on interviews with and the observation of 15 youth groups, including seven gangs, 108 respondents under the age of 30 (including 82 gang members or former members), 44 members of their families (siblings, cousins, or parents), and 10 people working for related institutions (e.g. social workers, school staff, etc.). In addition to the recorded interviews, the many informal, everyday discussions with respondents constituted a research source of supplementary information. The author's many roles in the city involved – i.e. resident, school monitor, citizens' group member, community organiser, chief counsellor of a day-camp, and sports coach – were undoubtedly helpful in enabling him to gain access to such a broad and potentially elusive range of respondents.

The November 2005 riots as observed from Villiers-sur-Marne

The riot-related events occurring in the deprived area of Villiers were relatively small scale, much to the surprise of local actors, considering that unfavourable socio-economic conditions, long-term negative relations between the police and resident youths and a well established network of local gangs had all recommended it as extremely violence prone. Before attempting to explain possible reasons for this low riot intensity, it is necessary to describe what exactly occurred from the end of October to mid-November in Villiers.

The main steps in the occurrence of the Villiers-sur-Marne riot were as follows:

1 27 October 2005: The electrocution of three teenagers chased by the police in Clichy-sous-Bois (the acknowledged trigger of the 2005 riots) becomes the number one topic of discussion of the youth of the Hautes-Noues *cité*.

2 28 October 2005: Two police vans and a station wagon with about 20 riot police officers (CRS) settle in the housing estate. The increase in pedestrian patrols and stop-and-search operations raises tension in the neighbourhood.

3 29–30 October 2005: The 'juniors' (adolescents who form an organised gang) increase in presence throughout the town, while donning masks to prevent facial identification. They take no action but prepare for its impending occurrence. They manufacture mini homemade bombs from citric acid and aluminium, which they explode in the most crowded and busiest areas. Across the remainder of the town, several controversial incidents (e.g. the burning of a car in a neighbouring locality, an arson attack on a school) are attributed to the Hautes-Noues youths. One gang, whose members are slightly older, takes advantage of the police focus on the 'juniors' by robbing a neighbourhood toy store and a tobacconist shop.

4 30 October (evening): A mosque in Clichy-sous-Bois is sprayed with tear gas, inducing a fresh wave of indignation in Hautes-Noues. Skirmishes with the police and the ritualised burning of dustbins become daily occurrences.

5 31 October to 2 November: Tension mounts as a consequence of the growing number of stop and search operations, and clashes between youth groups and the CRS.

6 3 and 4 November: The 'juniors' engage in a daily ritual of setting fire to dustbins, insulting police officers, and slinging stones, cans and other objects at them. For their part, the CRS discharge dozens of tear gas canisters. Stray gas enters surrounding civilian apartments, much to the outrage of the residents affected.

159

7 5 November: A car is set alight close to the main police station in Hautes-Noues.

8 9 November: Several youths head towards the shopping mall in a neighbouring city to loot it. The police act on prior intelligence (possibly an informer's tip-off) to evacuate the area before the youths arrive.

Gangs and their role in the riots

Having established the main components of the riot features which occurred in Villiers-sur-Marne, it is now necessary to outline the nature and structure of local teenage gangs and explain the precise nature of their involvement in the riot. As we have just seen, the level of disruptiveness was unexpectedly low. The fact that the Hautes-Noues estate on Villiers stayed relatively calm is arguably correlated to the nature of youth gang structures and to particular events impacting on the locality in the weeks directly preceding the onset of the nationwide riots.

Gangs and neighbouring groups

Gangs represent a major form of juvenile sociability within poor housing estates. What makes them particularly distinctive as social entities is the importance they attach to masculine and transgressive values and their permanent state of conflict with the remainder of society. Gangs are poorly structured and demarcated by porous boundaries, in which delinquency is not so much an instrumentally oriented activity as a mechanism for strengthening group cohesion, identity and insularity.

Alongside the permanent members of these gangs, there are other individuals whose membership is far more intermittent, who generally refrain from delinquent activity and are seldom at the forefront of riotous behaviour. Indeed, their participation in riot violence is typically less than wholehearted and based on the principle of 'going along with the crowd'. The typical educational profile of these youths tends to be of a higher calibre than that of the more committed gang members: by and large, their school attendance rates are better and they generally come from families whose income is relatively higher than the neighbourhood norm. Some are employed but mostly in short-term jobs. They are generally between 14 and 23 years of age (23 years old being the very limit of activity within a gang), and only a minority have police records, albeit for minor offences.

The dozens of interviews undertaken with rioters (both gang members and non-members of gangs) reveal that their participation in the disorder had a variety of underlying motives. Almost universally, the rioters claimed a sincere attachment to their neighbourhood and a consequent involvement in its affairs. They felt that they are linked by a collective destiny, resulting from such factors as their common perceptions of being marginalised by the dominant social order; poor schooling and inferior life chances; the stigma and discrimination attached to their social, migratory and religious origins; and the continuous state of conflict with the police. However, over and above these elements experienced in common by all rioters, there are differences of social backgrounds, especially between the gang members and the others, which surface in the course of collective action. From our observations made *in situ* during the riots, it appears that youth gangs are generally highly involved and in the forefront of the action: they provide initiative, leadership and technical orchestration in relation to the riots.

To understand this systematic involvement of gang members, one must take into account the specific nature of their biographical trajectories. In the main, such youths have all undergone painful experiences at school, so that their poor 'school record' (Millet and Thin 2005) is unerringly predictive of their future 'criminal record'. The 'future', as such, for these individuals already looks bleak – especially from their own perspective. They tend to come from low-income families living in precarious conditions in over-crowded lodgings shared with many other siblings. Indeed, strong correlations have been made in the academic literature between such factors as family size, number of siblings, a propensity to be absent from school, academic failure, gang delinquency and involvement in the riots (Lagrange 2007, 2008b; Mohammed 2007).

Another important part of this process is that the type of offences often committed by these youths (e.g. burglaries, destruction, harassment and breach of peace) inevitably result in frequent conflicts with neighbours, coupled with repeated encounters with legal authorities, such as the police, courts and prison personnel, which are invariably humiliating and/or violent, and which engender strong desires for retribution and revenge. At the most mundane level, they are frequently subjected to police controls and associated forms of bullying (such as offensive body searches, beatings, tear gas attacks, insults, and being targeted by flash-ball guns), and, in turn, it is they who most regularly provoke the police.

In comparison with other rioters, they are the most frequent recipients of the heavy legal sentences meted out for physical assaults and the destruction of such institutions as local police stations and, less frequently, schools. In their constant quest for public visibility, they embody the orthodoxy of a particular 'street code' and are the guardians of the neighbourhood reputation. Their prominent role in the riots is therefore something 'expected' of them for they are part of a wholesale local rejection of authority, embodied by such figures as the police and town mayor. In other words, the specific life experiences of these youth gangs help to explain their intense feelings of injustice and almost knee-jerk reactions to the police. Such analysis converges with the observations made by Jobard (2006: 74) when he affirms that there exists a fundamental political socialisation deeply marked by the intimate relationship with criminal justice. Judicial prosecution and protest are therefore not mutually exclusive; they are linked and feed off one another.

Gang involvement and the timing of the riots

Given that the prevalence of gang members is a key factor in explaining the intensity of particular French riots, it is possible to interpret the relative 'weakness' of the disorder in Villiers-sur-Marne in terms of a temporary diminution of the influence of local gangs occurring at the end of October 2005.

It was around about this period that gang membership had temporarily declined, due to the fact that mainstay members had not yet been rejoined by the youth who had not yet left school or vocational training. The judicial context was none too favourable, either. In the month preceding the deaths of Zyad and Bouna, five Villiers gang members (all youths aged 15 to 19) had just been found guilty by the courts of 'acts of violence committed by several perpetrators'. In two cases, prison sentences had been meted out, having a depletive effect on local confidence and morale. The depressed mood among gang members was compounded by two other factors: first, police repression was intensified around September 2005 in response to the rise in burglaries with assault and hold-ups in small local stores; and second, earlier that summer, a total of nine young men over the age of 18 each turned their backs on gang life to take up permanent 'careers' in the *adult* criminal underworld.

Gang involvement in the riots: visibility vs. presence

Surveys of rioters referred to by Mazars (2006) and Delon and

Mucchielli (2007) indicate that only a minority of rioters involved in the northern Paris *banlieue* were already in possession of criminal records. It was equally true that, in Villiers, very few of those sentenced for riot-related offences were already known offenders. However, such data does obscure the fact that, during the incidents of collective violence occurring in October–November 2005, gang members were simply more adept at avoiding arrest than their non-gang counterparts.

According to our observations, the total number of those arrested during the Villiers riots amounted to less than one tenth of all those who actually participated. The risk of being arrested was therefore never very high. The chances of this occurring were unequally distributed among participants: in order to escape the police, it helped to be in possession of a fine knowledge of the urban environment, a practised sense of evasiveness, and a modicum of self-control.

Thus, it was extremely useful to know about the existence of the various local hideouts, some public, others private (and it should be said that there was no shortage of residents prepared to hide fugitives from the police) For this drill, it was helpful to be familiar with entrance codes to all relevant buildings – a knowledge that tended to be more available to gang members used to being shifted by police from one building to another. In addition, prior experience of different types of police intervention enabled gang members to anticipate the timing and duration of police operations, to know where and when it was safest to confront the police and, alternatively, when it was more sensible to vanish. Lastly, cool-headedness was often a decisive factor in enabling an individual to avoid arrest – but here, too, this was something usually developed through repeated clashes with the police.

Riot-related offences

It is important for us to consider the possible meanings that could be attributed to the various misdemeanours occurring during the riots. For example, setting a car on fire could be simultaneously interpreted as a means of protest (revolt), provocation (taunting the law enforcement agencies), entertainment, vindictiveness, the settling of an account, or a lucrative initiative (perpetrating an insurance fraud). Observers and commentators always tend to assign one single meaning (e.g. political or criminal) to such acts, but this meaning does not necessarily correspond to the actors' intentions, which may often be more complicated and vary over time.

163

In a relatively little known article in France (despite its availability as a translation from the English), Keith (1990) analyses the list of individuals arrested during the Brixton riots of April 1981. It emerges from this study there were in fact two riots, involving two separate groups of participants: the first was a strictly localised confrontation with the police, involving a large variety of people within a very narrowly circumscribed area of Brixton; the other, which took place some distance away from the first, was an opportunistic reaction to the breakdown of law and order (Keith 1990: 29). The author shows that the young blacks were not the only ones involved, but that they were primarily prosecuted for *riot offences*, whereas the whites (who were generally older and lived some distance away from the epicentre of violence) were primarily charged and sentenced for what we will call *during-the-riots offences*. Riot offences are the 'disinterested' destruction and burning of private and public property, and verbal and physical violence against the government and related authorities. By contrast, during-the-riot offences are generally motivated by self-interest and typically involve looting or, very occasionally, an attempt at insurance fraud.

In fact, the autumn 2005 riots were notable for the absence of widespread looting behaviour (Lagrange 2008b). This was also true of Villiers-sur-Marne. However, as the following field notes make clear, some local youths were sorely tempted to engage in such behaviour:

Note on November 9 2005: the last collective movement takes place. Some regular members of a gang operating in the housing estate (of whom at least one participated in the burning of a car on November 5) are invited by others to participate in the looting of the Arcades shopping mall in the neighbouring town of Noisy-le-Grand (150 stores and 10 restaurants all in one place). They were contacted in the morning by their peers from the *cité* Pavé-Neuf in Noisy-le-Grand, and I was appraised of the presence of 'guys from the *cité* Fauvettes in Neuilly-sur-Marne' (unverified information). They had been told the same morning, and the meeting was fixed for around 6 p.m. next to the Hotel Mercure, near the entrance to the commercial complex. The youths receiving this information (whom I had seen at another location trying to gather a maximum number of youths during a police raid which had gone off badly), knew that this type of opportunity was likely to interest only those individuals who form part of the delinquent core. They were expecting a massive rejection of the idea of mixing two kinds of involvement in the disorder. Dozens of youths from the housing estate had been informed but refused to participate. Six individuals in two cars (intending to act!), accompanied by another car carrying the curious ('only there to watch!'), went to the commercial centre, only to discover that the sector had been exceptionally cordoned off by the police (who had received prior information). Hundreds of shoppers had already been evacuated. The small groups then turned back with the intention of warning off the last car that was supposed to be joining them.

It is further evident from the present study that the choice of the commercial targets was not a random matter: the only tobacconist to be affected in Villiers-sur-Marne during the autumn 2005 riot had long had an extremely negative reputation among young adults in the neighbourhood. This approximates to the situation in Brixton where the torching of a local public house was generally attributed to the fact that its manager had recently been denounced by the Commission for Race Relations (Keith 1990).

These examples go to show that raising the question of the political meaning of the riots themselves and more generally of disturbances that occurred in the wake of a riot, is all but an easy task. As far as Villiers is concerned, it requires us to address the relationship between routine and breakdown, between delinquency and politics, and between local gangs and local political actors. Therefore, in what follows, we shall take the liberty of expanding the focus by scrutinising some aspects of the city's life some months before the national wave of riots occurred.

The involvement of gangs in the local political arena

Numerous commentators have devoted themselves to determining whether or not the riots were primarily political or non-political in nature. A useful starting point for such discussion is provided by the French political scientist Jacques Lagroye, who emphasises that 'giving a political dimension to a social movements implies an effort at organisation and interpretation that alone can ensure its success, i.e. its demonstrative value and homogenisation around a political objective' (2006: 325). Thus there are differing thresholds and degrees of politicisation that range from the emergence of a subversive protest or a demand into the public sphere, to its eventual conversion into a political object, perennial and recognised. In regard to the French riots, it has been shown how this 'perennialisation' was achieved both locally and nationally by activists, associations and action groups acting as spokespersons (Kokoreff 2008) or 'brokers' (Sanchez-Jankowski 1991) between street actors and relevant political institutions.

By focusing on the gangs (or, more precisely, their delinquent members), it should be realised that, at the everyday level, their grievances and demands rarely progress beyond the primary stage of politicisation. However, this is not to suggest that rioting or looting are their only means of political engagement. To illustrate this, we will present two aspects of what we might call 'gang politics': first, the brutal code of the local gang economy that hinges on the economy of intimidation and threat; and secondly, the involvement of the same youths in a conventional political and citizens' mobilisation led by the neighbourhood activists.

Insecurity, power and intimidation

The process of (in the words of the gang members) 'applying pressure' or 'to pop up in force' (i.e. in large numbers) can be defined as a strategy aimed at influencing local institutions' policies and actors. The gangs studied by Sanchez-Jankowski alternated between postures of co-operation and mistrust vis-à-vis governments, in order to foster a climate of uncertainty and insecurity enabling them to retain future spaces for negotiation. Thus, when demands via the usual channels of communication were not met, 'the gangs could give vent to acts of destruction and vandalism in the neighbourhood' (Sanchez-Jankowski 1991: 325).

A similar pattern emerged in the post-riot phase in Villiers-sur-Marne. As a matter of fact, even if riots only generated a small amount of harm in Villiers, violent breakdown has always been seen and feared by local political elites as *the* means of expression by the youths, and constantly likely to occur. This perennial expectancy deeply structures the kind of interactions between the groups in the political arena, enhancing the political influence enjoyed by the gangs – even if, for the reasons seen above, their level of riotous activity had been rather muted by the national standards of November 2005. According to field notes logged in November *2006*:

The opening of ESCALE (*Espace Socio-Culturel et d'Aide à l'Emploi*[2] – Socio-Cultural Centre and Employment Assistance) was an important event for the deputy mayor of the town who had been pushing this project for quite a long time. An inaugural ceremony with great pomp was organised in the presence of Jean-Louis Borloo, the minister for (among others) *politique de la ville**, and several journalists. A few days after the inauguration, a section of the 'microbes' (the nickname of a gang of particularly active teenagers aged between 15 and 17) tried to steal the security guard's scooter and a Molotov cocktail was found near ESCALE. A complaint was lodged by the municipality. At the same time, the mayor[3] expressed some concerns, and delegated a woman heading an association ('Association Femmes-relais' – a women's help group) to call a meeting with the gang at ESCALE. Taken aback, the group attended the meeting and was welcomed by the mayor, the cabinet director, the director of city planning, and the youth co-ordinator. Instead of a reprimand, a detailed presentation of the advantages of the ESCALE was made for their benefit and they were asked what their expectations were with regard to the youth service (*'They asked us what we wanted!'*). The gang was recognised and invited in that capacity, just after an attempted misdemeanour, and offered space for negotiation.

The 'microbes' did not immediately realise the extent of the local political 'clout' they were now able to exercise. However, it was on the basis of experiences like this that the idea gradually dawned that, by causing social unrest, they were able to achieve collective benefits for themselves.

The older youths among them more readily understood that a reputation based on a notorious delinquent past (whether real, exaggerated or purely invented) could offer the basis for local power and give rise to such benefits as improvements in local housing, jobs and investment. What is more, they did not hesitate to use the 'juniors' to apply pressure whenever necessary. At Villiers-sur-Marne, such manipulation of the fear of disorder has always enabled about 15 delinquents and known ex-delinquents to carve out a place for themselves in the local government or secure municipal accommodation via a process of patronage.

It should also be pointed out that professionals and elected representatives responsible for the local population, especially its youth element, are also vulnerable to these forms of intimidation. Such individuals aspire to avoid harassment or assault at their workplace, or else fear being the object of the type of local mistrust which might undermine their work. But there are also those who have an entirely selfless interest in establishing cordial relations with the public and maintaining the civil peace. Social workers are likely to see the achievement of these objectives as a sign of their good work, the elected representatives as a sign of the population's satisfaction and the effectiveness of the services.

Violence and disruption, or the common belief by local politicians that social breakdown is always a possibility, can induce the *politicisation* of rioters, or possible rioters, however young they may be. Such politicisation must be understood here as part of a process of being incorporated as a political actor by local elites – even if that process appears confined to acts of patronage stimulated by the fear and pressure brought to bear by the local youths.

Conventional politicisation: the alternative to the riots

Over and above these discrete brokerages based on the threat of collective disorder and the individual dangers posed to local stakeholders, deviant actors also engage in more conventional political processes. Martin Sanchez-Jankowski describes the different modes of activity engaged by 'his' gangs during election time. With regard to the posses observed in Villiers, these engagements are selective, reactive and require a favourably disposed local political configuration.

This is what happened in April 2005 in the Hautes-Noues housing project, some months before the autumn riots. The starting point for this was the publication of a report by the mayor of Villiers-sur-Marne, Jacques-Alain Bénisti (UMP), for the attention of Dominique de Villepin, the then Home Minister,[4] on the prevention of delinquency. This document was circulated on the Internet some months later and caused an immediate nationwide scandal on account of its two central theses. For the first of these, Mr Bénisti claimed that there is a direct link between delinquency and whether or not the parents in question predominantly speak a language other than French within the home. The second thesis was concerned with the possible reform of the norm of client confidentiality subscribed to by social workers, so as to oblige them to disclose relevant information to the police. This report was a document scarcely read by the inhabitants, who nevertheless heard a lot about it from the internet and via word of mouth.

This had a direct bearing on the following events of March/April 2005, which are described in field notes written at the time:

The local movement took off with an interview posted on the website [Afrik.com] on 15 March 2005.[5] The mayor's remarks in it were simplified, the text much shorter and the proposals shocking. The parents from Sub-saharan Africa and the Maghreb countries were explicitly targeted. The use of the word 'Bamboula' instead of 'Bambara' angered all those who read it.[6] On the youths' side, the decision to act was taken one Sunday afternoon during a very well attended football game organised by an association. One of the militants of this association printed and made about a dozen copies of the interview. From the outset, there was consensus on the decision to act, but there were differences on what means to employ. Some proposed setting fire to the mayor's Peugeot car. The suggestion to act according to the rule of law ('do things properly') carried the day. The proposition resulting from the debates[7] (proposed by a militant and supported by a prominent figure from the local criminal scene) consisted of selecting extracts of the report and the interview, making 1,500 photocopies of these and putting them into the letter boxes of the people living in the housing project. One group was given the task of writing the text, another (all girls) that of photocopying and the job of distributing the tracts fell to the volunteers. The majority of the latter were part of the neighbourhood gangs (those between 18–20 years of age were more motivated).

The next day, a group was formed. Some specially targeted inhabitants of Hautes-Noues who wanted to demonstrate in order to make themselves heard, and delegated a group of negotiators (whom I eventually accompanied) to lay down their demands. On their side, the representatives of the Green and the Socialist parties[8] proposed to write a letter to the Prime Minister and the President of the Republic, and to circulate a petition. The members of the group were adamant that the principle of a public meeting was non-negotiable. The two parties were eventually obliged to accept this. A new text was drafted in the name of the 'group for human dignity', and distributed across the town.

The meeting in question took place on Saturday, 9 April at 11 a.m. Days earlier, the youths gathered under the leadership of gang members, who co-ordinated the distribution of leaflets while others participated actively in the informal meetings and initiated contacts with passers-by. As if to wrong-foot his possible detractors, the day before the meeting, the mayor distributed a letter denouncing the 'lies' levelled by his accusers. In the letter, he reiterated his 'regard' for the migrant families in *cité* Hautes-Noues, before inviting all interested citizens to attend a counter-meeting in the local cinema hall, situated no more than 150 metres from the site of the demonstration. The 'group for human dignity' responded by despatching someone to film the small group of about 20 people present at the counter-meeting (some of whom were young UMP militants[9] from the town and others retired Maghrebians who managed the mosque, while a handful more were municipal employees living in the housing project who had been urgently rounded up by the mayor).

By 11.45am, there were some 200 persons, chiefly neighbourhood residents, attending the demonstration in opposition to the mayor. Of the youths now present in force there were around 30 gang members. Also present in small number (a total of about four) were out-of-town activists from the *Mouvement des Indigènes de la République* (MIR) and the anti-fascist movement *Ras L'Front*.[10] These militants were completely unknown to the neighbourhood demonstrators, who made no attempt to communicate with them and who left them entirely to their own devices.

After the rally, dozens of people rushed to the cinema hall where the mayor was now holding court. The resulting face-off was tense but devoid of explicit threats or insults. Indeed, by 2pm, most of the young adults had returned to the housing project. The afternoon was then devoted to exchanging accounts of the event, amidst a general atmosphere of satisfaction.

The April rally made a lasting impact on local political life. The support of delinquent gang members – especially those regularly involved in local drug trading – was a key factor in encouraging the support of younger community members. The involvement of the gangs also demonstrated to a wide audience their commitment to their families, the people of the neighbourhood and what may be described as their own 'territory'. Not least of all, the demonstration underlined that the youths were an integral part of the neighbourhood and certainly enhanced their local reputation.

Fundamentally, the collective experience of 9 April was also something which helped to determine the relative calm of November 2005, together with the more conjectural factors already evoked. The demand for respect and recognition expressed by the residents' collective had now achieved an audience. This acquisition of a political 'voice' proved instrumental in such gains as the allocation of new jobs in a recently opened social centre to local residents of Maghrebian origin. The success of the political mobilisation also caused local players to openly question the riot as the only expression of political grievance.

Conclusion

The different forms of the mobilisation of gangs described in this chapter highlight the collective rationality of violence occurring during riots. Over and above the demand for respect and recognition which is expressed in this subversion of the social order, collective mobilisation of the youth from poor neighbourhoods has been seen to have a more or less lasting impact on their immediate environment. This chapter has further shown how the engagement of gang members may just as easily take the form of conventional political activity, such as public demonstrations, calls for national press release, work for the weakening of a local public opinion, or a more unconventional resort to violence and/or intimidation.

Moreover, the recurrence of riots reveals their intrinsic limits. They are reactive and situational, carried out by vulnerable people who lack political leverage and enjoy little access to national political structures. At the local level, the scarcity of economic and political resources limits the emergence of enduring and autonomous political movements, while it is fair to say that the established powers enjoy a much greater scope of resources in order to isolate or co-opt the emerging figureheads of protest (Jobard and Linhardt 2008). Nevertheless, as we have witnessed in this chapter, the politicisation resulting from lived experience of individual violence or collective breakdown is not easily extinguished. An arrest, a judicial condemnation, or even incarceration, will not necessarily anaesthetise the potential for an individual to revolt, however young he may be.

Notes

1 Hautes-Noues *cité* (a ZUS area) has been targeted by different *politiques de la ville* programmes over the last 25 years and was elected to be an ANRU site some months before the 2005 riots. Many indicators are typical for this kind of problematic area: one third of the *cité* inhabitants

are under 20 years old, one third of household's parents are foreigners (and one third of the foreign residents are unemployed), almost 40 per cent of inhabitants below 25 years old are unemployed. According to Lagrange's predictive model (this volume), Hautes-Noues *cité* should have had one of the highest levels of disorder during the 2005 riots – this proved not to happen in actuality.

2 A municipal building newly erected that houses youth and employement services, the local mission, various departments, a boxing ring and multi-purpose rooms.

3 Who is also a representative in the *Assemblée nationale* (French Parliament).

4 In May 2002, a government was formed by the new president, Jacques Chirac (UMP Party, winner of the presidential elections against Le Pen), in which Nicolas Sarkozy was the Home Minister and Dominique de Villepin, Minister for External Affairs. Sarkozy left the Home Ministry at the end of 2004, which was taken over by de Villepin. But the failure of the referendum on the European Union in May 2005 led President Chirac to form a new government, in which de Villepin was the Prime Minister and Sarkozy again the Home Minister.

5 http://www.Afrik.com/article 8205.html.

6 Bambara is one of the most spoken languages in Mali. 'Bamboula' is a derogatory racist expression found in French slang.

7 This was initially held in the gymnasium then continued over several days in the streets, building lobbies and in the youth centres.

8 Two parties from the national Left-wing coalition government (1997–2002), led by the Prime Minister Lionel Jospin.

9 UMP is the hegemonic conservative party in France, founded by Jacques Chirac after beating Jean-Marie Le Pen in 2002. The local mayor Jacques-Alain Benisti is a UMP member and MP.

10 The *Mouvement des Indigènes de la République* is a national movement founded at the beginning of 2005 that took an anti-colonial stance, imputing most of the problems of suburban youths in France to the colonial legacy. *Ras L'Front* is one of the principal anti-Front National organisations in France, created in the mid-eighties (see Chapter 11).

Chapter 14

The French police and urban riots: is the national police force part of the solution or part of the problem?

Christian Mouhanna

Introduction

This chapter examines the role of the police in the 2005 French riots. The police occupy a central role in the French state. Bearing this in mind, and given recent criticisms of their conduct in relation to the youth of the *banlieues*, it seems pertinent to ask such questions as: was police authority in any way responsible for triggering the riots in France? And what lessons should the police be drawing from the riots? We shall endeavour to answer these questions on the basis of 15 years of fieldwork studies on the police, the gendarmerie and their relationships with the residents of several so-called sensitive urban zones, and information mustered by the author during his time spent as Chief of Research at the Ministry of the Interior.

The policing context

Although the October–November 2005 events created a cataclysmic worldwide stir, they are part of an indisputable continuity. French *banlieues* have regularly been hit by riots of this type since the beginning of the 1980s, and more so since the early 1990s. Periodically, a neighbourhood goes up in flames, police patrols are attacked and, police stations and schools burnt out. Initially confined to the suburbs of big cities (like Paris, Lyon, Lille, Toulouse), in the past few years these types of riots have also occurred in middle-sized cities (for example, Thonon les Bains and Saint Dizier, both with fewer than 30,000 inhabitants, and Vitry le François, which has fewer than 20,000). Even outside these periods of extreme crisis, the burning of cars is normative – more than 40,000 cars were officially reported as having been 'torched' in 2007 alone. Relations between the police and the youths who live in these neighbourhoods are permanently on edge. The former try to keep these sectors 'under control', as they say, by increasing the prevalence of patrolling officers and having them carry out more intensive and extensive controls, involving stop-and-search operations, which the latter invariably find humiliating.

But police sovereignty over this territory is tenuous at best. Not infrequently, insults are hurled at the police, their cars are routinely spat upon, and various projectiles are lobbed at them from tall buildings. Officers interviewed over the 15-year research period regularly confessed to strong feelings of fearfulness. While it is true that authoritative institutions as a whole are affected by acts of rejection and contempt, as we can glean from the burning of schools and aggression against teachers, there is no doubt that the police are the primary focus of this hatred. Of course, it is perfectly understandable that the forces responsible for maintaining law and order, and enforcing the respect for the rules and regulations of society, should occasionally generate resentment. What we are nonetheless witnessing in the *banlieues* is a situation of permanent hostility on the part of people objecting to the siege-like presence of the police and their apparent indifference to the need to maintain any reasonable relationship with local residents.

A further key dimension to be considered concerns the political usage of the police in French society. It is imperative to understand that, in France, most police forces are under the central authority of the Minister of the Interior. This legally enshrined subservience was gradually reinforced as part of a politically opportunistic strategy adopted in 2002 by the then Minister, Nicolas Sarkozy, with the aim of succeeding to the Presidency of the Republic on the basis of a strong law and order platform (Monjardet 2008). In this respect, the riots occurred amidst fierce antagonism between Mr Sarkozy – 'France's first cop' – and the youths of the *banlieues*.

The French national police force: the solution

The French police and the gendarmerie have a long tradition of combating riots and civil disorders of all kinds. Some 17,000 officers from *Gendarmerie Nationale*[1] and 14,000 officers from *Police Nationale*[2] serve in detachments designated here as 'riot police forces' (known respectively as '*Gendarmerie mobile*' and 'CRS' forces). These personnel may be sent by the Home Ministry to any part of French territory where an alert has been sounded (Bruneteau 1996; Fillieule and Jobard 1998). These police and gendarme reserve forces do virtually nothing else except control riots, monitor demonstrations, and patrol 'risky' areas. Being permanently on hand, these forces constitute a rapid response mechanism geared to intervening rapidly and ensuring physical control of any urban territory.

French police strategy is based above all on the logic of *space saturation* techniques. In practice, this typically involves deploying enough troops to instantly make their presence felt, and showing through frequent use of stop-and-search that the state (in the form of its police) is now in full control of the area.[3] This symbolic use of force is customarily preferred to the alternative tactic of arresting the more dangerous delinquents. Negotiation, mediation and prevention are alien, some might say altogether forbidden, practices. The use of these special police forces is clearly designed to achieve a balance of (physical) power favourable to the state.[4] Each time a riot takes place, the appearance of this massive and intimidating police presence makes it possible to confine the incidents in question to a particular urban zone and to suppress all rioting within a matter of few days.

This strategy – relatively simple and effective in the short term because it allows a speedy response to complex problems – has rubbed off on other, non-specialist police officers. Thus, small law and order units have been created at the *département* level[5] and even the local urban police forces are now trained to 'tackle' riots and disorders, in preference to talking to or negotiating with their civilian adversaries. The maintenance of public order and tight control of protesters are considered major priorities at all levels of policing. During his stints as Minister of the Interior (from May 2002 to March 2004, and June 2005 to March 2007), Nicolas Sarkozy consolidated French commitment to the space saturation model by devoting more resources to law enforcement personnel, equipment and strategies whilst abandoning all reference to problem-solving or neighbourhood policing (Goldstein 1990; Johnston 2005).

Ever since the 1960s, the riot police's broad objective has been not only to restore order whenever it is was threatened (during demonstrations, for example) and to protect public institutions (such as police headquarters and the Ministry, or prefectures in any of the 100 *départements*), but also to prevent any deaths from occurring as a consequence of police actions. This objective is partly humanitarian but is also political in orientation: public authorities have long appreciated that the violent deaths of demonstrators are capable of bestowing added legitimacy on the cause for which they have 'sacrificed' their lives.[6] The prime goal of the riot police is therefore always to arrest the rioters without ever killing or seriously wounding them, and we should note that, up to press, police forces have generally succeeded in this objective. Thus, during the 2005 riots, more than 11,000 policemen intervened on a nightly basis in riots right across France, while other reserve forces were constantly on alert. More than 200 policemen and gendarmes were wounded in the process. However, despite being exposed in extreme cases to deadly projectiles and rifles, the police chose not to return fire at the rioters. With the exception of the youths whose electrocution triggered the riots, no one died in the clashes and police strategy was therefore vindicated.

In 2005, the entire French political class concurred that police commitment had made it possible to maintain law and order and praised them on their overall efficacy. Hard-line policies sponsored by the Interior Ministry were regarded as having been validated by the restoration of peace. The Minister himself used this 'victory' to consolidate his image as the dependable custodian of law and order. Such discourses and policies also reinforced the collective spirit of the police and the gendarmes who saw themselves as the 'guardians of the Republic' and 'the last bastion of civilisation against barbarity'.[7] As far as onlooking French politicians were concerned, the fact that they knew now that they could rely on a suitably strong police force enabled them to avoid a more penetrating and potentially discomfiting assessment of the functioning of French society.

The French national police force: the problem

The police were by no means the single cause of the tension and disorder in the lead up to the riots. It is fair to say, however, that they invariably played a part in the triggering of such disorders. A familiar scenario was repeated in every instance. A young man or an adolescent was killed or wounded during a police intervention in a sensitive urban place. The news very quickly spread among the youths of this sector, most of whom automatically blamed the police for these atrocities, who were seen as enjoying a 'licence to kill'. The fact that police conduct is so often the catalyst of these riots is no accidental matter. The riots form part of a permanent state of conflict between the police and local youths in which even the former appear to take on the guise of one organised gang regularly confronting another (Mohammed 2008; Mouhanna 2006).

While the specialist riot police are regularly subjected to processes of critical reflection, resulting in recommendations for their improvement, the same cannot be said of the regular police, who are widely regarded as impervious to public or political influence, save for that emanating from the Interior Ministry. The various attempts to make the police more publicly accountable have been resisted on the grounds that the police profession itself is the only one truly qualified to deliberate on physical intervention and criminal investigation. Used to being only accountable to a single central authority, the police consider the public unfit to co-operate with them on aspects of local security. This avowedly centralised ethos has several important implications for public order management.

The first such implication is that police officers tend to be recruited nationwide through a centralised authority. Most new police recruits come from peaceful parts of the country and are sent to places far removed (both in terms of distance and in character) from their actual regions of origin. For many, this means deployment in the *banlieues* where, faced with local hostility, they make no determined attempt to forge a lasting relationship with neighbourhood residents. Without being prepared to tackle or understand the local population, these young police officers do not try to network with the inhabitants. On the contrary, they leave their place of work as soon as possible, returning to their home towns after four days of service for the two days of rest that follow. It is normative for such officers to be transferred to a less demanding beat at the end of two or three years of 'frontline' service. In the *département* of Seine-Saint-Denis (where Clichy-sous-Bois is located), the police officers posted there in 2005 had been there less than two years and their average age was 26.[8]

It is striking to see, when travelling in a patrol vehicle, the extent to which most police officers regard themselves as outsiders in these neighbourhoods, referring to the residents as 'them' and 'these people' and applying a range of belittling terms to describe the youths who live there. The younger officers making up the great majority of police personnel in the sensitive sectors know few residents by name – apart from, that is, from those few delinquents who regularly pass through the local police station. Officers therefore are permanently suspicious of every civilian they encounter, seeking first and foremost to ensure their own protection (Mouhanna 2000).

The lack of empathy towards the residents of the deprived neighbourhoods is also due to the racial and social prejudices widely prevalent in police stations. These prejudices are encouraged by the manner in which the police and police work are organised, in that the control strategies that officers are routinely asked to exercise primarily target people who are racially and socially marked out as 'young men of migrant origin'. The police are genuinely convinced that this type of person is primarily responsible for disorder and delinquency, and that it is therefore legitimate to concentrate all efforts in their direction. The recent tightening of policy in shift on the fight against illegal immigration has enhanced this police focus on ethnic minorities. Such sections of society find themselves subjected to greater numbers of identity checks than corresponding white peers, regardless of whether they are French citizens or not.

The modern emphasis on reactive methods of policing is exemplified by a preference for using 'fire-brigade' tactics in relation to even the most mundane security issues. Rather than carrying out a patient and carefully constructed operation based on the thorough investigation of a specified subject, the police are more liable to act without due focus and discretion. Thus, police personnel, comprising local police officers and reinforcements from riot police units, will typically surround an entire neighbourhood for up to several days. Each person, whatever their age, will be stopped on the roadside until their identity has been verified and the reasons for their comings and goings ascertained. Needless to say, the impact on local youth is considerable. It is extremely rare for this type of control to result in the identification of criminals (as the police themselves will readily concede) but that is not the point. Such operations are principally designed to demonstrate that the police institution 'has the neighbourhood well in hand' and is capable of impressing and intimidating the people. As the former Interior Minister Charles Pasqua once remarked, 'Fear of the gendarme is the commencement of wisdom'.[9] However, actual experience has consistently shown that repressive measures of this type seldom result in submission to authority. Rather, they invariably provoke a vicious circle of resentment and retaliation (Mouhanna 2000a).

In practical terms, those youths, finding themselves frequently stopped and checked, invariably turn rebellious and proceed to vent their anger and indignation by harassing, insulting and even abusing police patrols acting in isolation of their colleagues. This type of assault not only enhances the feelings of prejudice commonly experienced by officers in the *banlieues*, but also encourages police interventions of dubious legality, stemming from the desire for violent reprisal. On their side, the youth from the deprived neighbourhoods feel persecuted by the police and react to stop-and-search operations by stone throwing or ambushes.

The upshot of all this is a situation of latent and permanent conflict, with occasional interspersions of violence on both sides. Where the police are concerned, this state of affairs not only reduces the legitimacy of their actions but forces them assume the customs and manners of a gang – quite literally, to the extent that plain-clothed officers often resort to wearing 'uniforms' which duplicate the fashion sense of local youths. The way that the police talk to people in deprived areas undergoes a similar transformation, symbolising a lack of respect for the inhabitants, and contravening a formal obligation referred to in the Code of ethics (*Code de déontologie*) adopted in 1986. Hence, the use of '*tu*' (i.e. the less formal 'you') employed in relation to the youths – and, increasingly, the older inhabitants as well – has become habitual.

Another significant factor which helps to explain the distance between the police and the residents of the poor neighbourhoods is the increasing use of technologies that enable the police to avoid human contact. The search for information is now done more through computers and dossiers than through conversation. As a result, interaction that could have led to better interpersonal understanding is becoming a rarity. Officers complain that the 'people do not speak to them any more', though in reality the police are no longer listening.[10]

The politicisation of the police system?

Any notions of the police being in the service of, or accountable to, the public are largely incompatible with the French model of policing. Most police officers would not consider that they are in the service of the citizenry. This general attitude is reinforced within the tough suburbs due to the fact that, in police eyes at least, there exists a segment of the population that does not qualify for full rights of citizenship because it is essentially 'foreign' in its origins.

The whole issue of 'law and order' invariably assumes a salient position on the French political agenda. In the three years predating the French riots, the then Minister of the Interior, Nicolas Sarkozy, staked out his claim for political popularity on the basis of his self-professed determination to be resolute on matters of security and order (Monjardet 2008). This image was partially constructed on the basis of such hardline measures as shelving any plans he may otherwise have had to introduce a system of reforms aimed at a citizens' oriented police 'neighbourhood policing', or *'police de proximité'* (Mouhanna 2008), and reaffirming through bonus payments and promotion schemes a commitment to more reactive ('fire brigade') modes of policing. Relatedly, Mr Sarkozy made classic use of the image of *banlieue* youths as society's 'enemies within' to designate them as the primary target of police action. Grassroots-level police officers were immediately wary of the possible consequences of the Minister's hardline rhetoric. As one of them confided in interview, 'he is playing this game to get re-elected. In the meantime, I am on my own with my colleague on the beat, and we will be the ones who are going to pay the bill.' But even those officers most concerned by this political transparency were eventually goaded into confrontation, not only by those more senior than themselves, but also by the youths who came spoiling for a fight.

We have stressed the historical continuity of the events of late 2005 in terms of the police-youth relations. However, these events also marked an important turning point in the direction of nationwide security policy. The simultaneous occurrence of the riots in more than 300 *communes* on French territory caused widespread surprise and anxiety. Far from being the fallout of a political organisation capable of co-ordinating this type of revolt, such action was relatively spontaneous and allowed to spread unchecked. In several areas, the central authorities could not financially afford to send the type of reinforcements demanded of them by the police commissioners and prefects. Other local officials breathed huge sighs of relief on discovering that not all neighbourhoods in their sector had erupted into violence. Had they done so, the whole security system would have been entirely overwhelmed. The weakness of the police, and, consequently, of the State, became clear to some of the people. Both at the strategic as well as the symbolic level, the classic system of maintenance of public order was undermined not only in the eyes of the prefects and the police officers, but probably in the eyes of the people as well.

Alongside feelings of relief and even victory experienced by some politicians and senior administrators,[11] there was also concern for the disruption observed locally. Thus there began a veritable 'arms race' designed to re-equip the police with a range of hardware, including helicopters, drones, and non-lethal weapons such as Flashballs or Tasers. From a political point of view, the central government cordoned itself off from any possibility of engaging in constructive dialogue on police repression with members of the rough neighbourhoods. Having refused to enter into a dialogue before the riots when it was arguably much stronger, it was even less inclined to do so now, especially as the new President of the Republic, Mr Sarkozy, had fashioned his whole image and legitimacy on an unwillingness to compromise.

The enhanced centralisation and politicisation of national-level security issues inevitably produced practical consequences for police work. Instead of letting beat constables adapt to local realities, the latter found themselves committed to obeying national directives. In its drive to demonstrate 'positive results', the government has been cultivating what is now referred to in police circles and the law itself as an 'efficiency culture' (*culture du résultat*). All police stations are now obliged to provide statistics which will hopefully indicate that criminality is on the decline and that clearance rates are better. This new public management approach is not concerned with satisfying public demands (Matelly and Mouhanna 2007). Despite the 2005 riots, a large part of the public thinks that everything is fine and that criminality is on the decline. For those living inside the *banlieues*, it is not certain whether this is truly the case, particularly as minor (and largely unreported) riots regularly occur to remind us all that tensions run just as high as ever.

The police, for their part, were initially receptive towards this 'numbers game', especially as good figures achieved by methods fair or foul were linked to potential wage rises. Officers soon became disgruntled, though largely because the authoritarian approach characterising the last few years had proven dangerously confrontational. It was also quickly realised that the police officer who managed a local criminal justice problem without having to make an arrest was no longer given credit for his or her actions. By contrast, those colleagues choosing to haul in perpetrators of even the most minor misdemeanour stood to be commended – and in the long term, possibly promoted – for their conduct in the field.

The political appropriation of law and order issues not only fails at the end of the day to produce real improvements in security, but also has the effect of aggravating local tensions. As in other countries, massive and uncompromising police actions have been used as a smokescreen for hiding deeper, underlying problems; but perhaps more than in other countries, France uses law enforcement to prevent crucial questions from emerging as well as to stifle grievances. That is why in those sectors where such problems are particularly manifest recurring police-community conflict will remain inevitable.[12]

Notes

1 Out of 84,000 policemen all ranks taken together (not including auxiliary staff).

2 Compared with 64,000 policemen of all ranks serving in the police stations.

3 During the November 2007 riots in Villiers-le-Bel, a town of 27,000 inhabitants, more than 1,000 policemen took control of the town's sensitive zone (Lagrange 2008a).

4 See, for example, the Sevran operation, conducted on 24 April, 2008: 350 policemen were mobilised for a single operation in one neighbourhood. Result: five people were stopped and checked, one weapon and 800g of cannabis were seized. Many incidents of this kind have been recorded previously. A similar police operation is described in details in Jobard and Linhardt 2008: 87–90.

5 France is divided into 100 *départments*. Each of these *départements* is administered by a *préfet* who represents the central state authority and who is accountable for the maintenance of public order. It is the *préfet*, and not the local authorities, who directs police operations. In addition, in France there are approximately 400 police districts, headed by a police commissioner, but always under the more or less direct authority of the prefect.

6 The best known example of a death dates back to the student demonstration of 6 December 1986. Malik Oussekine, a young man of Maghrebian origin, died after he was beaten up by policemen from a motorcycle squad, which was subsequently dissolved. The political future of the government at the time, led by Jacques Chirac, was considerably affected by this sensational event (Fillieule and Jobard 1998: 82).

7 Words recorded by the author during interviews with the police.

8 According to a note sent by the 93rd *département préfét* to the Ministry of the Interior chief of staff, 13 June 2006 (*situation de la délinquance en Seine Saint Denis*).

9 Charles Pasqua on the TV political show, *L'Heure de Vérité*, channel A2, 2 July, 1986. Charles Pasqua is considered to have been one of the most influential political mentors of Nicolas Sarkozy.

10 Statements collected by the author.

11 On several occasions, a number of police chiefs and administrative officials proudly announced that 'victory in some suburban cities' had been won 'thanks to the helicopters that had paralysed the rioters' (interviews conducted by the author).

12 Thus, in Grigny, to the south of Paris where the police had been fired at in 2005, seven pistol shots were fired at 30 to 40 young rioters by some of the 20 officers present, who had been targeted by the rioters. See Bronner 2008.

Chapter 15

The 2007 presidential election and the 2005 urban violence in French 'deprived urban areas'

Christine Fauvelle-Aymar, Abel François and Patricia Vornetti

What is at stake in the analysis of voting patterns in deprived urban areas?

Although voting is an individual act, it is strongly influenced by the context in which the voter makes his or her choice. Whatever their individual characteristics – whether they are young or old, university graduate or not, employed or unemployed – voters behave differently depending on their place of residence. The demographic structure, social composition, economic conditions, spatial configuration, etc., characterising the electoral environment all influence people's decisions whether or not to vote or abstain, and their ultimate choice of party and/or candidate. In this sense, electoral behaviour is necessarily territorial.

Discussions of the possible impact of the territorial context on voting behaviour are generally absent from studies of French electoral activity, despite the fact that they once held a central place in French political science (Siegfried 1913). This absence is all the more surprising given that the significance of local environmental factors has been acknowledged in numerous Anglo-Saxon studies.[1] For example, a study by Butler and Stokes (1969) shows that British workers who live in 'middle class' constituencies are less likely to vote Labour and more likely to vote for the Conservative party than those who reside in other types of constituencies. In the French case, the works of Braconnier and Dormagen (2007) and Badariotti and Bussi (2004) stress the importance of ecological analysis in the understanding of electoral behaviours.

The territories we have chosen to analyse in this article[2] are those that French public policy makers have designated as urban priority areas. Such localities are known as *Zones Urbaines Sensibles* (ZUSs), or deprived urban areas. The 1996 law on *Politique de la ville* created these zones and defined them as being 'characterised by the presence of large complexes, degraded housing and a major imbalance between housing and employment'. Approximately 8 per cent of the population today lives in 751 ZUSs in France. The specific features of these territories constitute an ideal ground for an ecological analysis of political behaviours. Their residents in particular live under tough socio-economic conditions. According to the last census of 1999:[3]

- unemployment affects one out of four workers in the ZUSs (i.e. nearly twice the national average);
- more than one adult out of three has less than a primary level of education (against one out of five at the national level); and
- more than one family in four is a single-parent family (nearly twice the national ratio).

These territories made headlines in the autumn of 2005 by becoming the scene of urban violence. In the aftermath of these events, several associations called for registration on the electoral rolls – hitherto, massively incomplete in the case of deprived urban areas[4] – in anticipation of the 2007 presidential elections. Such activity enhanced the salience of suburban issues insofar as the political agenda for the 2007 presidential election was concerned.

Analysis of the results of the presidential election in ZUSs is interesting, not only in terms of its capacity to help us to better understand the link between territory and voting behaviour, but also to the extent that it enables us to address the possible relationship between urban violence and voting. Having outlined the scope of our study we will then set out the details of our analysis by examining in turn the issue of abstention and the electoral choices made by voters in the 2007 presidential election in comparison with the previous one (2002) and with the 2002 and 2007 parliamentary elections. We will then try to determine any possible influence of the 2005 riots on voting in the 2007 presidential election. Finally we draw the main conclusions of the study.

Scope of the study

The principal difficulty when analysing the voting pattern in ZUSs arises from the fact that the spatial configurations of such areas do not correspond to the electoral districts of which they form part. Therefore it became necessary to first reconstitute the results of the elections occurring in these spaces.

Identification of the electoral results in ZUSs

The lowest administrative level for which electoral results are available is that of the polling station. The management of polling stations comes under the auspices of the municipal administration. The delimitation of polling stations is not controversial since any redefining of the perimeter of polling stations has to be carried out within the existing boundaries of legislative constituencies. The issues at stake in the definition of a portion of a *commune* as a priority area (i.e. as a ZUS) are of a completely different order, given that it enables the implementation of specific public measures in this area (e.g. tax exemption, better employment and business development and other assistance mechanisms) and leads to an increase of government funding into the *commune*. The geographical delimitation of ZUS is thus the outcome of intense negotiations between the *communes* and the central administration. At times they have resulted in very simple and coherent boundaries (Figure 15.1); at others, much less so by comparison (Figure 15.2).

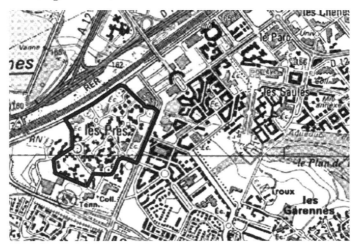

Figure 15.1 Example of a simple spatial delimitation of a ZUS. ZUS Les Prés de Montigny-le-Bretonneux (Yvelines)
Source: Délégation Interministérielle à la Ville (DIV): http://i.ville.gouv.fr/

185

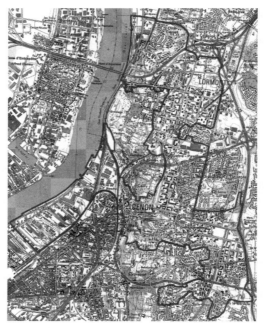

Figure 15.2 Example of a complex spatial delimitation of a ZUS. ZUS 'Hauts de Garonne-Bastide (Queyries-Brazza)' belonging to the *communes* of Bordeaux, Cénon, Floirac and Lormont
Source: Délégation Interministérielle à la Ville (DIV): http://i.ville.gouv.fr/

Thus the spatial delimitation of ZUSs is not linked to the electoral divisions marked out by the municipalities.[5] In order to give an electoral identity to the ZUSs, it was necessary to classify the polling stations of the *communes* we studied.

The polling stations of each *commune* containing a ZUS can be of three kinds. They can be:

- entirely composed of registered voters residing in the ZUSs – polling stations of the BI type,
- composed exclusively of registered voters living outside the ZUS – polling stations of the BE type,
- composed of a mix of voters registered in and outside the ZUS – polling stations of the BM type.

The following diagram (Figure 15.3) helps to better understand this typology of polling stations.

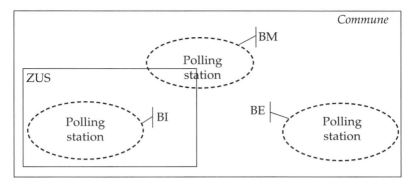

Figure 15.3 The classification of the polling stations in a given *commune.*

The election results that can be ascribed to ZUS voters are those observed in the BI polling stations. The comparison between these results and those from the BE stations enables us to situate the ZUS electorally in relation to the *communes* they belong to. The 'mixed' polling stations (BM) have to be excluded from the analysis as they include voters residing inside and outside the ZUS.

The ZUS sample

We have randomly selected a sample of ZUSs from among those having more than 1,800 inhabitants in the 1999 census (i.e. a total of 613 ZUSs out of the 751 existing ZUSs). The selection was carried out on a *commune*-based classification and all the ZUSs of each selected *commune* were included in the sample. The selection then comprised about 250 ZUSs. The classification of polling stations resulted in the elimination of about one fifth of this selection. Finally, the study sample is composed of 196 ZUSs (i.e. more than 30 per cent of all the ZUSs in the same demographic category) belonging to 108 *communes,* which makes for a total of 576 polling stations entirely located in ZUSs.[6]

The elections covered

The present analysis of electoral behaviour in ZUSs focuses on the 2007 presidential election. However, in order to fully appreciate the general trends, we will do a two-fold comparison: first, with another type of election (the 2007 parliamentary election); and second, with earlier elections (the 2002 parliamentary and presidential elections). This two-fold comparison will only be undertaken in relation to abstention patterns. With regard to voter choices, the comparison will be limited to the last presidential election. Attempting to compare voting preferences in a national poll (presidential election) with those made in a local one (parliamentary election) is rather hazardous since, in the first case, candidates are the same everywhere; while in the second case, voters deal with different political alternatives, depending on the electoral district in which they live, with the number and political affiliation of local candidates greatly varying from one district to another. Moreover, party coalitions change from one parliamentary election to the next, whereas some parties vanish or merge with other ones. The comparison of voter choices between territories, between elections or over time, is thus rather difficult to interpret in the case of parliamentary elections.

Abstention patterns in the ZUSs

At the national level, turnout at the 2007 presidential election rose greatly in comparison with 2002, and then declined at the parliamentary election. We will start by determining whether abstention in ZUSs followed a similar trend. We will then try to evaluate the discrepancies in the turnout levels as well as in their trends, between the ZUSs and the rest of the *communes* in which they are located.

From the 2002 to the 2007 presidential election

The upsurge in electoral mobilisation during the last presidential election was especially marked in ZUSs. In comparison with 2002, not only was there a drop in the level of abstention – more than 15 percentage points in the first round and nearly six points in the second round – but this feature was more apparent in ZUSs than at the national level. The abstention differential between ZUSs and the country as a whole thus decreased from 2002 to 2007 but it remained equal to more than four percentage points in the first as well as the second rounds (Table 15.1).

We should further note, however, that the relative dispersion of the abstention rates in ZUSs[7] was greater in 2007 than in 2002, especially in the first round (the mean deviation between the different abstention rates in ZUSs was 25 per cent of the average rate in 2007 against 16 per cent in 2002). It would seem that the 2002 non-voters did not mobilise in the same proportion in the various ZUSs in 2007.

Table 15.1 Evolution of abstention in ZUSs

	Presidential			Parlia-mentary 2007	Difference Parl. /Presid.
	2002	2007	Difference 2007/2002		
1st round					
Average rate†	36.0%	20.8%	−15.2	49.9%	+29.1
Minimum rate	22.7%	12.2%	−10.5	33.7%	+21.5
Maximum rate	64.9%	52.3%	−12.6	86.4%	+34.1
Coefficient of variation	0.159	0.249	+0.09	0.145	−0.104
Difference ZUS − France (in % points)	7.6	4.6	−3.0	10.4	+5.8
Odds ratios of turnout in 2007 compared to 2002		1.24		0.90	
2nd round					
Average rate†	26.2%	20.5%	−5.7	50.3%	+29.8
Minimum rate	16.0%	12.6%	−3.4	35.0%	+22.4
Maximum rate	48.2%	46.2%	−2.0	77.8%	+31.6
Coefficient of variation	0.192	0.218	+0.03	0.137	−0.081
Difference ZUS − France (in % points)	5.9	4.5	−1.4	10.3	+5.8
Odds ratios of turnout in 2007 compared to 2002		1.08		0.97	

†The average rates correspond to the average of the abstention rates observed in the ZUSs. Taking account of the fact that polling stations have a similar number of registered voters, this simple average is very close to a weighted average.

If turnout rose almost everywhere (in more than 95 per cent cases of the ZUSs comprising the sample), the increase was quite diverse from one ZUS to another, rising by as much as 28 percentage points between the two first rounds and up to 18 points between the two second rounds.

From the 2007 presidential election to the 2007 parliamentary polls

Two factors emerge from the comparison of the two types of elections that were held in 2007 (see Table 15.1 above).

First, voter mobilisation in ZUSs was much higher in the presidential election than in the parliamentary elections, with an average difference in abstention between the first rounds of each election amounting to 29 percentage points. Second, there was very little change in abstention in ZUSs between the two rounds of each election (–0.3 for the presidential election, +0.4 for the assembly polls).

The two factors highlighted here (a greater electoral mobilisation in the presidential than in the parliamentary elections, and a more noticeable difference between the types of election than between the rounds of each election) represent typical outcomes of French elections. In this sense, electoral turnout behaviour in ZUSs conforms to the one that is generally observed, even if, in terms of level, differences are more clear cut.

The 'odds ratios' of electoral turnout in 2007 in relation to 2002 (see Table 15.1, above)[8] underline the peculiarity of the first round of 2007 presidential election. This round is the only one for which the chances of a ZUS voter going to the polls were larger in 2007 than in 2002. The increased mobilisation in ZUSs for the presidential election was not repeated during the ensuing parliamentary elections. The fact that the ZUS abstention rate moved closer to the national average in the 2007 presidential election cannot be thus interpreted as the beginnings of a convergence movement of ZUS voters' electoral behaviour with that of residents of other territories.

The ZUSs and their communes

The preceding developments showed that ZUSs deviate from the national average both in terms of abstention levels as well as regarding the magnitude of turnout change from one election to another. Here we ask whether or not they also deviate from the wider territories in which they are located. In order to address this question, we will look at the differences in abstention rates between each ZUS and the rest of its host *commune*. The advantage of this type of calculation is that it neutralises the eventual influence of communal factors (which would operate in the ZUS as well as in the rest of the *commune*) of the sort found in the analysis of Butler and Stokes (1969). The results are given in Table 15.2 below.

Whatever the election concerned, ZUS voters, on the whole, abstain more than the other voters of their *communes* (the average difference amounts to 7–8 points in the parliamentary, and 4–5 points in the presidential elections). The value of the maximal positive difference can be very high: the rate of abstention in a ZUS can hence be more than 40 points higher than that observed in the rest of the *commune* (in the 2007 parliamentary elections). Electoral patterns in ZUSs thus differ from the territories in which they are situated.

Table 15.2 Abstention in and outside of ZUSs

| | Parliamentary | | Presidential | |
	2002	2007	2002	2007
1st round				
Maximal positive difference	24.4	43.6	33.1	30.1
Maximal negative difference	−8.3	−7.1	−7.7	−5.7
Average difference	7.6	7.8	5.3	4.1
Coefficient of variation	0.79	0.85	1.05	1.04
Coefficient of correlation ZUS/ outside ZUS†	*0.42*	*0.41*	*0.35*	*0.58*
Odds ratios of turnout in ZUS/ outside ZUS	0.84	0.83	0.91	0.93
2nd round				
Maximal positive difference	32.8	36.0	23.2	25.1
Maximal negative difference	−7.1	−6.7	−6.2	−5.0
Average difference	7.0	6.6	4.5	3.7
Coefficient of variation	0.88	0.89	0.98	1.05
Coefficient of correlation ZUS/ outside ZUS††	*0.47*	*0.54*	*0.52*	*0.52*
Odds ratios of turnout in ZUS/ outside ZUS	0.86	0.85	0.92	0.94

†The differences are calculated as the difference, for each ZUS, between the abstention rate in the ZUS and in the rest of the *commune*.
††The coefficients of correlation are all significant at the 1 per cent level.

The odds ratios of voter turnout in and outside of ZUSs confirm this greater propensity for ZUS voters to abstain. In fact, all the odds ratios are significantly less than 1, indicating that ZUS voters are more likely to abstain than the other residents of their *communes*. We should note, however, that behavioural differences are less important in the presidential election than in the parliamentary equivalent.

Voting trends in the presidential election

For the reasons given on pp. 187–188, we shall only consider ZUS voting preferences in relation to the presidential elections. We will first ascertain the voting trends in ZUSs in the 2007 presidential election. Then we will study the evolution taking place between 2002 and 2007. We will conclude by comparing the ZUSs with the *communes* in which they are located.

Rioting in the UK and France

The scores obtained by the political 'families' in ZUSs in the 2007 presidential election

In the first round of the 2007 presidential election, left-wing parties exhibited a clear lead in the ZUSs, to the extent that they totalled more than 40 per cent of the votes and were ahead of right-wing parties by nearly 20 percentage points. The centrist party came next (with 15 per cent of ZUS votes), followed by the extreme right (10 per cent). The extreme left is the political 'family' whose score in ZUS was the lowest (see Table 15.3 below). It seems that ZUS voters responded to the call for 'useful votes'[9] by concentrating their votes on the main candidates of the two major parties, with Ségolène Royal and Nicolas Sarkozy receiving more than 60 per cent of the ballots between them.

In the second round, Royal easily maintained her lead within the ZUSs by winning three out of every five votes. In fact, her score was much higher (by more than 10 points) than the total votes accumulated by the left and extreme left parties in the first round. These surplus votes probably came from a split in the votes received by François Bayrou (the centrist candidate) in the first round. If we assume that there was a 'perfect' transference of votes between the two rounds – that is, all the left and extreme left votes being transferred to Ségolène Royal and all the right and extreme right votes to Nicolas

Table 15.3 Results of the 2007 presidential election in the ZUSs

In % of expressed votes	1st round	ZUSs 2nd round	France 1st round	2007–2002 2nd round	Difference (1st round) ZUSs	France
Extreme left	8.3		7.1		–3.8	–3.3
Left	42.6		29.4		–1.2	–3.0
S. Royal	*38.5*	62.2	*25.9*	46.9	*+16.8*	*+15.0*
Centre	14.8		18.6		+10.4	+11.8
Right	23.6		34.5		+4.5	+3.4
N. Sarkozy	*21.9*	37.8	*31.2*	53.1	*+7.1*	*+11.3*
Extreme right	10.6		10.4		–9.9	–8.8

Note: In the 2007 presidential election, the extreme left includes O. Besancenot, J. Bové, A. Laguiller and A. Schivardi; the left includes M.-G. Buffet, S. Royal and D. Voynet; the centre F. Bayrou; the right P. de Villiers, F. Nihous and N. Sarkozy; the extreme right J.-M. Le Pen. In 2002, L. Jospin was the candidate of the main left party (Socialist Party) and J. Chirac the candidate of the main right party (RPR).

Sarkozy – then 75 per cent of the votes of the centrist candidate in the ZUSs would be passed on to the left candidate.

Evolution of voting patterns from the previous presidential election

At the national level, the 2007 presidential election was chiefly marked by three evolutionary departures from trends shown in the previous election: the implementation of the 'useful vote' strategy, which resulted in the elimination of minor candidates; the breakthrough made by Bayrou; and the decline of the extreme right. These evolutions can also be seen in the ZUSs incorporated in our sample (see last columns of Table 15.3 above).[10]

In ZUSs, as in the country as a whole, the centrist party represented by Bayrou, improved its score by more than 10 percentage points, while the two extreme parties, both left and right, showed a marked decline (3–4 points for the extreme left and 9–10 points for the extreme right).[11] In ZUSs as elsewhere, right-wing parties gained points whereas the left regressed. At the national level the progress made by right-wing parties was of the same order as the decline of left parties (around three percentage points), while in ZUSs, gains by the right were disproportionately larger than losses incurred by the left.

The ZUSs and their communes

Table 15.4 compares the average score of the different candidates in the 2007 presidential election within ZUSs with the scores they achieved in the rest of the *communes* in which the ZUSs are located.

We will start by observing that the scores recorded in the rest of the *communes* in which ZUSs are situated do not conform to the national averages.[12] ZUSs are located in *communes* whose voters are more inclined to vote for the left – and less so for the right – than the average French voter. This characteristic is reinforced for ZUS voters in comparison to voters living in the rest of their *communes*. Hence, the left performed much better in ZUSs than in the rest of the *communes*, while the right made a relatively poor showing, with an average difference, in both cases, of around eight percentage points in the first round of the 2007 presidential elections and nearly 10 in the second round. Extreme parties also registered better scores in ZUSs (+1.5 points of difference for the extreme left and for the extreme right) at the expense of the centrist party (approximately –4 points). The calculation of the odds ratios clearly shows that the ZUS voters were less attracted by right and centrist candidates, compared with the other voters in their *communes*[13]

193

Table 15.4 Scores in and outside of the ZUSs in the 2007 presidential election.

	ZUS		Outside ZUS		Odds ratios ZUS/outside ZUS†		Change in the difference ZUS – outside ZUS compared to 2002††
	1st round	2nd round	1st round	2nd round	1st round	2nd round	
Extreme left	8.3		6.7		1.56		−0.5
Left	42.6		34.5		1.34		+4.2
S. Royal	38.5	62.2	30.3	50.6		1.30	
Centre	14.8		18.5		0.67		−0.8
Right	23.6		31.2		0.77		−2.6
N. Sarkozy	21.9	37.8	29.1	49.4		0.72	
Extreme right	10.6		9.1		1.35		−0.5

†Meaning of the odds ratios: OR > 1: a voter registered in ZUS is more likely to vote for the political group than a voter living outside ZUS. OR < 1: a voter registered in ZUS is less likely to vote for the political group than a voter living outside ZUS.

††This column gives the average change, between the first rounds in 2002 and in 2007, in the difference for each ZUS between the score of the political group in the ZUS and its score outside the ZUS.

Despite this, voting patterns exhibited in ZUSs are not unconnected with those of the *communes* to which they belong. Thus, ZUSs that vote more for extreme parties (right or left) tend to belong to *communes* that also vote more for these same parties, with the correlation between the ZUS and the *communes* votes being the largest for extreme parties.

Finally, concerning the evolution of the difference in electoral choices between the residents of the ZUSs and of the rest of their *communes* between the 2002 and 2007 presidential elections, we note that the difference has only increased for left votes (see last column of Table 15.4). The left has regressed more in the rest of the *communes* than in the ZUSs, such that the difference has increased (by more than four points). Conversely, the scores achieved by the right in the ZUSs came closer to those realised in the rest of the *communes*, with the right votes having increased more in the ZUSs than in the wider *communes*. For the other three political groups, there was very little variation in the difference of votes in and outside of ZUSs from 2002 to 2007.

The 2007 presidential election in ZUSs and the 2005 urban riots

Urban deprived areas provided a fertile ground for the riots that occurred in France towards the end of 2005. These incidents gave a boost to electoral mobilisation campaigns by voluntary associations working in such neighbourhoods and ensured that the suburbs featured high on the 2007 electoral agenda. It is therefore especially pertinent to assess whether or not the 2005 riots may have influenced electoral behaviours in the ZUSs in which they occurred.

The study proposed here of the relations between the results of the 2007 presidential election and the 2005 urban violence in ZUSs is carried out by using the ordinary least squares method of regression. The conclusions will be presented once we have described the indicators of urban violence and the methodology employed in our analysis.

Methodology

The urban violence occurring late in 2005 is measured according to statistics compiled by the national police administration from 27 October to 20 November 2005. Three types of violent offences are listed:

- the number of burnt cars
- destruction of, or damage to, *public* property
- destruction of, or damage to, *private* property.

We consider that the sum of these three categories constitutes 'urban violence'. In those ZUSs in our sample for which this data is available[14], the burning of cars accounted for the majority of the incidents recorded (72 per cent), the destruction of private property about 15 per cent and the destruction of public property a little less than 12 per cent.

We also use an indicator of the intensity of the riots, defined for each ZUS as the share of the autumn urban violence in the overall 'expressive' delinquency that occurred in 2005.[5] Our chosen method of analysis involves regressing[16] each electoral variable observed in the first round of the 2007 presidential election (i.e. rate of voter turnout and scores of political parties) on two other variables, namely the same electoral variable, but observed in the first round of the 2002 presidential election, and one of the indicators of urban violence (i.e. either one of the offence categories or the sum of them expressed in terms of rate per 1,000 inhabitants, or the indicator of riot intensity). This rigorous and simple approach is based on the hypothesis that a certain type of electoral result observed in the first round of the 2007 presidential election is largely explicable in terms of the corresponding result observed in the first round of the previous presidential election, and by the level of urban violence in 2005. By introducing the lagged value of the dependent variable in the regression, we were able to account for the influence of the structural factors of electoral behaviours whose impact varies little from one election to another. It should be stressed that our analysis is carried out on aggregated data (per ZUS) and not on individual data. This characteristic has important implications for the interpretation of the results. Indeed, it precludes the drawing of any conclusions concerning individual behaviours. The correlations arrived at are calculations involving entire entities – for example, between the turnout registered in a ZUS and the rate at which certain types of offence occurred within it at the time of the riots. But the correlations between the individual observations forming these wholes cannot be determined. If, for example, the rate of turnout is negatively linked to that of car burning, we can in no way infer that the typical perpetrators of this kind of infraction were apt to abstain more than any others. The correlation merely signifies that in ZUSs, the level of turnout is lower the higher the rate of the car burning that occurred.

Moreover, the veracity of the estimated results is dependent on the validity of the indicators of urban violence we employed. Crime statistics issued by the police have to be taken with a high level of caution, since they say more about what the police do and are told to do, than they do about the actual crime.[7]

The impact of the 2005 riots on voting in the 2007 presidential election

The results of the regressions are presented in Table 15.5.

Voter turnout in the 2007 presidential election in ZUSs does not seem to have been affected by the overall level of urban violence in 2005, even if the rate of damage to private property had a significantly negative impact. On the contrary, the intensity of the 2005 riots had a positive effect on voter turnout. All other things being equal, in ZUSs where violence was particularly severe (in comparison with the usual level of delinquency prevailing in the ZUS), turnout in the 2007 presidential election was also greater.

This increase in turnout in the ZUS where riots were more intense did not benefit the extreme right party. In fact, quite the opposite occurred. The extreme right recorded lower scores in ZUSs where the number of incidents per 1,000 inhabitants was higher. Conversely, the left scored better in ZUSs where the level of violence was more salient.

Table 15.5 Results of the estimation of the impact of urban violence

| | | Electoral variable (1st round of the 2007 presidential) | | | | |
		Turnout rate	Extreme left votes	Left votes	Right votes	Ex- treme right
Rate/1000 inhabts.	Burning of cars	n. s.	n. s.	+ *	n. s.	– ***
	Damages to public property	n. s.	n. s.	n. s.	n. s.	n. s.
	Damage to private property	- **	n. s.	+ *	- **	n. s.
	2005 autumn urban violence	n. s.	n. s.	+ **	n. s.	- ***
	Intensity of the 2005 autumn urban violence	+ ***	*n. s.*	*n. s.*	*n. s.*	– **

Note: the coefficient is not statistically significant at the 1% level.

*** (*resp.* ** *and* *) indicates that the coefficient is statistically significant at the 1% level (resp. 5 and 10% level). The R² varies between 0.41 (for the estimation of the extreme left votes) and 0.67 (for the estimation of the left votes). The number of observations varies between 130 and 156 due to data availability.

Conclusions

The preceding analysis of the results of the 2007 presidential election enables us to highlight several observations regarding electoral behaviours in ZUSs. The first two are concerned with voter turnout and the following two with voter choices.

1 The level of abstention in ZUSs was higher than the national average and also exceeded that occurring in the rest of the *communes* in which the ZUSs are located.
2 The abstention patterns of ZUS voters differ according to the type of election. ZUS residents mobilise themselves for elections of prime importance, such as the presidential election, but appear less concerned about more local, and less personalised, elections. This selective abstention, which varies according to the type of election, is common to all voters. However, it is more pronounced among ZUS voters.
3 Within ZUSs, there was a clear swing in favour of the left and – more so than anywhere else – right-wing candidates. Centrist candidates, by contrast, tended to receive fewer votes. This was a constant trend in ZUSs, whatever the election.
4 There was an evolution in voter preferences in the 2007 presidential election towards useful voting strategies. This tendency, which was just as evident in ZUSs as elsewhere, led to the elimination of minor candidates, the breakthrough made by centre Bayrou, and the decline of the extreme right.

Finally, as a result of our close examination, we can safely say that ZUS voters are just like any others. The electoral results recorded in ZUSs are no doubt special (cf. points 1 and 3). But the evolution from one election to another is the same as elsewhere (cf. points 2 and 4). We can therefore consider that the specific features of ZUS electoral results are above all a consequence of the singularity of these territories, and that they are related to the special characteristics of the environment confronted by the residents of the ZUSs.

The analysis of the impact of urban violence on voting in the ZUSs leads to the same sort of conclusion. It would seem that the riot episode had a local impact on the electoral choices in the presidential election that followed. In places where the explosion of violence was particularly severe compared with the usual level of delinquency, a greater number of voters went to the polls for the presidential election and these voters were less inclined to vote for the extreme right.

There are not enough elements to undertake a more detailed interpretation of these correlations. Data is scarce at the level of the deprived neighbourhoods. This is truly unfortunate, for a much deeper understanding of implications of these life spaces for political understanding and behaviour would provide us with even more interesting insights than we have been able to unravel here.

Notes

1 See Fauvelle-Aymar and François (2006) for a list of these works. See also Darmofal (2006) for a description and analysis of electoral turnout based on aggregate data.
2 And which have been the subject of several studies by the authors, see Fauvelle-Aymar, François and Vornetti (2005, 2006).
3 These are the most recent figures available for ZUSs.
4 See especially Pan Ké Shon (2004), who shows that the different positions with regard to electoral registration are due to the individual characteristics of the residents of these neighbourhoods.
5 It can even happen that a ZUS spans several *communes*. This can be seen, for example, in the ZUS Hauts de Garonne-Bastide that stretches across four *communes* (Bordeaux, Cenon, Floirac and Lormont). The contours of the ZUS are shown in Figure 15.2.
6 The list of towns and ZUSs in our sample can be found on the following website: http://ses.telecom-paristech.fr/francois/supports/listeZUS.pdf
7 As measured by the coefficient of variation.
8 The odds ratio is obtained by comparing the occurrence of a particular phenomenon (electoral turnout) between two groups or, as in this case, $OR = \dfrac{p_1/(1-p_1)}{p_2/(1-p_2)} = \dfrac{p_1(1-p_2)}{p_2(1-p_1)}$ at two different moments (in 2002 and 2007). It is defined as with p_1 being the rate of turnout in ZUS in 2007 and p_2 in 2002. If the OR is equal to 1, then the chances of ZUS voters going to the polls are the same in 2002 as in 2007. If it is less (resp. greater) than 1, there are fewer (resp. more) chances of ZUS voters going to the polls in 2007 than in 2002.
9 The 'useful vote' is a mobilisation rhetoric used in this election by the Socialist Party to rally voters. In 2002, the Socialist party candidate, Lionel Jospin (the incumbent Prime Minister) did not obtain the required number of votes to maintain his candidature in the second round. The two who qualified were the right-wing candidate, Jacques Chirac, and the extreme right candidate, Jean-Marie Le Pen. The explication given afterwards by the Socialist Party was that many leftist voters had voted for other left wing candidates or for extreme left candidates in the first round.

10 The comparison here only relates to the first round in view of the atypical circumstances of the second round of the 2002 presidential election, which pitted a right-wing candidate (J. Chirac) against an extreme right candidate (J.-M. Le Pen).

11 The odds ratios of vote choices in ZUS in 2007 as compared with 2002 confirm these changes:

	Extreme L	Left	Centre	Right	Extreme R
OR 2007/2002	0.67	1.01	3.35	1.16	0.48

Thus there was three times more chance of a ZUS voter voting for the centrists in 2007 than in 2002, and 50 per cent less chances that s/he would vote for the extreme right.

12 See Table 3 for national scores.

13 The comparison between voting patterns of ZUS residents and those of voters living in the rest of the *communes* leads to the same conclusions with respect to the 2007 parliamentary elections. The limits indicated above (sections 2.3) do not apply here, given that the two types of voters are confronted with the same political offer.

14 That is in 156 ZUSs.

15 'Expressive' delinquency comprises offences that are not aimed at the appropriation of somebody's property (robbery), but which involve damage to property (mutilation, destruction) and assault on persons symbolising authority (such as policemen). They are listed by the police and gendarmerie services in a statistical table called *État 4001*. It should be noted that our indicator of the riots intensity constitutes an approximate measure given that the various types of offences included under 'expressive' delinquency are not the same as those figuring in the urban violence category.

16 Using the ordinary least squares method.

17 For a discussion of the problems caused by the measurement of crime, see in particular Collectif (2004), Névanen *et al.* (2006) and Robert (2008). In France, unlike in Great Britain (and its British Crime Surveys), police statistics are used to measure crime and delinquency nationwide, and not victimisation surveys.

Part IV

Other International Comparisons

Chapter 16

A North American example: the 2001 Cincinnati riot and a subsequent peacemaking initiative

David Waddington

Introduction

Given the extensive and well documented history of collective violence in twentieth-century urban America (Gilje 1996; Gurr 1989), some readers may find it surprising to discover that the United States has witnessed only sporadic instances of rioting since the 'long, hot summers' of the 1960s, of which the infamous Los Angeles, California riot of 1992 was easily the most destructive and spectacular, and the Cincinnati, Ohio riot of 2001 the most notable to have occurred since the start of the new millennium (Waddington 2007). This chapter is dedicated to exploring the nature and underlying causes of the Cincinnati disorder, and to describing and evaluating an innovative, court-sponsored scheme for promoting more harmonious police-community relations in the so-called Queen City. The purpose of the chapter is to provide a further comparative basis for understanding the French riots and to explore the feasibility of utilising the peacekeeping initiative in the French social context. Each of these aspects of discussion will be returned to in the conclusion of this book.

Macdonald *et al.* (2007: 2571) emphasise how:

> It is important to underscore why Cincinnati is an appropriate setting for testing the relationship between race and perceptions of injustice by the police. The city's proximity to the former slave state of Kentucky resulted in a steady influx of escaped slaves entering the city prior to the Civil War. With the fall of the Confederacy, many freed slaves went to the city in search of work and to avoid further persecution. This led to conflict

between immigrant workers and freed slaves in 1884 that erupted into the most deadly race riot in the history of the US, leaving 84 dead and scores more injured. Like many other US cities, Cincinnati witnessed racial conflict during civil rights protests in the late 1960s when the city recorded two race riots.

These authors explain how, in April 2001, Cincinnati became 'one of the few cities since the 1960s to have a major riot over racial grievances related to the police' when two days of protest and disorder were activated by the shooting of an African American civilian (Timothy Thomas) by a white officer (Patrolman Stephen Roach) during a police chase. A fuller description of this triggering incident is provided by Rothman and Land (2004: 36–7), who recall how:

On [Saturday] April 7 2001, just after 2 a.m., off-duty police officers spotted Thomas, who was wanted by the police for 14 misdemeanors warrants, many of which were traffic-related. They reported this to on-duty officers, who pursued Thomas on foot. One officer, Stephen Roach, ran down a dark alley with his gun drawn. He did not know the nature of Thomas's warrants, and in a sudden confrontation, Roach fired and fatally wounded Thomas. The officer at first claimed he saw what looked like a weapon and fired in self-defense. Later he claimed it was an accident. To many in the African American community it looked like murder and yet another example of police overuse of force.

Two days later, a demonstration by angry protesters (including the deceased's mother) in front of City Hall was followed by a similar gathering outside the Over-the-Rhine police station, where protesters threw stones before being dispersed by police in riot gear (Waddington 2007). Violence resumed during the following afternoon when a section of a 50-strong demonstration by young African Americans ran amok in the downtown area of city, overturning rubbish bins, smashing shop windows, restaurants and bars, and assailing white motorists. Sixty-six arrests were made as police – some on horseback and others firing tear gas canisters – eventually regained control. Later that day (10 April), a renewed police crackdown resulted in 82 further arrests. This was followed in the early hours of 11 April by the imposition of a city-wide curfew between the hours of 8pm and 6am, rigidly enforced by 125 state troopers specially imported for that purpose (ibid.).

As Macdonald *et al.* explain, a few weeks prior to the Cincinnati riot, the city and its police had been subjected to a federal lawsuit filed by the Cincinnati Black United Front (BUF) and the Ohio chapter of the American Civil Liberties Union (ACLU), alleging a 30-year pattern of police racial abuse and discrimination. A District Court recommendation that all parties resort to a formal conciliation procedure as an alternative to litigation resulted in a so-called Collaborative Agreement (CA). Cincinnati Police Department (CPD) and city authorities were initially reluctant to engage in collaboration but the rioting induced a change of heart (Rothman and Land 2004: 37). As such, 'Policy reforms laid out in this document included the formation of a community group for operational reform; a revision of the police's use of force policies; and the creation of a citizen-complaint panel that was independent of the police department' (Macdonald *et al.* 2007: 2571). In the remainder of this chapter, we explore in more detail the causal context of the riot. This is followed by an outline and appraisal of the Cincinnati Collaborative Agreement.

The causal context of the riot

At the time of the Cincinnati riot, the city had a population of 330,000 of which 43 per cent were African Americans (Waddington 2007). The 7,600-strong Over-the-Rhine neighbourhood constituted one of the most densely concentrated black communities in the city. According to Maag (2006),

> As Over-the-Rhine's white families left for the suburbs after World War II, its buildings attracted black families displaced when Interstate 75 tore though the nearby West End neighborhood ... It gradually became a slum in what the Census Bureau has found is the sixth most segregated city in the nation. By 1990 the neighborhood's median family income was $4,999, census figures show. It was the most dangerous part of the city, according to Police Department records, with almost 22,000 calls for emergency services, 8 murders and 306 robberies in 2001.

The gradual demise of the city's manufacturing base in the 1990s had resulted in heavy job losses among African American males just when funding for youth employment projects was being withdrawn. One symptom of the resulting impoverishment was an accompanying rise in drug-related arrests, averaging 2,500 since 1995 (Sokhey 2007).

The related police enforcement operation cannot be separated from commercial and political processes encouraging the 'gentrification' of the Over-the-Rhine locality in the 1990s as a solution to its social and economic problems.

Leibowitz and Salmon (1999) trace the process by which the 'chronic indecision' that was symptomatic of a 'leadership vacuum' in City Hall led to the instigation in the early 1990s of a new public-private organisation, Downtown Cincinnati Incorporated (DCI). Spurred on by the local media, the DCI broke with the city's longstanding local tradition of public service provision and community development by working towards a '20/20 Vision' of the downtown area, incorporating 'speciality retail outlets, the performing arts, a museum, two professional sports stadiums and expanded convention facilities as well as a plethora of upscale restaurants, bars and nightclubs' (ibid.: 250). Leibowitz and Salmon insist that such a vision promised few benefits in terms of jobs or consumption opportunities for adjoining ethnic minority neighbourhoods like Over-the Rhine. Worse still, 'the concept of development advocated through this program constitut[ed] a redefinition of downtown which effectively eras[ed] these existing residents from the area's future' (ibid.: 252).

The late 1990s heralded the anticipated proliferation of new internet- and entertainment- and leisure-based firms into Over-the-Rhine, and saw its corresponding gentrification, marked by an influx of new professionals. Before long, the CPD was being pressurised by these newer residents and the local political and business communities into ridding the area of its drug-using and petty criminal fraternities. Officers were also constantly working towards specified quotas of arrests. The police responded zealously to such pressure. Between 1996 and 2000, the CPD invoked a 'draconian local ordnance', empowering them to exclude from the locality for up to 90 days any person caught drug-dealing (Cottle 2001). The problem with this approach was that, typically, 'police officers cruised the area, more concerned with catching troublemakers than with building relationships with its people' (Waddington 2007: 68).

This new development was the latest twist in a long saga of negative police-community relations extending from the post-riot era of the 1960s. Between 1967 and 2000, the Cincinnati Police Department had been subjected to 17 official investigations alleging various forms of racial misconduct, ranging from allegedly unjust shootings of African Americans to unfair employment practices involving the hiring and promotion of African American police officers. Of the total of 214 recommendations arising from these reports, very few were implemented. Parallel to these issues were the controversy and concern surrounding the frequent killing of African American men by police officers: there had been a total of 14 such fatalities between February 1995 and March 2001.

It was against this background that, on 5 March 2001, the Ohio chapter of the American Civil Liberties Union (ACLU) and Cincinnati Black United Front (BUF) filed a class action lawsuit to the US District Court for the Southern District of Ohio, alleging systematic discrimination on the part of the CPD. Such action was provoked by the experience of Mr Bomani Tyehimba, an African American businessperson who had complained that his civil rights had been violated when two police officers handcuffed him and needlessly pointed a gun at his head during a traffic stop in 1999. As plaintiffs, the BUF and ACLU were protesting that civil rights violations of this nature and regular police killings of African Americans 'were not an aberration, but part of an illegal but common pattern and practice of discrimination by the Cincinnati Police Department' (Rothman 2006: 110). The Legal Director of the Ohio ACLU was adamant that the 'drug exclusion war' embarked on by the CPD between 1996 and 2000 formed part of a 'tapestry of abuses' against African Americans, representing 'one more way in which over-policing has brought the community to the brink' (quoted by Waddington 2007: 68).

The collaborative agreement

It was scarcely a month before the Cincinnati riot that the ACLU/BUF class action against the CPD was placed before US District Judge, Susan J. Dlott, a former domestic relations lawyer. Dlott's prior legal experience had convinced her that the best way of achieving lasting solutions to conflict was to involve the people concerned in the process of defining the actual problem and exploring possible solutions. Her approach to dealing with the class action was therefore to advocate an 'Alternative Dispute Resolution' (ADR) approach to resolving the chronic problem of police-community relations, predicated on 'collaborative problem solving and negotiation' (Rothman 2006: 110). Judge Dlott confidently envisaged that a carefully handled ADR procedure would 'provide an opportunity for the parties and the court to create a national and international model for other communities' (ibid.: 111).

All parties agreed to depart from litigation in favour of collaboration. A sum of $100,000 dollars was donated with this objective in mind by the New York-based Andrus Family Fund (AFF), a charitable organisation committed to fostering innovative approaches to community reconciliation. This money was used alongside matched funding from city authorities to sponsor a pluralistic dialogue. Following an AFF recommendation, Judge Dlott appointed Jay Rothman, president of the ARIA Group (an Ohio-based conflict resolution training and consulting company), to act as co-ordinator or 'special master' of the project. By the end of March 2001, an advisory group had been set up, consisting of attorneys and other representatives acting on behalf of the parties to the initial lawsuit (namely, the Cincinnati BUF, the ACLU, the Cincinnati City and Police Administration, and the Cincinnati Fraternal Order of Police).

Amidst the added urgency generated by the April riot, the advisory group chose to divide up the local population into eight separate categories of 'stakeholders' (or 'identity groups') for the purpose of consultation. These were: African Americans; city employees; police and their families; white citizens; business, foundation, and education leaders; religious and social service leaders; and youth and other minorities. The co-operation of the local media helped to ensure that all residents and/or employees of the city were invited to complete a questionnaire which aimed to elicit 'their goals for the future of police-community relations in the city, why these goals were deeply important to them, and how they thought these also could be achieved' (ibid.: 115). This exercise achieved 3,500 responses, including 750 returns from local youth. There then followed a series of four-hour 'dialogue and agenda-setting meetings' which were attended by a total of 800 people drawn from the various identity groups.

Pressure was already mounting for some tangible signs of progress. In the immediate wake of the riot, the CPD rank-and-file, 'subtly encouraged by supervisors and the police union' (Osborne 2007), reacted to the enhanced criticism and scrutiny of their methods by embarking on a 'slowdown' of their activities. This action included among its measures a 35 per cent reduction in arrests and a similar decline in the issuing of tickets for traffic violations (McLaughlin and Prendergast 2001). Towards the end of the year, tension was rekindled in Cincinnati when Officer Roach was found not guilty of negligent homicide in relation to his attempted arrest of Timothy Thomas, and two other white officers were acquitted following allegations of their part in the death of a black man who had died of asphyxiation while in police custody in November 2000. These proved the final straws for the Cincinnati BFU, who called for an economic boycott of their city – a sanction which quickly resulted in the cancellation of visits by top musical entertainers (Sokhey 2007).

Following pressures from the District Court for a breakthrough to be achieved, the ARIA Group distilled the feedback they had received from the identity groups into a set of shared goals. This outcome was formally endorsed by an 'Integration Group', comprising 5–10 representatives from each of the eight identity groups, which met in December 2001. Thereafter, the following five goals were submitted as the intended basis of a collaborative agreement, to a 'Settlement Group' consisting of formal negotiators acting on behalf of each of the main parties:

1 Police officers and community members will become proactive partners in community problem solving.
2 Build relationships of respect, cooperation, and trust within and between police and communities.
3 Improve education, oversight, monitoring, hiring practices, and accountability of the Cincinnati Police Department.
4 Ensure fair, equitable, and courteous treatment for all.
5 Create methods to establish the public's understanding of police policies and procedures and recognition of exceptional service in an effort to foster support for the police. (quoted by Rothman and Land 2004: 38)

Negotiations towards a settlement spanned January to April 2002. The content of the final agreement incorporated not only the five goals specified by the identity group meetings, but also recommendations arising from a related investigation by the Civil Rights Division of US the Department of Justice (DOJ) into allegations of racial bias and abuse by CPD officers. The DOJ review had been carried out in the summer and autumn of 2001 on the authorisation of the city mayor. Both Judge Dlott and the main parties to the class action had agreed that any DOJ recommendations would be included in the final Collaborative Agreement (ibid.: 39).

The final version of this document was authorised by all parties on 3 April 2002. It established two key areas of future activity to which both the police and local citizenry were expected to make significant contributions. The first of these, community problem-oriented policing (CPOP), would involve both parties working co-operatively in the resolution of problems relating to crime, disorder and the quality of life. To this end, weekly meetings would be held involving the implementation of 'scanning, analysis, response and assessment' (SARA) techniques, where citizens and officers would engage in the analysis of problems and the formulation, execution and evaluation of the strategies used to solve them. In the meantime, a Mutual Accountability Plan (MAP) would be established as the basis of eliciting a variety of data from which to measure such relevant issues of concern as citizen satisfaction with police procedures and behaviour, officer safety and job satisfaction, the demographics of traffic stops, etc.

Among its other measures, the CA provided for the instigation of a civilian review board charged with investigating complaints against the police. Relevant investigations would be carried out independently of police supervision and board members would be invested with powers of subpoena. Another important innovation was the Cincinnati Community Police Partnering Center, which was set up for the purpose of training civilians and officers in use of CPOP and SARA. City authorities invested $5 million to ensure that the CA would be as effectively implemented as possible. Judge Dlott also appointed a former US Attorney for the State of Michigan, Saul Green, as official Monitor of the agreement. It would be his responsibility to 'review all data relevant to implementation of the agreement and to report the results to a court-appointed "conciliator" who would evaluate the Monitor's reports, instruct parties on how to improve compliance and give the parties an opportunity to cure any flaw before the court becomes involved in the enforcement process' (Taslitz 2003: 247).

Evaluating the collaborative agreement

A general indication of the possible utility of the collaborative agreement may be gleaned by consideration of yet another controversial police-civilian encounter occurring in Cincinnati. Comparisons both with the 'Rodney King incident', that was so pivotal to the Los Angeles riot (Waddington 2007), and the fatal shooting of Timothy Thomas were inevitably evoked when it emerged that a 41-year-old African American resident of the city had died as a result of a beating by two white police officers which was captured on videotape by cameras positioned on top of a police cruiser. This incident occurred around 6am on Sunday morning, 30 November 2003, shortly after staff at a fast food restaurant had called paramedics to the assistance of a 350-pound black man, Nathaniel Jones, who had suddenly collapsed just outside the premises.

Jones, who was later found to have an enlarged heart and traces of cocaine and PCP, or 'angel dust', in his bloodstream, is reported to have grown sufficiently violent with the paramedics to cause them to radio for police assistance. Two white officers were first to arrive on the scene, one of whom asked Jones to tell him what was going on. Videotape evidence suggested that Jones had been unwilling to co-operate:

> 'White boy, red neck!' Jones shouted while moving toward the officer. 'Back up! Back up!' the officer said. Seconds later, Jones lunged forward and threw a right fist at the officer, touching off the struggle in which officers James Pike and Baron Osterman wrestled Jones to the ground and began attempting to handcuff him, pummelling him with their nightsticks more than 30 times while trying to subdue him. Throughout the violent struggle, officers shouted at least 16 times: 'Put your hands behind your back.' They finally succeeded in handcuffing Jones only after four additional officers arrived and helped restrain him. (Horstman 2003)

It quickly became apparent, though, that Mr Jones had now ceased breathing and subsequent attempts to revive him proved in vain. Controversy surrounding his death was intensified by the fact that there was a 37-second gap occurring at the outset of the police videotape of the incident, arousing suspicion that police may have deliberately concealed the fact that their actions had been provocative (ibid.).

Unlike the case of the earlier death of Timothy Thomas, this fatality did not precipitate a riot. It is conceivable the existence of measures introduced under the CA may have helped to offset the occurrence of disorder. A joint ACLU Advisory Panel and Plaintiff/ACLU Class Counsel report (2004) later emphasised how the Cincinnati Citizen Complaint Authority (CCA) investigation into the conduct of the seven officers had resulted in 'severe' disciplinary procedures being invoked against three officers found guilty of using excessive force, and in recommendations for re-training in first-aid procedures being made with regard to all seven attending officers. The report then concluded with on a reassuringly optimistic note: 'Our collaborative agreement is the path to restoring trust and reducing the risk that this will happen again. Let's recommit ourselves to vigorous enforcement of that agreement' (ibid.: 12).

Further anecdotal evidence suggests that the introduction of the CA and its various provisions has done little to ameliorate the problems initially giving rise to the Cincinnati riot of 2001. Such indications suggest that other possible factors – notably, the enforced relocation (and consequent demoralisation) of black residents of Over-the-Rhine – may well have been more significant.

La Botz (2007) reports that, six years after the riot, 27.8 per cent of the population of Cincinnati were living in poverty (the figure for African Americans was closer to one third), making it third poorest American city after Detroit and Buffalo. The city's unemployment for African Americans stood at 10 per cent (compared with 5 per cent for whites), although it was far higher, at 30 per cent, among black teenagers. According to Maag (2006), it was not long after the riot before 40 per cent of Over-the-Rhine's property stock was standing vacant. Since then, however, entire blocks have been bought up by the Cincinnati Center City Development Corporation (3CDC), created in 2003 on the basis of $80 million investment by city corporations. In one 18-month period alone, 3CDC bought up 100 buildings and 100 vacant lots in Over-the-Rhine, with plans to develop 96 new condominiums on Vine Street, the neighbourhood's central thoroughfare. Crack houses have correspondingly disappeared and crime been dispersed into neighbouring areas (ibid.).

Such a development has been greatly accelerated due to the efforts of Operation Vortex, which is, according to La Botz, 'a joint effort by the Cincinnati Police Department and the Hamilton County Sheriffs to drive criminals out of Over-the-Rhine in order to make the area more attractive to investors and developers'. La Botz maintains how:

> Those developers ... smile upon the removal of poor blacks to make way for the creative class, the young, the hip, the childless, the folks with surplus expendable income. The operation has turned Vine Street, Over-the-Rhine's principal thoroughfare, into the main street of a ghost town and has driven crime into nearby communities and even into the suburbs. (La Botz 2007)

Each Vortex unit consists of 50 officers (including a captain, lieutenant and five sergeants) deployed to aggressively target particular areas with a zero tolerance attitude to street crime and drug trafficking. The initiative is actually an extension of the so-called Take Back Our Streets programme implemented in May–June 2006, when an 'Over-the-Rhine Task Force' accumulated 1,050 arrests in a six-week period, though some 700 of these were for minor misdemeanours, an outcome which provoked allegations by civil libertarians of police harassment: 'In fact, Operation Vortex is so controversial that leaders in one of Cincinnati's most crime-plagued neighborhoods – the Avondale Community Council – recently asked that the tactic not be used there, contrary to the department's plans' (Osborne 2007).

Osborne insists that the CA has been generally plagued by recurring instances of police foot-dragging and lack of co-operation. For example,

> In March 2005, Dlott ruled that the city and its police department had breached the deal when Streicher and police supervisors blocked a court-appointed monitoring team from viewing police training and accessing records at police headquarters. The team also complained that Streicher and his assistant, Lt. Col. Richard Janke, were persistently rude and uncooperative. Dlott warned city officials to improve their behavior or face stricter oversight and the levying of fines. A crucial sticking point centered on CPOP and how much involvement the public should have in shaping how officers do their jobs. Streicher wanted a more limited role that focussed on using residents to patrol their neighborhoods and report crimes and suspicious activity to the police. Plaintiffs insisted on enforcing a provision to create the Police Community Partnering Center to oversee the department's CPOP efforts and to coordinate similar efforts among civilian groups and others (ibid.)

This attitude is apparently consistent with earlier expressions of police sentiment. The CA project master has complained on record of police resistance to a preliminary period of 'problem definition' on the grounds that it would simply result in adversarial 'finger pointing' by non-police participants. On a more specific note, the CPD and their attorneys refused, outright, to discuss the highly salient and contentious issue of 'racial profiling' because they were unwilling to recognise the actual existence of such a problem (Rothman 2006). It was at this point that Rothman chose to shift the process onto a more forward-looking, goal-oriented direction, rather than risk its complete derailment. With hindsight, he clearly believes that he capitulated prematurely: 'I did not spend adequate time explaining how a problem framing process need not be adversarial, but rather can reveal mutual misunderstandings and foster new trust, thus in itself leading to new attitudes and problem solving relationships' (ibid.: 112).

Rothman also feels that the ADR process represented a 'lost opportunity' to ensure local citizens' ownership of the strategies for reversing negative police-community relations and maintaining their future commitment. The consultation of the eight identity groups had been a very useful exercise in that:

> It surfaced issues of frustrations and threats and gave voice to people's stories of hurts and aspirations for a better future. But then it rather quickly (in hindsight, I would say prematurely) moved into a bargaining mode as the lawyers sat down to hammer out an agreement. (ibid.: 121)

Consequently, it became exceedingly difficult to maintain public interest, commitment and participation: when an email was circulated early in 2006, inviting respondents to the original questionnaire to re-engage in the process, only a fraction of them responded (ibid.).

The CA expired in mid-2007, though city authorities and the plaintiffs agreed to extend it by one year. The 2007, third annual end-of-year CA Evaluation Report, prepared as usual by members of the RAND Corporation (Schell *et al.* 2007), emphasised that Cincinnati's black citizens were still experiencing longer police traffic stops than their white peers; were more likely to have their vehicles searched for drugs, weapons and stolen items; and were more likely to see their fellow passengers subjected to police questioning. The report further observed that 75 per cent of all those subsequently arrested are black, and that 75 per cent of incidents in which force is used are those involving black citizens.

The CA Monitor responded with the observation that:

> [T]he formidable efforts of the last five years cannot be deemed a success unless the department is able to address the daily interactions between police officers and African American residents, as found by RAND in this report. These problems have been raised in the earlier RAND reports, but there is no longer time to debate over what steps to take. The dynamic between the African American community and the police must be addressed now. (Green and Jerome 2007)

Though such comments may suggest that the CA is most fundamentally a failing initiative, all parties remain adamant that it would be wrong to underestimate the importance of the Cincinnati Partnering Center. Great optimism resides in the fact that 'Cincinnati is the one place in the country where citizens and police are sitting together on a regular basis to address issues with civility and respect' (Rothman 2006: 127).

Conclusion

In common with countless preceding examples occurring in Britain, France and the USA, the 2001 Cincinnati riot was provoked by a highly controversial triggering incident (in this case a fatal shooting) involving a police officer and an ethnic minority male. The killing of Timothy Thomas followed decades of alleged abuse and discrimination by the CPD in relation to Cincinnati's Over-the-Rhine and other highly segregated 'outcast' black communities. The onset of heavy job losses and withdrawal of youth programmes provoked a corresponding rise in drug-related crime. The attempted 'gentrification' of Over-the-Rhine was accompanied by an insistence among the incoming business community that the area be purged of its drug-using element. Police engagement in a 'drug exclusion war', involving 'draconian' legal measures, led to the alienation and resentment of a substantial section of the local population – hence the predisposition to riot.

It remains uncertain to what extent the Collaborative Agreement, an innovative attempt to ensure constructive dialogue, co-operation, mutual understanding and joint decision-making between the CPD and its civilian constituency, ever had the requisite design features to succeed in such objectives. Despite promising beginnings, there are signs that police foot-dragging and obstructionism soon resulted in civilian apathy and demoralisation where the CA was concerned. The recent inception of Operation Vortex, with its zero tolerance orientation towards street crime, has 'succeeded' not only in re-charging the type of disaffection that produced the 2001 riot but also in driving it out of the area.

Chapter 17

Why are there no riots in Germany? Mutual perceptions between police forces and minority adolescents

Tim Lukas

Introduction

From the 1980s onwards, France has faced a series of violent riots in urban agglomerations, culminating in the autumn 2005 riots which continued for several weeks and spread to most of France's major cities. The situation in France has attracted attention across the length and breadth of Europe. Along with previous riots in Great Britain, the French riots provided the basis for German media speculation as to whether similar disorders might well occur in their country. Despite some smaller incidents which occurred in Bremen and Berlin during the course of the 2005 events in the French suburbs, German policy-makers and social scientists initially agreed on the assumption that the situation in both countries has almost nothing in common.

However, in November 2006 the public arrest of two children stemming from a Turkish background in the Berlin borough of Kreuzberg led to a spontaneous clash between an upset crowd of Turkish juveniles and the police. Albeit that this incident represented a singular case and comparable events have failed to materialise thus far, French circumstances were then predicted to breed in Germany as well (see, for example, *Der Spiegel* 16 November 2006).

Structural integration

Since most of the rioters in France and Britain were from migrant backgrounds, academic and public debates in Germany on the riots predominantly oscillated around the question of the structural integration of second generation migrant youth, basically identifying three dimensions of access to the German mainstream society, namely in the fields of citizenship, education and housing.

Regarding the legal form of integration, it was repeatedly mentioned that, despite their migrant origins, most of the rioters actually held French citizenship due to a republican understanding of citizenship in France. Migrants from the former colonies usually become French citizens without having to overcome difficult legal barriers. Also in Great Britain the equalisation of immigrants appears fairly advanced, with a rather liberal citizenship law in line with ambitious racial anti-discrimination policies across many areas of society in order to promote equal rights and opportunities for ethnic minorities. However, in Germany politicians still have difficulties accepting the reality of being an immigration country – causing corresponding consequences for the legal integration of immigrants: no formal commitment to equality, no universal identity of citizenship and thus a politics of naturalisation which lags far behind those of France and Great Britain (Drewes 2007). For example, unlike Maghrebian juveniles in France or Asian youths in Britain, most of the Turkish adolescents in Germany still do not hold German citizenship and many of them cannot relate to the society they were born into and in which they live (Lehnartz 2008).

Besides the legal status, what is also crucial for the societal integration of migrants is education. In Great Britain, some ethnic minority groups (particularly those of Pakistani descent) achieve educational results well above the average for the autochthonous population. Comparing France and Germany, nearly 50 per cent of the Maghrebian juveniles could be assigned to higher levels of educational attainment, while in Germany Turkish pupils are far more concentrated at lower levels (European Commission 2001).

Yet another indicator of integration is housing. Since the concentration of migrants in German cities has increased over the past years, socio-spatial segregation processes have ensued, with parts of the cities becoming more and more 'foreign'. Unlike in France or Great Britain, migrants in Germany usually concentrate in inner-city quarters, which theoretically have the distinct advantage of providing a mixture of functions and an infrastructure to conduct local business. Large suburban housing estates in comparison offer almost nothing of that sort. The functional disposition as a dormitory town has few possibilities for labour and leisure activities. However, it is also the case in German cities that social exclusion more and more often coincides with geographical exclusion (Häußermann

2007). Large high-rise housing estates at the fringes of cities are increasingly becoming the last resort for people with no other choice, the cumulation of disadvantaged and discriminatory circumstances (Lukas 2007).

One might assume that all these conditions rather militate for an increased likelihood of riots breaking out in Germany. Paradoxically, the opposite is true. That begs the crucial question of why French and British cities face violent protests, while German cities appear rather quiet and peaceful in comparison. Given the weak explanatory value of earlier German debate, I would now like to consider another argument, which has not yet attracted sufficient public attention and which needs further research in the future: the relationship between ethnic minorities and the police.

Police and minorities

As the French riots and many other events have demonstrated, the 'flashpoints' (Waddington *et al.* 1989) of collective unrest have mostly resulted from police actions. Whether the situation involves juveniles who were electrocuted while fleeing from the police (as in Paris in 2005) or whether children were handcuffed and arrested (as in Berlin in 2006) – collective protest is almost always triggered by police measures, their simple presence or even an accident involving the police (Cox and Fitzgerald 1996). Retrospectively analysing French riots between the years 1990 and 1995, Peralva (1997) found an important proportion of cases where police forces cast the first stone by conducting ID checks or chasing suspected juveniles. Lapeyronnie (2006) has indicated the deterioration of the relationships between the police and residents as an underlying root cause of riotous behaviour. American researchers have further insisted on the general importance of hostile contacts as an important factor for understanding the triggering of major crises (Snyder 1979). Finally, Haan and Nijboer (2005) have shown that the police's bad reputation and the absence of trust towards the legal system influence not only the emergence of riots but also the nature and extent of violent conflicts between youths and the police. Against this background, incidents like 'demonstrative' arrests of youths in the presence of their peer groups could often lead to large-scale violence.

In France, contacts between the police and adolescents have created a climate conducive to 'mutual mistrust' (Lapeyronnie 1998: 301) and stoke juvenile hatred towards the police who are generally perceived as a 'symbol of an inequitable, racist and unacceptable system' (Dubet 1997: 225) which promises but in practice does not allow 'egalité'. In this context of extremely deteriorated relations, all the police need to do is appear on the scene for this to be interpreted as a provocation, sparking off spiralling confrontations (Jobard 2002).

The relationship between, and mutual perceptions of, police and migrant adolescents and the behaviour of police forces are therefore crucial elements in any analysis of the causes of collective youth unrest. However, collective violence, while an important research topic in itself, is also an indicator of more general and equally consequential social problems relating to system legitimacy and trust in institutions (Tyler 2004).

Police-minority relations play an important role in international empirical research on the police, particularly in the USA and Great Britain (Benedict et al. 2000; Decker 1981; Smith et al. 1999). Whereas conflicting evidence exists regarding the relative impact of demographic factors such as education, income and gender, it is in fact age and race that have repeatedly been found to affect citizens' attitudes toward the police. Young people are usually more likely to adopt negative attitudes toward the police than older citizens, and members of ethnic minority groups are more likely to view the police less favourably than natives. In a review of recent public opinion surveys on police satisfaction in England and Wales, Skogan (1996) asserts that there is a disproportionate decline in satisfaction with policing among racial minorities and a particular likelihood of young, single and unemployed black men to feel unfairly treated when stopped by the police. Clancy et al. (2001) point in the same direction when analysing data from the 2000 British Crime Survey (BCS). They found that confidence in the police and satisfaction with experience of the police is consistently lower among minority ethnic groups and among young people from minority groups in particular. However, based on current 2004/05 BCS data, Jansson (2006) finds people from all black and minority ethnic groups as having *higher* levels of confidence in the police compared with white respondents.

Qualitative studies on police perceptions in France highlight mutual resentment between the police and adolescents in disadvantaged urban neighbourhoods. Attending the daily life of adolescents in a Parisian *cité*, Marlière (2005) observes insults, mockery and physical fights as characterising ordinary contacts between young residents and police forces. Analysing anonymous grievances against the French police, Body-Gendrot and Withold de Wenden (2003) found that 56 per cent of the callers complained of having received unequal treatment through the police due to their real or assumed origin. Examining youths of Maghrebian descent, Sicot (2000) suggests that juveniles of immigrant origin tend to feel that French policemen are unfair and discriminatory in their performance. Within the framework of a survey on self-reported delinquency that was conducted in Grenoble and Saint-Etienne and comprised 2300 young people aged 13 to 19, Roché (2001) found that males of North African origin displayed a stronger antagonism to the police than other respondents.

Mutual perceptions between the police and minority adolescents in Germany

Although there is a strong research tradition in Germany devoted to the experiences of minorities in the criminal justice system at large – mainly stimulated by the pivotal question of discriminatory and selective treatment of minorities at all stages of law enforcement (Albrecht 1997, 2002; Mansel and Albrecht 2003; Pfeiffer *et al.* 2005) – empirical research into the relationships between migrants, ethnic minorities and the police in Germany is still in its infancy. For a long time, the role of the police in empirical and social scientific research was predominantly linked to the control of community disorder and the prevention of crime. In this regard, research on the police was merely research for the police (Ohlemacher 1999). It was during the 1990s that independent research on the police was first established in Germany (Liebl 2006). In this context, the role of policing diverse and multicultural societies became a subject of scientific interest. A number of studies have investigated the extent of ethnic or racial prejudices and discriminatory attitudes and agreed on the finding that xenophobic attitudes are widespread among German police forces (Franzke 1993; Jaschke 1997; see, however, Mletzko and Weins 1999).

While these studies have almost always focused on perception patterns of police forces, little is known in Germany about the experiences and perceptions of juvenile migrants with regards to their interaction and experiences with the police. Neglecting this perspective, however, runs the risk of reducing a complex relationship of interactions to the self-descriptions and attributions of only one of the concerned parties; or as Anhut and Heitmeyer (2000: 557) assume: 'Conflicts are not based on attitudes and behavioural patterns of one side only, but result from reciprocity and interactions'. Some current studies have therefore examined the previously neglected perspective of minorities and particularly adolescent minorities' attitudes towards the German police.

Within the scope of the so-called 'foreigner survey', which was conducted nationwide on behalf of the German Youth Institute (DJI), approximately 2500 foreign (i.e. Italian, Greek and Turkish) young people aged between 18 and 25 were interviewed with respect to the degree of trust they place in societal institutions and organisations, such as the government, political parties, courts of justice and the police. Although it could be shown on the surface that a relatively high percentage of German and non-German young people shared a strong or very strong trust in the courts and the police (Weidacher 2000: 142), a detailed examination of the collected data provides a divergent impression. Re-analysing the DJI data, Gesemann (2003: 209 ff) emphasised the differences between the various nationalities. A high degree of similarity within the answer patterns holds true for Greek and Italian migrants as well as for western German respondents. However, by way of contrast, eastern German and Turkish interviewees expressed less trust in police forces (see Figure 17.1).

In contrast, a local study from Duisburg found higher levels of trust in the police forces among Turkish compared with native respondents (Schweer and Strasser 2003; Schweer and Zdun 2005). Even the entire group of migrants revealed a stronger satisfaction with the work of

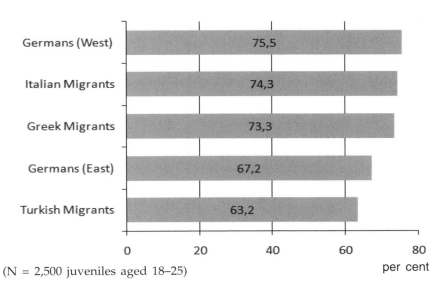

(N = 2,500 juveniles aged 18–25)

Figure 17.1 Share of respondents who trust the police: German Youth Institute Study, 1996/97

the police as compared with the autochthonous group (see Figure 17.2). Poor police acceptance among German-Russians is principally explained by negative or vicarious experiences with the police in their home countries.

These findings are mirrored by another survey among adolescents and young adults in North Rhine-Westphalia in which Turkish respondents showed higher levels of trust in judicial institutions (including the police) than native Germans and ethnic Germans from Russia (Heitmeyer *et al.* 2005). Further, Oberwittler (2007) found no significant differences in feelings of discrimination by the police among native and migrant adolescents in an urban sample when controlling for neighbourhood disadvantage which is significantly linked to lower trust.

Most surveys find that sex, age, educational level and place of residence are important influences on trust of police. Gesemann (2003: 210) identifies highly educated male juveniles, aged 20 to 23 and living in urban agglomerations as demonstrating the lowest levels of police trust. Whereas Turkish migrants aged under 30 display the least faith in the police force, senior citizens emanating from the first generation of Turkish immigrants are more trusting of the police (*Die Tageszeitung* 24 July 2006).

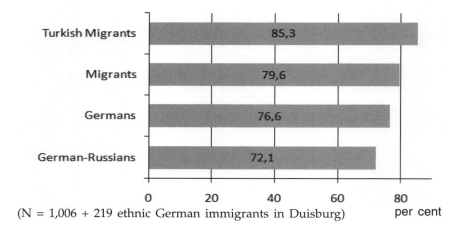

(N = 1,006 + 219 ethnic German immigrants in Duisburg)

Figure 17.2 Share of respondents who trust the police: University of Duisburg-Essen Study 2001–2004

However, research in the USA found that the underlying social conditions and demographic factors are significant for public dissatisfaction only in combination with concrete experiences of discriminatory police actions (Winfree and Curt 1971). Skogan (2005, 2006) suggests that differences in treatment provides the main link between social factors and views of the police. Police legitimacy strongly depends on whether people believe the police force has acted fairly and openly with them (Tyler 2004).

Thus, what is known about the actual experiences of and interactions between (migrant) adolescents and the police in Germany? Heitmeyer *et al.* (1997: 270) demonstrated the normal course of discrimination experienced by Turkish juveniles in Germany. More than 34 per cent of the interviewed adolescents in a standardised survey declared that they 'often'/'very often' have had experiences of unfair treatment at the hands of the police. However, data obtained from the annual multi-topic survey published by the German Centre for Studies on Turkey arrives at the conclusion that contacts with police forces are one of the fields of experience where discrimination plays only a minor role (Sauer and Goldberg 2006). Ethnic discrimination is more likely in areas of life which are characterised by a high degree of economic competition and conflicts for limited resources (see Figure 17.3).

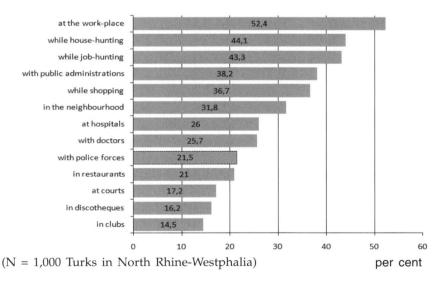

(N = 1,000 Turks in North Rhine-Westphalia)   per cent

Figure 17.3 Experienced discriminations in different areas of life (German Centre for Studies on Turkey 2005)

Qualitative studies, using interview approaches and field observations, have provided a deeper insight into everyday adolescent-police interactions. Gesemannn (2001) found that negative experiences with police performance play an important role in the interviewees' daily lives. ID checks, personal searches and arrests are regarded as ethnic discrimination and thereby ascribed to their non-native status. Nonetheless, given the actual existence of delinquent foreigners, problems with the police are predominantly regarded as a logical consequence of the police's mission to control crime. Schweer and Zdun (2005) highlight that strong language, which might be interpreted as discrimination, usually mirrors the 'code of the street' (Anderson 1999) used by police officers as an attempt to gain respect in the 'street corner society' (Whyte 1996/1943). Hüttermann (2000) points in the same direction when observing a sub culture of 'street corner police' which seek to get in contact with juveniles who frequent public spaces. In adjusting their behaviour to the (body) language of their clientele, the police gain access to juvenile and minority subcultures which, in the end, serves to smooth out interactions and prevent larger conflicts (Gesemann 2003). Police forces in Germany, according to this view, are not really detested by minority youths but rather perceived as an opponent and strategic partner in the competition for social acceptance (Hüttermann 2000).

Conclusion

Deteriorated relationships between migrant youths and the police are a fundamental characteristic of riot-affected countries like Great Britain and France. In Germany, research did not find evidence of strong resentment of the police among migrant adolescents or serious confrontations between both groups. Given various aspects of failed foreigner integration policies which apply to Germany as well, it does not seem to be too farfetched to say that the generally reasonable police-minority relationship is the reason behind the absence of riots in this country.

Nevertheless, this should not hide the fact that in Germany as well as in other countries, the contact between police forces and migrant adolescents appears potentially conflict-laden too. However, German society has cultivated a culture of 'round tables', which are usually applied to integrate opposing interests by means of reconciliation and conflict resolution. For example, after the clash of Turkish juveniles and the police in the Berlin borough of Kreuzberg, mediation talks were immediately initiated to bring together the concerned parties and to de-escalate the situation (*Berliner Zeitung* 22 November 2006). As a result, the opponents agreed on peaceable terms and the police executives decreed a new guideline, stipulating that future patrols in the area will be conducted only by officers who are familiar with the place. Police officers who do not know the area will be exposed and sensitised to the area's particularities (*Die Tageszeitung* 12 December 2006).

The experiences made in French suburbs seem to speak for this approach. The assignment of a centrally organised police apparatus, which could hardly be appreciative of the local peculiarities of the respective residents, amplifies the already – quasi naturally – existing discrepancy between youths and the police and between migrant youths and the police in particular (Althoff 2006).

However, approaches aiming at the reduction of negative and stigmatising attitudes require more than just the acquisition of intercultural knowledge during the police training. With regards to an enduring understanding in migrant-police relationships it seems indispensable to increasingly recruit ethnic minorities into the police apparatus. Concerning this matter, we face a 'shambles' (Jaschke 2006) in Germany: the current proportion of ethnic minorities in the police ranks is just above 1 per cent nationwide, in several federal states it is even far below that (Behr 2007). Although politicians and police constantly emphasise the need for more officers of foreign descent (*Der Tagesspiegel* 18 November 2006), the present politics of engagement sets the bar for migrant applicants so high that they actually bring about assimilation where they otherwise call for diversity. Nevertheless, the recruitment of ethnic minorities into the police force appears promising not only against the background of intercultural problem solving (Holdaway 1991), but also as demanded in terms of providing equal opportunities and equal treatment of migrants as well as promoting structural integration of immigrants into the labour market.

With regard to the prevention of large-scale youth violence this could be a starting point for future police policies. If we could manage to improve the relationships between the police and migrant youth in this way, then it seems reasonably likely that also in the future we will be able to wonder why there are still no riots in Germany.

Part V

Conclusions

Rioting in the UK and France

respect Thomas refers to th
lives'. Indeed, both con
multiculturalism on th
have chosen to self-
connotations co
especially at s
Pearce obse
2001 riot
an ex
of

Chapter 18

Conclusions

Fabien Jobard, Mike

Introduction

The foregoing chapters have largely focused on the various recent cases of public disorder in England and Wales and France as separate countries and, to some extent, cultural entities. In contrast, the purpose of this concluding chapter is to examine the main common themes. To this end, we initially dwell on those contributions which focus on the 2001 and 2005 riotous events in England and Wales, plus our two other national case studies, namely the USA and Germany. We then move on to discuss the primary themes emerging from the French studies, before exploring in more detail a central issue concerning multiculturalism and race relations. We conclude by focusing on the French situation and discussing some important policy implications arising from our findings.

Overview of chapters on England and Wales, the USA and Germany

One of the main themes identified throughout the majority of the chapters concerns *multiculturalism*. The multiculturalism ideal and the appreciation of difference has been a decided policy adopted in the UK, certainly from the 1960s. Kalra and Rhodes, however, suggest that, post-2001 riots, this has been increasingly questioned on the basis that such notions have perhaps allowed, or even *created*, the development of communities being segregated by ethnicity. In this

229

...e Cantle report's depiction of 'parallel
...ributions mention arguments opposed to
...e grounds that minority ethnic populations
...segregate from mainstream society. Such negative
...ncerning multiculturalism have been directed
...gregated Muslim communities. Thomas and Bujra and
...ve though that, rather than an underlying concern of the
...s being to preserve such segregated communities, they were
...ression for recognition on the part of South Asian communities
...qual inclusiveness *within* a multicultural society. Further, Kalra
...nd Rhodes and Thomas put forward the argument that segregation
in inner-city areas has largely been determined, or at least enhanced,
by institutionally racist local government housing policies.

The segregation issue is explored further by a number of the
contributions in respect of the apparently divisive post-1981 policy of
local authority allocation of resources according to 'ward level indices
of multiple deprivation'. It has been argued here that not only has
this had the effect of enhancing racialised geographical communities
(even if, to take Kalra and Rhodes' point, they are in reality more
'symbolic landscapes' rather than firm geographical boundaries)
between minority ethnic populations and white communities, as
came to the fore in the 2001 riots, but also *within* respective minority
communities, as instanced by King's examination of the 2005 riots in
the Lozells area of Birmingham. Here, grievances surfaced between
the South Asian community who where seen as being more effectively
organised in obtaining local authority resources than the longer-term
resident African-Caribbean community.

Crucially, Thomas focuses on the post-2001 'watershed' policy of
Community Cohesion and on assertions that such a policy is not only
contrary to the principles of multiculturalism, but integrationalist to the
extent of (to mis-use a quote from one of Bujra and Pearce's interview
respondents) a 'melting pot'. His contention though, evidenced in
his study of youth work in Oldham, is that Community Cohesion
and multiculturalism are not necessarily mutually exclusive; indeed,
Community Cohesion can be utilised to recognise rather than subsume
multiculturalism/diversity. In other words, Community Cohesion can
serve to enhance 'core values' while recognising diversity. Despite
this though, Thomas suggests that the negative impact of Community
Cohesion policies is the withdrawal or non-renewal of local authority
funds for mono-ethnic/religious community projects.

In contrast to the above contributions, but still within this primary
theme, Lukas refers to the relatively exclusionary situation that

exists in Germany for minority ethnic communities. He suggests that notions of neither multiculturalism nor integrationalism/citizenship are applicable here, but that the term 'marginalisation' is more accurate. Indeed, he points to an increasingly social and geographical segregation for such communities.

A second major theme is that of police-community relations. This is especially relevant within Lukas' account as to why there have been no major riotous eruptions in Germany in comparison with the UK, France and elsewhere, despite the general lack of incorporation of its minorities. In this respect he focuses on a developed system of police-community 'round table' communication and mediation practices. Police-community relations is also an issue that runs throughout Bujra and Pearce's examination of the 2001 Bradford disturbances, which points to an apparent dichotomy between diversity-sensitive policing and the policing operational logic directed at the universal. They argue that it was a combination of the latter, which necessitates equality of treatment rather than being sensitive to the individual culture, and police 'ethnic framing' that led to an escalation of the conflict. Waddington's focus on the Cincinnati riots of 2001 also highlights the issue of police-community relations as being subject to ongoing tension for at least the previous 30 years. A way forward was not only the recognition of this fact, but an attempt at conciliation by the formulation and enactment of a 'collaborative agreement' between the police and the various community stakeholders. However, his findings show that while a written agreement was reached, the police would seem to have been somewhat recalcitrant in putting their part of the equation into practice. King's contribution also highlights a police attempt at mediation between conflicting groups, to which they would have no lines of communication due to the criminal and underground nature of the latter, through the utilisation of an independent mediation service.

A third (related) theme is that of racialised territories, 'turf' or territorial boundaries. We referred earlier to Kalra and Rhodes' suggestion of racialised *symbolic* rather than *actual* geographies, and many of the contributions stress the importance of spatiality in relation to the disorders. Bagguley and Hussain, as well as Bujra and Pearce, raise this as a dominant issue in respect of the Bradford 2001 riots, as do Kalra and Rhodes in relation to Oldham and Burnley. Associated with this, and something that must be a concern for future policy, is that despite there being no recent re-escalation of conflict to the extent as seen in these instances, the underlying situations continue.

In this respect, King as well as Kalra and Rhodes, point to the present realities of 'slow rioting' and ongoing tensions.

Chapters on the French riots

Placing the English and the French contributions side by side, it is remarkable to note how the topics addressed in the two countries regarding contemporary riots are similar and yet contrasting. They are similar in the sense that the core issues are embodied by police-public relationships, by race-relations and/or multiculturalism, and by territory in combination with identity. But those concepts relate to different realities on either side of the Channel, and their importance for an understanding of the causes of the riots must be differently ordered.

The undisputed *immediate* cause for the riots in France was the police. Triggering events have been of different kinds in the UK (racial conflicts, BNP's involvement, etc.), but Hamidi shows that major French riots from the beginning of the 1990s onwards have systematically stemmed from (rumours of) deadly police encounters. Not only have the deaths of two young boys in Clichy during a police chase been the starting point of the riots in 2005, but the mismanagement of the riot police sent to the trouble-spots over the weekend after the fatal incident (the shooting of a tear gas canister into the local mosque) appeared to be the triggering event that led to the spread of rioting nationwide. The police, then, can be seen as the key player in riot processes in France. However, there are a number of associated amplificatory factors: the central organisation of the French police and, more conjecturally, its over-politicisation by the then Minister of Interior and President in waiting, Nicolas Sarkozy, have made the police a metonymic figure in the eyes of the *banlieues* youths. In this respect, the police are, on the one hand, seen as embodying the policies that Sarkozy represents, and on the other hand as embodying the whole French polity.

Mouhanna highlights in his conclusion two major consequences of this growing importance of the police in the *banlieues*. The first one is the over-investment of policy-makers in an attempt to 'secure' the *cités* from ongoing disorder – but in a typical 'means over ends syndrome' (Goldstein 1979), it is argued that the police are mainly deployed in the *cités* on a self-preservation basis, i.e. a spiralling militarisation producing a lasting reinforcement of riot police forces and the multiplication of local paramilitary police units. In this respect,

Mouhanna shows how much the elected local and central authorities relied on the police during the *banlieues* riots in 2005, reinforcing both the myth of the 'thin blue line' protecting the Republic from chaos and conversely increasing the growing dependence of the elected bodies on the police. The ongoing presence of the police in the *banlieues* has an immediate impact on the way that politics is organised at the local level. On the basis of long-term in-depth observation in one *banlieue* town, Mohammed shows the extent to which violence has become a routinised political tool over the last decades in some *cités*. The local mayor (being also an MP), although infamous in France for his explanation of the riots as being rooted in polygamy, devotes a part of the town's resources to the local gang leaders in order to avoid major disturbances that could jeopardise the local balance of powers. Mohammed demonstrates, then, the extent to which small-scale riots or disorders actually belong to routine politics in French *cités*, as a means to force local authorities to divert subsidies from the city centre to the *cité* or to specific (ethnic) groups residing in the *cité*. Unlike the UK, in France these resource allocation processes rely more on bargaining processes and trials of strength, rather than being based on routine multiculturalist policies.

The above example indicates that law-and-order issues are not solely used as a one-sided form of political domination. Mohammed's focus on the local impacts of law and order shows the integration of extraordinary and daily collective violence into routine politics. In this respect it not only illustrates the dissolution of normative boundaries in the local polity but, as in some English towns, the 'slow rioting' that occurs on a routine basis in the *banlieues*. On the basis of interviews conducted after the 2005 riots in Saint-Denis (the main town of the first riot-torn *département*), Kokoreff argues that core rioters were actually tied into different networks of local actors, such as social workers, school teachers, communist or Left activists and local politicians. His contribution indicates that riot-prone territories are actually places in which the use of collective violence is subject to a deliberative engagement with those mediators, and thereby eventually play a role in local politics.

Local area studies like those conducted by Mohammed and Kokoreff also shed a new light on the nature of the national wave of rioting in 2005. An overly dominant focus on the respective roles played by the central police and by Nicolas Sarkozy as symbols of the youths' hatred by the media and wider academic literature has tended to mask the fact that this universal episode contains hundreds of different local and, indeed, parochial events, with each location unveiling its specific set of causes and forms of collective violence. One salient aspect of this localised nature is the fact that local politics, local identities and territories now deter national political activists from the local scenes. Both Kokoreff and Mohammed show how these apparently politicised territories refused to open to national migrants' or race-related political movements like MIR or CRAN, thus contributing to (despite their apparent national character) the scattering of the different local revolts. Historical insights offered by Hamidi, who depicts the growing distance in France throughout the 1980s and 1990s between rioters, political movements and institutionalised parties, help to understand the salience of a long-term disenchantment of the mundane world experienced by the *banlieues* youths – a disillusion long sustained by the instrumental use of local political forces by the hegemonic *Parti socialiste*. In an attempt to give a broader insight on the links between collective violence and politics in France, Fauvelle-Aymar, François and Vornetti focus on votes cast in a sample of ZUS areas (considered to be among the most deprived urban areas in France), where the overall votes achieved by Sarkozy have been the lowest recorded in France. Their logistic regressions indicate that, all else being equal, turnout in the 2007 French presidential election was greater in those ZUSs hit by rioting, and that the left candidates, notably the main opponent Ségolène Royal, scored better in those ZUSs marked by the intensity levels of the daily recorded violence.

Unlike the UK riots, the 2005 French episode and its 300 affected areas offer a basis for the use of explanatory tools used to understand the causes of the US riots. As expected, Lagrange discovers that riots are more likely to occur in poor urban areas (ZUSs), specifically the ones most affected by youth unemployment and by renewal programmes launched by ANRU. Further, the 2005 riots were apparently massively driven by major social factors in which 'race' (as this term is used in the USA) does not play a role in itself, but migration waves do. More accurately, it appears that the riots were strongly linked with the intensity of racial segregation (measured on the basis of proxy variables). Such a finding highlights the dialectical roles of territories and race in the causation of the French riots. Due to the legal restrictions on administrative data in France, Lagrange's findings shed an ambivalent light on the race-related aspects of the 2005 riots. On the one hand, one can consider that segregation towards sub-Saharan families has played a central role; while on the other hand, one can point to the position that recent waves of immigration are the key factor here, since newcomers (today mainly from sub-Saharan Africa) are settled in the most deprived areas of the *banlieues*. In addition to the central role played by the law and order policies, one further policy has recently gained a major place among the significant contextual variables of collective violence in urban France. As Epstein explains, the urban renewal policy has, since the beginning of the 2000s, not only become the main instrumental policy aimed at dealing with urban misery and urban disorders, but could indeed be one of the most salient determinants of future riots in France.

Policy and political implications

It is often asked whether riots are ultimately worthwhile for those who engage in them. Piven and Cloward (1991: 456) answer this question resoundingly in the affirmative:

> Lower-stratum protestors have some possibility of influence ... if their action violates rules and disrupt the workings of an institution on which important groups depend. When lower-stratum groups form organizations and employ conventional political strategies, they can easily be ignored. But institutional disruptions cannot so easily be ignored. Institutional disruption provokes conflict; they arouse an array of 'third parties', including important economic interests, and may even contribute to electoral dealignment and realignment. To restore institutional stability and to avoid worsening polarization, political leaders are forced to respond, whether with concessions or repression.

As far as riots in the UK are concerned, the early 1980s disorders had a positive effect on, for instance, policing (Police and Criminal Evidence Act 1984) and on race relations (Thomas, this volume). But the impact of the ever-recurring French riots on politics and policies gives rise to a more pessimistic view than the one defended until now by the two American authors[1]: in France, repetitive riots since the beginning of the 1990s seem to have produced nothing but a strong contribution to political shifts within the French public sphere (impacting on fear of crime, fear of immigration, hate crime, extreme-right voting patterns, etc.) which finally nurtured and legitimated law-and-order policies as the main strategic option. Nevertheless, some empirical evidence could suggest a more ambivalent view on the policies instituted – without referring again to the introduction of *politique de la ville*, which represented a real if not very successful

235

policy shift in France, one can add that major police abuses of force that ignited large-scale rioting during the 1990s and 2000s led to the introduction of human rights provisions in the Police Acts (in 1986 1993 and 2000) and also the creation of a national civilian review board (2000).

It is important therefore to take a closer look at the effects of the 2005 riots on French polity (in terms of both politics and policy) in order to assess the extent to which it is worth rioting in France, or the degree to which it simply results in self-destructive nihilism (Marx 1970). Even if it is too soon to give a definitive assessment on the impact of the nationwide 2005 riots in France, we can observe most assuredly that: (a) race-relations policies follow from the riots, and simultaneously; (b) such policies instituted still seem to follow the path taken from the 1990s onwards, and (c) a policy process unable to deter further riots in France.

Race relations and multiculturalism

In such an ideological context, it appears to be quite difficult to assess both the state of race relations in contemporary France and the possible impact that the riots have had on them. In an enlightening French-English comparative study, Garbaye (2005: 10) recently pointed to the main differences as far as political inclusion of minorities in each country is concerned: 1) Due to earlier immigration flows, the fact that Commonwealth migrants gained citizenship from the first generation onwards, and the impact of earlier riots, the formation of an immigrants' political elite 'took place much earlier' in Britain than in France; 2) British minority politicians frequently have a career as (Labour) party activists behind them, while their French counterparts 'are more frequently picked by party-list makers among local personalities with little political clout'; and 3) The formation of a political elite in Britain 'was accompanied by the formulation and implementation of anti-discrimination policy agendas in Britain, which has not been the case in France'.

Things are changing on both sides of the channel, and violence in general and riots in particular have been playing a significant role in both cases, threatening to shatter the rigid boundaries separating the two 'models'. In England, 'signs of a return to a more assimilationist perspective appeared in the early 2000s' (Garbaye 2005: 17), exemplified by the oath of allegiance to 'British values' defended by Home Secretary David Blunkett in 2004, and the promotion of 'Community Cohesion' programmes by the Commission for Racial Equality from

2004 onwards (as discussed by Thomas in this volume). In France, for the first time ever, the 2005 riots have undoubtedly introduced an agenda shift marked by the prioritisation of racial issues in the policy process. Meanwhile, Sarkozy's presidency results from his long (and successful) strategy to gain *Front National* supporters 'back' to the Conservative party and from his relentless ideological manipulation of social fears resulting from 2005 riots and disorders. Therefore if the riots had an impact on the political agenda in France, its meaning is far from univocal.

The 2005 riots undoubtedly took place in a critical juncture marked by a rise of racial and culturally related issues. Already in 2001, a law recognised that the slave trade in which France took part constitutes a crime against humanity. In February 2003, *Ni Putes Ni Soumises* (NPNS) was founded in order to promote a hardline assimilatory discourse as a way to protect Muslim women in the *banlieue* from (Muslim) male violence. The intense media coverage of NPNS increased when, in 2003, they pronounced that the Muslim headscarf was a 'symbol of the submission of women in places where the State should guarantee a strict gender equality' (as quoted in the women's magazine *Elle* in November 2003), thereby launching a national controversy which ended with a law being passed in 2004 banning the wearing of headscarves in schools (Jelen 2005). For their part, the Parliament passed a law on 23 February 2005 mentioning the 'positive role' played by the French in their former colonies.

The headscarf controversy and the debate launched on the law on the former colonies encouraged the foundation by immigrant activists in January 2005 of the *Mouvement des Indigènes de la République* (MIR) with the objective of fighting against the contemporary 'postcolonial State' of France that allegedly treats immigrants as mere 'natives'. Two weeks after the 2005 riots had subsided, a Representative Council of Black Associations (CRAN) was founded to promote blackness in French politics and culture, and to insist on the introduction of racial administrative statistics and more urgent positive action. Controversies between the right-wing majority, anti-racist assimilationist movements such as NPNS and radical movements like MIR or CRAN or grassroots activists like MIB intensified to such a degree as to force 'race relations' (to use an English term) to the forefront of public debate (Ancelovici 2008: 87–89; Dufoix 2005) and resulted in 'ambivalent policy-making in the domain of multiculturalist policies' (Lépinard 2008: 100).

The 2005 riots took place within the context of the above heightened controversies and had immediate consequences. President Jacques Chirac, who had already inaugurated a national day celebrating the abolition of the slave trade and, in December 2004, set up the Equal Opportunities and Anti-Discrimination Commission (HALDE) as an independent statutory authority aimed at identifying and deterring racial discrimination. Chirac also lent his support to a 'law on equal opportunities', introduced in January 2006, in order to fight 'discrimination' and help youths 'from immigration or overseas territories', a phrase which broke with decades of euphemistic references like 'youths from *deprived* territories'. Following his election in June 2007, Chirac's successor Nicolas Sarkozy appointed three minority members to his government, among them the founder of NPNS, Fadela Amara, and displayed some sympathy towards grievances raised by CRAN. But Sarkozy also showed resolute tendencies towards Conservative nationalism by creating a Ministry dedicated to 'immigration and national identity', the only one of its kind in Europe – which promotes fierce anti-immigration policies and advocates uncompromising measures in response to rebellious youths.

At present it is too soon to assess the long-term consequences of the 2005 French riots on policy innovation. Meanwhile though, the shock provoked by the riots, the controversies launched by CRAN, MIR or NPNS and Sarkozy's opportunistic 'strategies of minority management' (Esman 2004: 52) both supports agendas aimed at reinforcing the electoral support displayed by former FN voters and visibly addresses race issues in such a way that even France's sacrosanct 'non-ethnic administrative data' (Simon 2008) is subject to public scrutiny. In this respect, the 2005 riots have, more so than their predecessors, resulted in increased controversy around multiculturalism and race relations, and in ambivalent, if not contradictory, policies.

On the (non-)impact of policies aimed at deterring riots

During the 2005 riotous period and its aftermath, possible explanations were put forward for the violence and destruction. Sociologists, media, opinion makers and politicians seemed to agree on the causes of the riots: the deepening social deprivation affecting the *banlieues*, its disastrous effects on male youths also reeling from negative relations with an increasingly militarised police force, and the inefficiency of policies designed to alleviate such problems, were all regularly featured in relevant discussions.

As usual in such tumultuous situations, some political and media pundits argued that the disorders had been deliberately provoked by 'Islamic fundamentalist extremists', were the consequence of provocative hip-hop lyrics, or were a by-product of polygamous Muslim families. These arguments were mainly delivered by the closest supporters of the law-and-order strategy deployed by Sarkozy (see Mohammed, this volume), who obviously needed to remain committed to the police – the 'thin blue line' protecting the French Republic from internal chaos. This blaming strategy (against deviant migrants or 'scum') also echoed the lasting strategy of the then president-in-waiting Sarkozy, aimed at 'siphoning off' (Mayer 2007) Far Right voters one and a half years prior to the presidential election (Cautrès and Cole 2008: 30).

However, such verbal escalation should not hide the fact that most French opinion makers sustained the view that riots were rooted in the social despair of *banlieue* youths, reactivated by violent encounters with the police. The opinion expressed below exemplifies the most common accounts concerning French riots and does not differ significantly from what many journalists and some academics have repeated since then. What is most surprising here is that this depiction of the riots is volunteered from within the intelligence service of the *Police nationale* itself:

> [The riots consisted of] an unorganized urban insurrection, lacking any obvious leadership or political agenda. The youths were spurred on by a strong sense of their identity which does not rest solely on their ethnic or geographic origins, but also on their social condition, as people rejected by French society. (2005, in Dufresne 2007: 137)

Of course, this sociogically oriented explanation of the riots was not shared by hardliners like Sarkozy, who reacted strongly to this assertion (Dufresne 2006: 131; Mucchielli 2009). But to focus unduly on Sarkozy's authoritative gesture would cause us to miss a crucially central point regarding the *locus* of the riots in the French 'polity'. As soon as Sarkozy was elected, he followed in the shoes of all his predecessors from 1981 onwards by announcing a substantial programme called *Plan Espoir Banlieue* ('Banlieue Hope Programme'), aimed at alleviating the underlying causes of riots by providing funding for, among other things, social programmes, urban planning, and better education in the most deprived areas.

Looking back at the last three decades of riots in France one can easily notice a kind of political cycle marked by a reiterating occurrence of riot/ineffectual policy/new riot, etc. Policy content has varied over the years, but the accompanying rationales seldom have. Here, for example, is what President François Mitterrand said in Lyon's *banlieue* two months after the eruption of the Vaulx-en-Velin riot in 1990:

> Tomorrow there could be horrible tragedies of the type which occurred in this very region ... It will be necessary to take from those who have much to give something to those who have nothing, lest the poorest localities flounder ... I have learned all my life that whoever owns something hates giving it back. [We should not] fear the hostility of those who own. (Body-Gendrot 2000: 71)

The Vaulx-en-Velin riot immediately induced the strong reinforcement of *politique de la ville* (Body-Gendrot 2000: 75). However, the effect of this innovation was merely to cushion the deep and lasting consequences of de-industrialisation on male youths from the *cités*.

Fifteen years later, Prime Minister de Villepin reacted to the recently occurring riots by introducing a law aimed at encouraging and supporting those individuals struggling to cope in an inhospitable labour market. Somewhat in contrast to the tone adopted by Mitterrand, de Villepin stated how:

> Our country has just gone through a hard time [i.e. the 2005 riots] and we need to act: We must refuse powerlessness and solve the problems experienced by the French people ... The crisis we have just endured unveils weaknesses and shortage. Discrimination, either of a direct or an indirect nature, is of particular concern for the people living in deprived neighbourhoods, for immigrants and their dependants and those who have arrived from our overseas territories ... Unequal opportunity specifically hits youths from the ZUSs ... But this crisis has helped us appreciate the numerous achievements we need to accomplish. We face a great opportunity, we must seize it. (Introduction to the Law on Equal Opportunities, presented to Parliament 16 January 2006)

Central to this law was a new work contract aimed at young employment seekers. The contract gave employers the means to dismiss employees more easily, thus encouraging them to take on young job seekers with less risk. Following waves of protest, Jacques Chirac abrogated the law in what was widely perceived as a 'humiliating reversal'. One side-effect of this defeat was to remove from contention Sarkozy's only real Conservative rival in his bid for candidacy in the Presidential race.

Following his election, Sarkozy introduced his 'Hope in *Banlieue* Programme' by arguing:

> Over the last 20 years we have learned one thing: it is not sufficient to create a *ministère de la ville*, and likewise nor does the inflow of money, nor housing refurbishment make the inhabitants not feel neglected, abandoned, put aside from the Republic, aside from its laws and the support it displays ... [Nevertheless] I do pay homage to all *ministres de la ville* ... since 1988 and who have ardently tried to convince the public about the intensity of the *banlieues* crisis. (Nicolas Sarkozy, speech introducing the *Plan Espoir Banlieue*, 8 February 2008)

This broad rhetoric has remained basically unchanged while the *politique de la ville* has followed its now ancient three-decades-long path. Such a policy has proven to be indispensable in the daily life of people living in the *cités*, but it remains incapable of solving what it was aimed to achieve: the disappearance of the riots. It all constitutes a neverending cycle that continues to reproduce itself amidst a growing authoritarian powerlessness, characterised by an overwhelming police militarisation and urban renewal measures based on a hollow political rhetoric.

The very essence of riots in France actually lies in their ritualised nature. Despite their spontaneity, riots are characterised by a high level of self-discipline: cars are set alight, street confrontations with the police happen in the strict confines of the *cités*, with no contagion to city centres like Paris and with no recourse to gunfire, and with no electoral mobilisation by the rioters and their peers in the local elections. Riots do not overly impact on the political balance of power in France. They are therefore dealt with as the one of the unavoidable costs of a social crisis in which the police are repeatedly brought in to play with a key containing role.

The show still goes on

Neither the intensification of the criminal justice system's efforts to manage criminality, nor the police militarisation process – nor, indeed, the successive programmes aimed at dealing with underlying causes of the riots – have deterred ongoing collective violence in the French *cités*. To conclude our discussions, three main post-2005 developments in France deserve special mention.

To begin with, there are now clear signs of a radicalisation of collective violence. First, there is a form of increased nihilistic violence illustrated in recent inter-youth fights during conventional protest, characterised by the observers as '*casseurs* versus protesters violence', or as *banlieues* youths versus secondary school and university students. During the protest movements in January–March 2005 (against the education reform) and in March 2006 (against the government's CPE initiative), hundreds of young protestors were harassed, assaulted, robbed and beaten up by gangs of youths[2] (Bronner 2006; Dufresne 2007; Kokoreff 2008). These events induced a resurfacing of *banlieue*-related fear and concern, since they provided evidence that, by attacking other young people who were partly demonstrating for *their* interests, the *banlieues* youth were intent on political self-destruction.

Secondly, signs of a radicalisation of police-youth confrontations in the French *banlieues* may be detected in localised breaks with such ritualised forms of riotous behaviour as hit-and-run fights with the police, setting cars and public buildings alight, and using non-lethal weapons against the police. On 25 November 2007, two helmetless black and Arab pupils riding a small motorbike collided with a police patrol car in the Paris *banlieue* Villiers-le-Bel and died instantly. Three nights of riots then occurred in the town during which the youths, quite predictably, threw stones, cobblestones and Molotov cocktails, but also made novel use of firearms (Lagrange 2007). The Villiers-le-Bel riot was significant in that, unlike in 2005, the police used their firearms in self-defence (Bronner 2008). Again, during a smaller-scale riot in Grigny in May 2007, police officers used their firearms several times; youths also fired at the police during a further confrontation in Grigny in March 2008. For the time being, such events are not very frequent and seem to occur only in *cités* like La Grande Borne which are characterised by both a persistently high level of deprivation and severely endemic conflict with the police.

Finally, some post-2005 riots have occurred that seem to confirm some of the main findings of quantitative analysis of the 2005 riots wave specifically regarding the geography of the riots (Lagrange 2006b). To date, five high-intensity riots (entailing more than one night of unrest) have occurred since that period: in Saint-Dizier (October 2007), Vitry-le-François (June 2008), Romans-sur-Isère (October 2008), Villiers-le-Bel (November 2007) and Grigny (March 2008). The most striking aspect of these is that, while the Grigny and Villiers riots occurred in classical large-scale *cités*, the first three occurred in very small estates, located in small cities isolated in rural areas characterised by a negative demographic growth. Also, looking at the geography and demography of the riots, one should note that Grigny and Villiers-le-Bel are both located in the furthest outskirts of the capital (respectively 25 and 18 km away from Paris), and marked by a large community of sub-Saharan African immigrants. It would certainly be too soon to draw generalisations from these latest events, as we still lack accurate information. Nevertheless, they do appear to represent an extension of the riot-like protests into the cities that could never have been contemplated several years ago.

What seems undisputed today is that France's turbulent *banlieues* have regressed into the same type of violence-prone condition that affected them at the outset of the 1990s. The apparent re-establishment of order in urban France must not obscure a possible radicalisation of collective violence, the like of which has been observed both during and after the 2005 episode. For the time being, one key institution remains constant to the riots. Indeed, we can safely predict that the political economy of the riots will stay unchanged so long as the police remain ready and able to contain the rioters within their territorial boundaries and without inflicting fatal casualties. The moving balance of 'ritualisation' and 'escalation' (Edelman 1969) observed during 2005 and after depicts today's riot-prone localities as 'murky areas' (Aureyo and Moran 2007: 245) where the balance of power between the political authorities, the rioters and the police is decidedly unstable.

In a recent major work, the American historian, Charles Tilly, pertinently remarked:

> I have omitted the widely used term 'riot' from the typology for a different reason: because it embodies a political judgment rather than an analytical distinction … . In cataloguing thousands of violent events – many of them called riots (or the local-language equivalent) by authorities and observers – from multiple countries over several centuries, I have not once found an instance in which the participants called the event a riot or identified themselves as rioters. (2003: 18–19)

What our cross-national insight into contemporary 'riots' in France and in the UK has shown is that, contrary to Tilly's assumption, collective violence, 'non-normative' or 'deviant' protest, and non-institutionalised action all constitute the protest repertoires of male youth struggling to survive within deprived urban areas. The forms and brutality of these actions may differ widely in both countries from night-brawls to inter-racial fights, deviant games such as car-burning or car-rodeos to scattered attacks against other youths that turn into organised confrontations with the police. However, no matter what their actual form may take, in both countries rioting appears to have become a major form of contentious politics; and in France at least, it appears to have produced both positive and negative dividends.

Notes

1 In her 2007 Presidential address to the American Political Science Society, Frances F. Piven clearly supports the positive impact of collective violence 'from below': 'Without the support of the rabble, the war with England could not have been won … [in the US] chattel slavery was not restored, the Southern apartheid system is dismantled, and while labor is taking a beating, there are still unions, and they may matter again in American politics' (Piven 2008: 1–2).
2 On how 'youth gang' must be defined, see Mohammed in this volume.

References

Abdallah, M. (2000) *J'y Suis, J'y Reste! Les Luttes de l'Immigration en France depuis les Années Soixante*. Paris: Éditions Réflex.

Abdallah, M. (2001) 'IM'média, l'immigration par elle-même', *Vacarme*, 17: 30–36.

Abudu Stark, M.J., Raine, W.J., Burbeck, S.L. and Davison, K.K. (1974) 'Some empirical patterns in a riot process', *American Sociological Review*, 39: 865–76.

ACLU (American Civil Liberties Union) Advisory Panel and Plaintiff/ACLU Class Counsel (2003) 'Nathaniel Jones, 04/17/62 – 11/30/03: What we have learned since November 2003', Report dated 21 August 2004. http://www.acluohio.org/issues/policepractices/Jones_Study_Guide_Final.pdf.

Albrecht, H.-J. (1997) 'Ethnic minorities, crime, and criminal justice in Germany', in M. Tonry (ed.) *Ethnicity, Crime, and Immigration. Comparative and Cross-National Perspectives*. Chicago and London: University of Chicago Press.

Albrecht, H.-J. (2002) 'Polizei, Diskriminierung und Fremdenfeindlichkeit in multi-ethnischen Gesellschaften', in A. Donatsch, M. Forster and C. Schwarzenegger (eds) *Strafrecht, Strafprozessrecht und Menschenrechte. Festschrift für Stefan Trechsel zum 65. Geburtstag*. Zurich and Geneva: Schulthess.

Alexander, C. (2004) 'Imagining the Asian gang: ethnicity, masculinity and youth after "the riots" ', *Critical Social Policy*, 24(4): 526–49.

Althoff, M. (2006) 'Die Ausschreitungen in den französischen Vorstädten. Zwischen Provokation, Erklärung und Deutung. Oder: was haben Frankreich und Holland gemeinsam?', *Kriminologisches Journal*, 38(2): 112–117.

Amin, A. (2002) 'Ethnicity and the multicultural city: living with diversity', *Environment and Planning A*, 34: 959–80.

Amin, A. (2003) 'Unruly strangers? The 2001 urban riots in Britain', *International Journal of Urban and Regional Research*, 27(2): 460–63.

Amrani, Y. and Beaud, S. (2004) *Pays de Malheur! Un Jeune de Cité Ecrit à un Sociologue*. Paris: La Découverte.

Ancelovici, M. (2008) 'Social movements and protest politics', in *Developments in French Politics*. Basingstoke: Palgrave MacMillan.

Anderson, E. (1999) *Code of the Street: Decency, Violence, and the Moral Life of the Inner City*. New York: Norton.

Anhut, R. and Heitmeyer, W. (2000) 'Bedrohte Stadtgesellschaft. Diskussion von Forschungsergebnissen', in R. Anhut and W. Heitmeyer (eds) *Bedrohte Stadtgesellschaft. Soziale Desintegrationsprozesse und Ethnisch-kulturelle Konfliktkonstellationen*. Weinheim and Munich: Juventa Verlag.

Appleton, J. (2005) 'What's behind the battle of Lozells?', *Spiked-Politics*, 26 October. http://www.spiked-online.com?Articles/0000000CADF2.htm.

Auyero, J. and Moran, T. (2007) 'The dynamics of collective violence', *Social Forces*, 85(3): 1341–67.

Bachmann, C. and Le Guennec, N. (1997) *Violences Urbaines. Ascension et Chute des Classes Moyennes à Travers 50 ans de Politique de la Ville*. Paris: Albin Michel.

Back, L. (1996) *New Ethnicities and Urban Cultures*. London: UCL Press.

Back, L. and Keith, M. (1999) '"Rights and Wrongs": youth, community and narratives of racial violence', in P. Cohen (ed.) *New Ethnicities, Old Racisms?* London: Zed Books.

Back, L., Keith, M., Khan, A., Shukra, K. and Solomos, J. (2002) 'New Labour's white heart: politics, multiculturalism and the return of assimilationism', *Political Quarterly*. 73(4): 445–54.

Backes, O., Dollase, R. and Heitmeyer, W. (1998) 'Wie groß ist die Fremdenfeindlichkeit in der Polizei? Eine Analyse zu Risikokonstellationen im Polizeialltag', *Newsletter Forschungsnetzwerk für ethnisch-kulturelle Konflikte, Rechtsextremismus und Gewalt*, 9: 4–11.

Badariotti, D. and Bussi, M. (2004), *Pour une Nouvelle Géographie du Politique*. Paris: Anthropos.

Bagguley, P. and Hussain, Y. (2003) 'The Bradford riot of 2001: a preliminary analysis'. Paper presented to the Ninth Alternative Futures and Popular Protest Conference, Manchester Metropolitan University, 22–24 April 2003.

Bagguley, P. and Hussain, Y. (2008) *Riotous Citizens: Ethnic Conflict in Multicultural Britain*. Aldershot: Ashgate.

Bauman, Z. (2004) *Wasted Lives: Modernity and its Outcasts*. Cambridge: Polity.

BBC News (2001) 'Police deny "no-go" areas for whites', 19 April 2001. http://news.bbc.co.uk/1/hi/uk/1285085.stm.

BBC News online (2005a) 'Man killed in Birmingham clashes', 23 October http://news.bbc.co.uk/1/hi/england/west_midlands/4367654.stm.

BBC News online (2005b) 'Residents' fear during violence', 23 October http://news.bbc.co.uk/1/hi/england/west_midlands/4368662.stm.

Beaud, S. (2002) *80% au Bac ... et Après? Les Enfants de la Démocratisation Scolaire*. Paris: La Découverte.

Beaud, S. and Masclet, O. (2006), 'Des "marcheurs" de 1983 aux "émeutiers" de 2005: Deux générations sociales d'enfants d'immigrés', *Annales*, 61(4): 809–43.

Beck, U. (1992) *The Risk Society: Towards a New Modernity*. London: Sage.

Béhar, D. (1995) 'Banlieues ghettos, quartiers populaires ou ville éclatée?', *Les Annales de la recherche urbaine*, 68–69: 6–14.

Behr, R. (2007) 'Die Besten gehören zu uns – aber wir wissen nicht, wer sie sind', in M.H.W. Möllers and R.C. Van Ooyen (eds) *Jahrbuch öffentliche Sicherheit 2006/2007*. Frankfurt/M.: Verlag für Polizeiwissenschaft.

Benabou R., Kramarz F. and Prost C. (2005) *The French Zones d'Education Prioritaire: Much Ado About Nothing?* London: Centre for Economic Policy Research, Discussion Paper 5085.

Benedict, W.R., Brown, B. and Bower, D.J. (2000) 'Perceptions of the police and fear of crime in a rural setting: utility of a geographical focused survey for police services, planning, and assessment', *Criminal Justice Policy Review*, 11(4): 275–98.

Benyon, J. (1984) 'The policing issues', in J. Benyon (ed.) *Scarman and After: Essays Reflecting on Lord Scarman's Report, the Riots and their Aftermath*. Oxford: Pergamon Press.

Benyon, J. (1987) 'Interpretations of civil disorder', in J. Benyon and J. Solomos (eds) *The Roots of Urban Unrest*. Oxford: Pergamon Press.

Benyon, J. and Solomos, J. (1987) 'British urban unrest in the 1980s', in J. Benyon, and J. Solomos (eds) *The Roots of Urban Unrest*. Oxford: Pergamon.

Berliner Zeitung (2006) 'Jugendliche und Polizei suchen das Gespräch. Runder Tisch im Wrangelkiez', 22 November.

Bertossi, C. (2007) *Distant Neighbours: Understanding how the French Deal with Ethnic and Religious Diversity*. London: Runneymede Trust.

Birmingham City Council (2006a) *Lozells and East Handsworth Ward*. http://www.birmingham.gov.uk/GenerateContent?CONTENT_ITEM_ID=11631andCONTENT_ITEM_TYPE=0andMENU_ID=5452.

Birmingham City Council (2006b) *Aston, Newtown and Lozells Area Action Plan: Sustainability Appraisal and Strategic Environmental Assessment Scoping Report*. http://www.birmingham.gov.uk/Media/Sustainability%20Scoping%20Report%20Sep%2006.pdf?MEDIA_ID=184243andFILENAME=Sustainability%20Scoping%20Report%20Sep%2006.pdf.

Black Radley Report (2007) *Lozells Disturbances: Summary Report*. Birmingham: Black Radley Ltd.

Blanchard, E. (2007) 'The Paris police and Algerians in Paris (1944–1956). Colonial context and equality of rights, the impossible implementation of ordinary policing', University of Leeds, UK (unpublished).

Bleich, E. (2003) *Race Politics in Britain and France: Ideas and Policymaking Since the 1960s*. Cambridge: Cambridge University Press.

BN Village (2005) 'Community warnings of possible repeat weekend attacks in Birmingham', Ligali Media Network, 29 October.

Body-Gendrot, S. (2000) *The Social Control of Cities? A Comparative Perspective*. Oxford: Blackwell.

Body-Gendrot, S. (2010) 'Police marginality, racial logics, and discrimination in the banlieues of France', *Ethnic and Race Studies*, forthcoming.

Body-Gendrot, S. and Withold de Wenden, C. (2003) *Police et Discriminations Raciales, le Tabou Français*. Paris: Editions de l'Atelier.

Bonelli, L. (2007) 'Policing the youth: towards a redefinition of discipline and social control in French working-class neighbourhoods', in S. Venkatesh and R. Kassimir (eds) *Youth, Globalization and the Law*. Palo Alto, CA: Stanford University Press.

Bornewasser, M., Eckert, R. and Willems, H. (1996) 'Die Polizei im Umgang mit Fremden – Problemlagen, Belastungssituationen und Übergriffe', *Schriftenreihe der Polizei-Führungsakademie*, 1/2: 9–165.

Bouamama, S. (1994) *Dix Ans de Marche des Beurs*. Paris: Desclée de Brower.

Boubeker, A. and Hajjat A. (eds) (2008) *Immigration en Lutte. Des Travailleurs Indigènes aux Héritiers de l'Immigration Postcoloniale*. Paris: Éditions Amsterdam.

Boulding, K. (1989) *Three Faces of Power*. London: Sage.

Bourne, J. (2007) *The Baby and the Bathwater: Community Cohesion and the funding crisis*. http://www.irr.org.uk/2007/November/ha000014.html.

Braconnier, C. and Dormagen, J.-Y. (2007) *La Démocratie de l'Abstention*. Paris: Gallimard.

Bradford Commission Report, The (1995) *The Report of an Inquiry into the Wider Implications of the Public Disorders in Bradford which Occurred on 9, 10 and 11 June 1995*. London: The Stationery Office.

Bradford Vision (2001) *Community Pride Not Prejudice: Making Diversity Work in Bradford*. Bradford: Bradford District Race Review.

Brah, A. (1993) '"Race" and "culture" in the gendering of labour market: young South Asian Muslim women and the labour market', *New Community*, 19(3): 441–58.

Bronner, L. (2006) 'Au coeur d'une bande du '9–3', le plaisir de la violence' http://www.theaugeanstables.com/2006/03/28/au-coeur-dune-bande-du-9-3-le-plaisir-de-la-violence/.

Bronner, L. (2008) 'Le jour où la police a tiré à balles réelles sur les émeutiers', *Le Monde*, April, 25.

Brown, (2007) 'God and man in the French riots', *American Foreign Policy Interests*, 29: 183–199.

Bruneteau, P. (1996) *Maintenir l'Ordre*. Paris: Presses de Sciences Po.

Burnett, J. (2004) 'Community, cohesion and the state', *Race and Class*, 45(3): 1–18.

Burnley Task Force Report (2001) *Burnley Speaks, Who Listens?* Burnley: Burnley Task Force.

Butler, D. and Stokes, D. (1969) *Political Change in Britain*. London: Macmillan.

Butt, N. (2006) 'Lessons learned? A study of how the police service identifies and deals with community conflict, using the Bradford riots of 2001 as a case study'. Unpublished MA thesis, University of Bradford.

Byrne, D. (1999) *Social Exclusion*. Oxford: Blackwell.

Campbell, B. (1993) *Goliath: Britain's Dangerous Places*. London: Methuen.

Cantle, T. (2001) *Community Cohesion. A Report of the Independent Review Team*. London: Home Office.

Cantle, T. (2005) *Community Cohesion. A New Framework for Race Relations*. Basingstoke: Palgrave.

Carling, A., Davies, D., Fernandes-Bakshi, A., Jarman, N. and Nias, P. (2004) *Fair Justice for All? The Response of the Criminal Justice System to the Bradford Disturbances of July 2001*. Bradford: University of Bradford.

Castel R. (2003) 'The roads to disaffiliation: insecure work and vulnerable relationships', *International Journal of Urban and Regional Research*, 24(3): 519–35.

Castells, M. (1977) *The Urban Question*. London: Hodder & Stoughton Educ (1st ed. 1972).

City of Bradford Metropolitan District Council (1989) *Crime and Disorder Audit 1998*. Bradford MDC: Strategic Management Unit.

Cautres, P. and Cole, A. (2008) 'The 2007 French election and beyond', in A. Cole, P. Le Galès and J. Levy (eds) *Developments in French Politics*. New York: Palgrave Macmillan.

Clancy, A., Hough, M., Aust, R. and Kershaw, C. (2001) *Crime, Policing and Justice: The Experience of Ethnic Minorities – Findings from the 2000 British Crime Survey*. London: Home Office Research Study 223.

Clarke, Lord T. (2001) *Burnley Task Force Report on the Disturbances in June 2001*. Burnley: Burnley Borough Council.

Cohen, P. (1996) 'All White on the Night? Narratives of nativism on the Isle of Dogs', in T. Butler and M. Rustin (eds) *Rising in the East? The Regeneration of East London*. London: Lawrence and Wishart.

Collectif (2004), 'Un autre regard sur la délinquance', Special Issue *Déviance et Société*, 28(3): 259–404.

Commission for Racial Equality (CRE) (1999) *Open Talk, Open Minds*. London: CRE.

Commission for Racial Equality (CRE) (2001) *A Place for Us All: Learning from Bradford, Oldham and Burnley*. London: CRE.

Commission on the Future of Multi-Ethnic Britain (CFMEB) (2000) *The Future of Multi-Ethnic Britain: The Parekh Report*. London: Profile Books.

Copsey, N. (2004) *Contemporary British Fascism: The British National Party and the Quest For Legitimacy*. Basingstoke: Palgrave.
Cottle, M. (2001) 'Did integration cause the Cincinnati riots?', *The New Republic*, 5 July 2001. http://www.highbeam.com/library/docFree.asp?d ocid=1P1:43909594&key=0C177A56741C1568120A3180569061F7D0C7E7878 0B0A.
Cox, S.M. and Fitzgerald, J.D. (1996) *Police in Community Relations: Critical Issues*. Dubuque: Brown.

Damamme, D. and Jobert, B. (1995) 'La politique de la ville ou l'injonction contradictoire en politique', *Revue Française de Science Politique*, 45(1): 3–30.
Darmofal, D. (2006) 'The political geography of macro-level turnout in American political development', *Political Geography*, 25: 123–50.
Davies, B. (1999) *A History of the Youth Service in England* (2 Vols.). Leicester: Youth Work Press.
Decker, S.H. (1981) 'Citizen attitudes toward the police: a review of past findings and suggestions for future policy', *Journal of Police Science and Administration*, 8(1): 80–87.
Delon, A. and Mucchielli L. (2007) 'Judicial processing of juveniles : the case of rioters 'déférés' in November 2005', *Penal Issues*. http://www.cesdip. org/spip.php?article320.
Denham, J. (2002) *Building Cohesive Communities: A Report of the Ministerial Group on Public Order and Community Cohesion*. London: Home Office.
Department for Communities and Local Government (DCLG) (2007a) *Preventing Violent Extremism: Winning Hearts and Minds*. London: DCLG.
Department for Communities and Local Government (DCLG) (2007b) *Commission on Integration and Cohesion: Our Shared Future*. London: DCLG.
Donzelot, J. and Epstein, R. (2006) 'Démocratie et participation: l'exemple de la rénovation urbaine', *Esprit*, 326: 5–34.
Donzelot, J. and Estèbe, P. (1994) *L'État Animateur. Essai sur la Politique de la Ville*. Paris: Seuil.
Donzelot, J., Mével C. and Wyvekens A. (2003) *Faire Société. La Politique de la Ville aux Etats-Unis et en France*. Paris: Seuil.
Dosanjh, B. (2006) *Beauty Queen*. Documentary. Director and producer: A Tang Hui film.
Drewes, S. (2007) 'Was erzählen Jugendunruhen über Integrationspolitik? Eine Einführung', in Heinrich-Böll-Stiftung (ed.) *Banlieue Europa. Jugendunruhen – Stadt – Migration*. Berlin: Heinrich-Böll-Stiftung.
Drury, J. and Reicher, S. (2000) 'Collective action and psychological change: The emergence of new social identities', *British Journal of Social Psychology*, 39: 579–604.
Drury, J. and Reicher, S. (2005) 'Explaining enduring empowerment: a comparative study of collective action and psychological outcomes', *European Journal of Social Psychology*, 35: 35–58.

Drury, J., Cocking, C., Beale, J., Hanson, C. and Rapley, F. (2005) 'The phenomenology of empowerment in collective action', *British Journal of Social Psychology*, 44: 309–328.

Dubet, F. and Lapeyronnie, D. (1992) *Les Quartiers d'Exil*. Paris: Le Seuil.

Dubet, F. (1997) 'Die Logik der Jugendgewalt. Das Beispiel der französischen Vorstädte', in T. von Trotha (ed.) *Soziologie der Gewalt*. Opladen: Westdeutscher Verlag.

Dufoix, S. (2005) 'More Than Riots: A Question of Spheres', http://riotsfrance. ssrc.org/Dufoix/.

Dufresne, D. (2007) *Maintien de l'Ordre: Enquête*. Paris: Hachette.

Duprez, D. and Kokoreff, M. (2001) *Les Mondes de la Drogue*. Paris: Odile Jacob.

Eatwell, R. (2004) 'The extreme right in Britain: The long road to "modernization"', in R. Eatwell and C. Mudde (eds) *Western Democracies and the New Extreme Right Challenge*. London: Routledge.

Edelman, M. (1969) 'Escalation and ritualization of political conflict', *American Behavioral Scientist*, 13: 231–45.

Edelman, M. (1977) *Political Language. Words That Succeed and Policies That Fail*. New York: Academic Press.

Epstein, R. (2005) 'Les politiques territoriales post-contractuelles: le cas de la rénovation urbaine', *Politiques et Management Public*, 23(3): 127–43.

Epstein, R. (2008) *Gouverner à distance. La rénovation urbaine, démolition-reconstruction de l'appareil d'Etat*. Paris: IEP, thèse de doctorat.

Esman, M. (2004) *Facing Ethnic Conflicts: Toward a New Realism*. Lanham, MD: Rowman & Littlefield.

Etzioni, A. (1995) *The Spirit of Community: Rights, Responsibilities and the Communitarian Agenda*. London: Fontana.

European Commission (2001) *Effectiveness of National Integration Strategies Towards Second Generation Migrant Youth in a Comparative European Perspective*. Final Report of Project ERB-SOE2-CT97-3055.

Evans, J. and Mayer, N. (2005) 'Electorates, new cleavages and social structures', in A. Cole, P. Le Galès and J. Levy (eds) *Developments in French Politics*. Basingstoke: Palgrave MacMillan (4th series).

Farrar, M. (2004) 'Social movements and the struggle over "race"', in M.J. Todd and G. Taylor (eds) *Democracy and Participation – Popular Protest and New Social Movements*. London: Merlin Press.

Fassin, D. (2006) 'Riots in France and silent anthropologists', *Anthropology Today*, 22(1): 1–3.

Faure, A. (2004) 'Spéculation et société: les grands travaux à Paris au XIXᵉ siècle', *Histoire, Economie et Société*, 3: 433–48.

Faure, A. (2008) 'La ségrégation, ou les métamorphoses historiographiques du Baron Haussmann', in M.C. Jaillet, E. Perrin and F. Ménard (eds) *Diversité Sociale, Ségrégation Urbaine, Mixité*. La Défense: Plan Urbanisme, Construction et Architecture.

Fauvelle-Aymar, C. and François, A. (2006) 'L'analyse électorale multi-niveaux, présentation et application au référendum français de 2005'. Paper presented at GAEL, 'Le renouveau des analyses contextuelles', Paris, 6 June.

Fauvelle-Aymar, C., François, A. and Vornetti, P. (2005) *Les Comportements Electoraux dans les ZUS à la Présidentielle de 2002 – Les électeurs des ZUS, des électeurs comme les autres*. Paris: Délégation Interministérielle à la Ville.

Fauvelle-Aymar, C., François, A. and Vornetti, P. (2006) *Le Vote des ZUS – Analyse des Elections Municipales de 2001 et Comparaison avec la Présidentielle de 2002*. Paris: Délégation Interministérielle à la Ville.

Favell, A. (1998) *Philosophies of Integration: Immigration and the Idea of Citizenship in France and Britain*. Palgrave: Macmillan.

Feldman, A. (1991) *Formations of Violence: The Narrative of the Body and Political Terror in Northern Ireland*. Chicago: The University of Chicago Press.

Fillieule, O. and Jobard, F. (1998) 'The maintenance of order in France. Towards a model of protest policing' in D. della Porta and H. Reiter, (eds) *The Policing of Mass Demonstrations in Contemporary Democracies*. Minneapolis: University of Minnesota Press.

Franzke, B. (1993) 'Polizei und Ausländer. Beschreibung, Erklärung und Abbau gegenseitiger Vorbehalte', *Kriminalistik*, 10: 615–19.

Fullilove, M. (1994) *Root Shock: How Tearing Up City Neighbourhoods Hurts America, and What We Can Do About It*. Oxford: One World.

Galland, O., Cicchelli, V., de Maillard J. and Misset, S., (2006) *Comprendre les Emeutes de Novembre 2005. L'Exemple d'Aulnay*. Paris: Cerlis.

Galland, O., de Maillard, J., Kokoreff, M. (2007) *Enquêtes sur les Violences Urbaines. Comprendre les Emeutes de Novembre 2005. Les Exemples d'Aulnay-sous-Bois et de Saint-Denis*. Paris: Documentation Française.

Garbaye, R. (2005) *Getting Into Local Power: The Politics of Ethnic Minorities in British and French Cities*. Oxford: Blackwell Publishing.

Geisser, V., Karam, K. and Vairel, F. (2006) 'Espaces du politique. Mobilisations et protestations', in E. Picard (ed) *La Politique dans le Monde Arabe*. Paris: Colin.

Gesemann, F. (2001) 'Wenn man den Polizisten nicht vertrauen kann, wem dann? Zur gegenseitigen Wahrnehmung von Migranten und Polizisten', in F. Gesemann (ed.) *Migration und Integration in Berlin. Wissenschaftliche Analysen und politische Perspektiven*. Opladen: Leske & Budrich.

Gesemann, F. (2003) 'Ist egal ob man Ausländer ist oder so – jeder Mensch braucht die Polizei. Die Polizei in der Wahrnehmung junger Migranten', in A. Groenemeyer and J. Mansel (eds) *Die Ethnisierung von Alltagskonflikten*. Opladen: Leske and Budrich.

Giddens, A. (1998) *The Third Way: The Renewal of Social Democracy*. Cambridge: Polity.

Gilje, P.A. (1996) *Rioting in America*. Bloomington and Indianapolis: Indiana University Press.

Gilroy, P. (1992) 'The end of anti-racism', in J. Donald and A. Rattansi (eds) *'Race', Culture and Difference*. London: Sage.

Gilroy, P. (2002) *There Ain't no Black in the Union Jack: The Cultural Politics of Race and Nation*. (Third edition). London: Routledge.

Goldstein, H. (1990) *Problem-Oriented Policing*. New York: McGraw-Hill.

Goodhart, D. (2004) 'The Discomfort of Strangers', *Guardian*, 24 February.

Green, S. and Jerome, R.B. (2007) 'City of Cincinnati independent monitor's response to RAND's third annual evaluation report: police-community relations in Cincinnati', December 2007. http://www.gabsnet.com/cincinnatimonitor/December%202007.pdf.

Greener, I. (2002) 'Agency, social theory and social policy', *Critical Social Policy*, 22(4): 688–705.

Greenhalf, J. (2003) *It's a Mean Old Scene: A History of Modern Bradford from 1974*. Bradford: Redbeck Press.

Gurr, T.R. (ed.) (1989) *Violence in America, Volume 2: Protest, Rebellion, Reform*. Newbury Park, California: Sage.

Haan, W. de and Nijboer, J. (2005) 'Youth violence and self-help', *European Journal of Crime, Criminal Law and Criminal Justice*, 13(1): 75–88.

Hajjat, A. (2006) 'L'expérience politique du MTA', *Contretemps*, 16: 76–85.

Hajjat, A. (2008) 'Révoltes des quartiers populaires, crise du militantisme et postcolonialisme' in A. Boubeker and A. Hajjat (eds) *Histoire Politique des Immigrations (Post) Coloniales: France, 1920–2008*. Paris: Amsterdam.

Hall, S. (2000) 'Conclusion: the multicultural question', in B. Hesse (ed.) *Un/Settled Multiculturalisms*. London: Zed Books.

Harvey, D. (2003) *Paris, Capital of Modernity*. London: Routledge.

Häußermann, H. (2007) 'Verwaltete Marginalität', in Heinrich-Böll-Stiftung (ed.) *Banlieue Europa. Jugendunruhen – Stadt – Migration*. Berlin: Heinrich-Böll-Stiftung.

Heitmeyer, W., Möller, R., Babka von Gostomski, C., Brüß, J. and Wiebke, G. (2005) *Integration, Interaktion sowie die Entwicklung von Feindbildern und Gewaltbereitschaft bei Jugendlichen deutscher und türkischer Herkunft sowie bei Aussiedler-Jugendlichen unter besonderer Berücksichtigung ethnisch-kultureller Konfliktkonstellationen (Längsschnittstudie). Zwischenbericht II.* (Unpublished).

Heitmeyer, W., Müller, J. and Schröder, H. (1997) *Verlockender Fundamentalismus. Türkische Jugendliche in Deutschland*. Frankfurt/M.: Suhrkamp.

Hewitt, R. (2005) *White Backlash: The Politics of Multiculturalism*. Cambridge: Cambridge University Press.

Hewstone, M., Tausch, N., Hughes, J. and Cairns, E. (2007) 'Prejudice, intergroup contact and identity: do neighbourhoods matter?', in M. Wetherell, M. Lafleche and R. Berkley (eds) *Identity, Ethnic Diversity and Community Cohesion*. London: Sage.

Hmed, C. (2006) '"Tenir ses hommes". La gestion des étrangers "isolés" dans les foyers Sonacotra après la guerre d'Algérie', *Politix*, 19 (76): 11–30.

Hmed, C. (2007) 'Contester une institution dans le cas d'une mobilisation improbable : la "grève des loyers" dans les foyers SONACOTRA dans les années 1970', *Sociétés Contemporaines*, 65: 55–81.

Holdaway, S. (1983) *Inside the British Police*. Oxford: Blackwell.

Holdaway, S. (1991) 'Race relations and police recruitment', *British Journal of Criminology*, 31(4): 365–82.

Home Office (2003) *Community Cohesion Pathfinder Programme: The First Six Months*. London: Home Office.

Home Office (2005) *Improving Opportunity, Strengthening Society: The Government's Strategy to Increase Race Equality and Community Cohesion*. London: Home Office.

Horstman, B.M. (2003) 'Divided: with race as their lens, many viewers draw opposite conclusions from the Nathaniel Jones tape. Why?', *Cincinnati Post* (online edition), 6 December, 2003. http://www.cincypost.com/2003/12/06/cbw120603.html.

House, J. and MacMaster, N. (2006) *Paris 1961: Algerians, State Terror and Memory*. Oxford: Oxford University Press.

Hundley, J.R. Jnr. (1968) 'The dynamics of recent ghetto riots', *Detroit Journal of Urban Law*, 45, 627–39. Reprinted as: Hundley, J.R. Jnr. (1975) 'The dynamics of recent ghetto riots', in R.R. Evans (ed.) *Readings in Collective Behavior*. Chicago: Rand McNally.

Hussain, Y. and Bagguley, P. (2005) 'Citizenship, ethnicity and identity: British Pakistanis after the 2001 riots', *Sociology*, 39(3): 407–25.

Hüttermann, J. (2000) 'Polizeiliche Alltagspraxis im Spannungsfeld von Etablierten und Außenseitern', in R. Anhut and W. Heitmeyer (eds) *Bedrohte Stadtgesellschaft. Soziale Desintegrationsprozesse und ethnisch-kulturelle Konfliktkonstellationen*. Weinheim and Munich: Juventa Verlag.

Independent Police Complaints Commission (2006) *Final Report into the IPCC Independent Investigation into the Appropriateness of the West Midlands Response and the Circumstances Immediately Prior to the Death of Aaron James*. IPCC reference: 2005/01279 (edited version).

Ireland, D. (2005) 'Why is France burning? The rebellion of a lost generation', *Axis of Logic*, 9 November 2005. http://www.axisoflogic.com/artman/publish/article_19897.shtml.

Jansson, K. (2006) *Black and Minority Ethnic Groups' Experiences and Perceptions of Crime, Racially Motivated Crime and the Police: Findings from the 2004/05 British Crime Survey*. Home Office Online Report 25/06.

Jaschke, H.-G. (1997) *Öffentliche Sicherheit im Kulturkonflikt. Zur Entwicklung der städtischen Schutzpolizei in der multikulturellen Gesellschaft*. Frankfurt/M. and New York: Campus.

Jascke, H.-G. (2006) 'Bloße Folklore wird hier nicht ausreichen'. http://www.heute.de/ZDFheute/inhalt/5/0,3672,3919589,00.html. (accessed 26 November 2008).

Jazouli, A. (1986) *L'Action Collective des Jeunes Maghrébins en France*. Paris: CIEMI, L'Harmattan.

Jazouli, A. (1992) *Les Années Banlieues*. Paris: Seuil.

Jefferson, T. and Grimshaw, R. (1984) *Controlling the Constable*. London: Frederick Muller.

Jelen, B. (2005) 'Leur histoire est notre histoire. Immigrant culture in France between visibility and invisibility', *French Politics, Culture & Society*, 23(2): 101–25.

Jobard, F. (2002) *Bavures Policières? La Force Publique et Ses Usages*. Paris: La Découverte.

Jobard, F. (2003) 'Research note. Counting violence committed by the police. Raw facts and narratives', *Policing and Society* 13(4): 423–28.

Jobard, F. (2005) 'Géopolitiques d'une banlieue militante. Une mobilisation politique en lointaine banlieue parisienne', *Contre-temps*, 13: 30–8.

Jobard, F. (2006) 'Sociologie politique de la racaille', in H. Lagrange and M. Oberti (eds) *Emeutes Urbaines et Protestation. Une Singularité Française*. Paris: Presses de Sciences-Po.

Jobard, F. (2008) 'The 2005 French urban unrests. Data-based interpretations', *Sociology Compass*, 2(4): 1287-1302.

Jobard, F. (2009) 'Rioting as a political tool: the 2005 French riots', *Howard Journal of Criminal Justice*, forthcoming.

Jobard, F., Linhardt D. (2008) 'Control and guardianship. A comparison between two surveillance spaces, Orly international airport and Dammarie's housing project', in M. Deflem (ed.) *Surveillance and Governance: Crime Control and Beyond*. Amsterdam: JAI Press.

Jobard, F. and Névanen S. (2009) 'Colour-tainted sentencing? Discrimination in court decisions concerning offences committed against police (1965–2005)', *Revue Française de Sociologie. English Annual Supplement*, 50, forthcoming.

Johnston, L. (2005) 'From "community" to "neighbourhood" policing: Police Community Support Officers and the "police extended family" in London', *Journal of Community and Applied Social Psychology*, 15, 241–54.

Juhem, P. (1998) *SOS-Racisme. Histoire d'une Mobilisation 'Apolitique'. Contribution à une Analyse des Transformations des Représentations Politiques après 1981*. PhD dissertation. Paris: Université Paris 10.

Juhem, P. (2000) ' "Civiliser" la banlieue. Logiques et conditions d'efficacité des dispositifs étatiques de régulation de la violence dans les quartiers populaires', *Revue Française de Science Politique*, 50(1): 53–72.

Juhem, P. (2004) 'L'autre musique. Le concert de SOS Racisme ou la victoire de l'apolitisme', *Vacarme*, 29: 19–21.

Kalra, V. (2000) *From Textile Mills to Taxi Ranks: Experiences of Migration, Labour and Social Chang*. Aldershot: Ashgate.

Kalra, V. (2002) 'Extended view: riots, race and reports: Denham, Cantle, Oldham and Burnley inquiries', *Sage Race Relations Abstracts*, 27(4): 20–30.

Kalra, V. (2003) 'Police lore and community disorder: diversity in the criminal justice system', in D. Mason (ed.) *Explaining Ethnic Differences: Changing Patterns of Disadvantage in Britain*. Bristol: Policy Press.

Keith, M. (1990) 'Que s'est-il passé? les émeutes de 1980 et 1981 dans les cités britanniques. Un essai d'analyse', *Revue Européenne de Migrations Internationales*, 6(3): 21–44.

Keith, M. (1993) *Race, Riots and Policing: Lore and Disorder in a Multi-Racist Society*. London: UCL Press.

Kepel, G. (1991) *Les Banlieues de l'Islam. Naissance d'une Religion en France*. Paris: Seuil.

King, M. and Brearley, N. (1996) *Public Order Policing: Contemporary Perspectives on Strategy and Tactics*. Leicester: Perpetuity Press.

King, M. and Waddington, D. (2004) 'Coping with disorder? The changing relationship between police public order strategy and practice – a critical analysis of the Burnley riot', *Policing and Society*, 14(2):118–37.

Kinsey, R., Lea, J. and Young, J. (1986) *Losing the Fight Against Crime*. Oxford: Blackwell.

Kirszbaum, T. (2004) 'Services publics et fractures de la ville: la "pensée publique" entre diversité, éclatement et souci du rapprochement', *Sociologie du Travail*, 46(2): 224–60.

Kokoreff, M. (2003) *La Force des Quartiers. De la Délinquance à l'Engagement Politique*. Paris: Payot.

Kokoreff, M. (2008) *Sociologie des Emeutes*. Paris: Payot.

Kokoreff, M. and Rodriguez, J. (2004) *La France en Mutations. Quand l'Incertitude Fait Société*. Paris: Payot.

Kraska, P.B. and Kappeler, V.E. (1997) 'Militarizing American police: the rise and normalization of paramilitary units', *Social Problems*, 44(1): 1–18.

Kundnani, A. (2001) 'From Oldham to Bradford: the violence of the violated', *Race and Class*, 43(2): 105–31.

Kundnani, A. (2002) *The Death of Multiculturalism*. London: Institute of Race Relations. http://www.irr.org.uk/2002/april/ak000013.html.

Kundnani, A. (2007) *The End of Tolerance: Racism in 21st Century Britain*. London: Pluto.

Laachir, K. (2007) 'France's "ethnic" minorities and the question of exclusion', *Mediterranean Politics*, 12(1): 99–105.

La Botz, D. (2007) 'Has it all come down to a jail? Cincinnati six years after the killings and the riots', *Counterpunch*, 5 October 2007. http://www.counterpunch.org/labotz10052007.html.

Lagrange, H. (2003) 'Crime and socio-economic context', *Revue Française de Sociologie, An English Annual Supplement*, 54: 29–48.

Lagrange, H. (2006) 'La structure et l'accident', in H. Lagrange and M. Oberti (eds) *Emeutes Urbaines et Protestation. Une Singularité Française*. Paris: Presses de Sciences-Po.

Lagrange, H. (2007) 'Déviance et réussite scolaire à l'adolescence', *Recherches et Prévisions*. CNAF: 82.

Lagrange, H. (2008a) 'Post scriptum to the riots 2005. November 2007 in Villiers'. http://academic.shu.ac.uk/aces/franco-british-riots/.

Lagrange, H. (2008b) 'Émeutes, ségrégation urbaine et aliénation politique', *Revue Française de Science Politique*, 58(3): 377–401.

Lagrange, H. and Oberti, M. (eds) (2006) *Emeutes Urbaines et Protestation. Une Singularité Française*. Paris: Presses de Sciences-Po.

Lagrée, J.-C. (1982) *Les Jeunes Chantent leurs Cultures*. Paris: L'Harmattan.

Lagroye, J. (2006) *Sociologie Politique*. Paris: Presses de Sciences-Po.

Lahire, B. (1998) *L'Homme Pluriel. Les Ressorts de l'Action*. Paris: Nathan.

Lapeyronnie, D. (1987) 'Assimilation, mobilisation et action collective chez les jeunes de la seconde génération d'origine maghrébine', *Revue Française de Sociologie*, 28: 287–318.

Lapeyronnie, D. (1992) 'De l'intégration à la ségrégation', *Cultures et Conflits*, 6: 73–89.

Lapeyronnie, D. (1993) *L'individu et les Minorités. La France et la Grande-Bretagne face à leurs Immigrés*. Paris: Presses universitaires de France.

Lapeyronnie, D. (1998) 'Jugendkrawalle und Ethnizität', in W. Heitmeyer, R. Dollase and O. Backes (eds) *Die Krise der Städte*. Frankfurt/M: Suhrkamp.

Lapeyronnie, D. (2006) 'Primitive rebellion in den französischen vorstädten: ein essay über die unruhen vom Herbst 2005', *Soziale Probleme*, 17: 63–89.

Lea, J. (2004) 'From Brixton to Bradford: Ideology and discourse on race and urban violence in the United Kingdom', in G. Gilligan and J. Pratt (eds) *Crime, Truth and Justice: Official Inquiry, Discourse, Knowledge*. Cullompton: Willan.

Lea, J. and Young, J. (1982) 'The riots in Britain 1981: urban violence and political marginalisation', in D. Cowell, D. Jones and J. Young (eds) *Policing the Riots*. London: Junction Books.

Lea, J. and Young, J. (1993) *What Is To be Done About Law and Order? Crisis in the Nineties*. London: Pluto Press.

Leeds, E. (1996) 'Cocaine and parallel polities in the Brazilian urban periphery: constraints on local-level democratization', *Latin American Research Review*, 31(3): 47–83.

Le Galès, P. (2008) 'Territorial politics in France: le calme avant la tempête?', in A. Cole, P. Le Galès and J. Levy (eds) *Developments in French Politics*. Basingstoke: Palgrave MacMillan (4th series).

Le Galès, P. and Mawson, J. (1995) 'Contracts versus competitive bidding: Rationalizing urban policy programmes in England and France', *Journal of European Public Policy*, 2(2): 205–241.

Le Goaziou, V. and Mucchielli, L., (eds) (2006) *Quand les Banlieues Brûlent… Retour sur les Emeutes de Novembre 2005*. Paris: La Découverte.

Lehnartz, S. (2008) 'Deutschland, du Opfer', *Frankfurter Allgemeine Sonntagszeitung*, 28 January.

Leibowitz, J. and Salmon, S. (1999) '20/20 vision? Interurban competition, crisis and the politics of downtown development in Cincinnati, Ohio', *Space and Policy*, 3(2): 233–55.

Lépinard, E. (2008) 'Gender and multiculturalism: the politics of difference at a crossroads', in A. Cole, P. Le Galès and J. Levy (eds) *Developments in French Politics*. London: Palgrave Macmillan.

Liebl, K. (2006) 'Polizeiforschung revisited: die Tagungen des Arbeitskreises "Empirische Polizeiforschung"', *Kriminologisches Journal*, 38(2): 128–45.

Linhart, V. (1992) 'Des Minguettes à Vaulx-en-Velin: les réponses des pouvoirs publics aux violences urbaines', *Cultures et Conflits*, 6: 91–111.

Local Government Association (LGA) (2002) *Guidance on Community Cohesion*. London: LGA.

Loveday, B. (2000) 'Must do better: the state of police race relations', in A. Marlow and B. Loveday (eds) *After Macpherson: Policing after the Stephen Lawrence Inquiry*. London: Russell House.

Lowles, N. (2001) 'BNP profiting from hate', *Searchlight*, July.

Lukas, T. (2007) *Crime Prevention in High-Rise Housing. Lessons from the Crime Prevention Carousel*. Berlin: Duncker & Humblot.

Maag, C. (2006) 'In Cincinnati, life breathes anew in riot-scarred area', *New York Times*, 29 November 2006. http://www.nytimes.com/2006/11/25/US/25cincy.html?fta=y.

Macdonald, J., Stokes, R.J., Ridgeway, G. and Riley, K.J. (2007) 'Race, neighbourhood context and perceptions of injustice by the police in Cincinnati', *Urban Studies*, 44(13): 2567–85.

Maibach, G. (1996) *Polizisten und Gewalt. Innenansichten aus dem Polizeialltag*. Reinbek: Rowohlt.

Mallory, M. (2006) 'Mayor Mallory, Manager Dohoney and Chief Streicher expand police patrols in neighborhoods', *Press Release for Mayor Mark Mallory*, City of Cincinnati, 29 September 2006. http://www.cincinnati-oh.gov/mayor/downloads/mayor_pdf14659.pdf.

Mansel, J. and Albrecht, G. (2003) 'Migration und das kriminalpolitische Handeln staatlicher Strafverfolgungsorgane. Ausländer als polizeilich Tatverdächtige und gerichtlich Abgeurteilte', *Kölner Zeitschrift für Soziologie und Sozialpsychologie*, 55(4): 679–715.

Marlière, E. (2005) *Jeunes en cité. Diversité des trajectoires ou destin commun?* Paris: L'Harmattan.

Marx, G. (1970) 'Issueless riots', *Annals of the American Academy of Political and Social Science*, 39(1): 21–33.

Masclet, O. (2003) *La Gauche et les Cités. Enquête sur un Rendez-Vous Manqué*. Paris: La Dispute.

Matelly, J.H. and Mouhanna, C. (2007) *Police, des Chiffres et des Doutes*. Paris: Michalon.

Mathieu, L. (2006) *La Double Peine*. Paris: La Dispute.

Mauger, G. (2006) *Les Bandes, le Milieu et la Bohème Populaire. Études de Sociologie de la Déviance des Classes Populaires (1975–2005)*. Paris: Belin.

May, S. (1999) 'Critical multiculturalism and cultural difference: avoiding essentialism', in S. May (ed.) *Critical Multiculturalism*. London: Falmer.

Mayer, N. (2007) 'Comment Nicolas Sarkozy a rétréci l'électorat Le Pen', *Revue Française de Science Politique*, 57(3/4): 429–45.

Mayer, N. and Tiberj, V. (2002) 'Do issues matter? Law and order in the 2002 French presidential election', in M. Lewis-Beck (ed.) *The French Voter: Before and After the 2002 Election*. Basingstoke: Palgrave Macmillan.

Mazars, M. (2006) *Les 'Violences Urbaines' de l'Automne 2005 Vues du Palais de Justice. Etude de Cas. Les Procédures Judiciaires Engagées au TGI de Bobigny*. Paris: Centre d'Analyse Stratégique.

McGhee, D. (2005) *Intolerant Britain: Hate, Citizenship and Difference*. Maidenhead: Open University Press.

McGhee, D. (2006) 'The new Commission for Equality and Human Rights: building community cohesion and revitalising citizenship in contemporary Britain', *Ethnopolitics*, 5:(2): 145–66.

McGhee, D. (2003) 'Moving to "our" common ground – a critical examination of community cohesion discourse in twenty-first century Britain', *The Sociological Review*, 51(3): 366–404.

McLaughlin, E. (2007) *The New Policing*. London: Sage.

McLaughlin, S. and Prendergast, J. (2001) 'Police frustration brings slowdown: Arrests plummet from 2000; officers seek jobs in suburbs', *The Enquirer*, 30 June 2001. http://www.com/editions/2001/06/30/loc_police_frustration.html.

McPhail, C. (1971) 'Civil disorder participation: a critical examination of recent research', *American Sociological Review*, 36, 1058–73.

McPhail, C. (1991) *The Myth of the Madding Crowd*. New York: Aldine de Gruyter.

Millet, M. and Thin, D. (2005) *Ruptures scolaires. L'école à l'épreuve de la question sociale*. Paris: Presses universitaires de France.

Mletzko, M. and Weins, C. (1999) 'Polizei und Fremdenfeindlichkeit. Ergebnisse einer Befragung in einer westdeutschen Polizeidirektion', *Monatsschrift für Kriminologie und Strafrechtsreform*, 82(2): 77–93.

Modood, T., Berthoud, R., Lakey, J., Nazroo, J., Smith, P., Virdee, S. and Beishon, S. (1997) *Ethnic Minorities in Britain – Diversity and Disadvantage*. London: PSI.

Mohammed, M. (2008) 'Youth gangs and "Trouble in the Projects"', *Penal Issues*. http://www.cesdip.org/spip.php?article332.

Mohammed, M. and Mucchielli M. (2006) 'La Police dans les "Quartiers Sensibles". Un profond malaise', in L. Mucchielli and V. Le Goaziou (eds) *Quand les Banlieues Brûlent. Retour sur les Emeutes de Novembre 2005*. Paris: La Découverte.

Mohammed, M., (2007) *La Place des Familles dans la Formation des Bandes de Jeunes*. Doctoral thesis. Guyancourt: Université Versailles Saint-Quentin.

Monjardet, D. (2008) 'How to assess a law enforcement policy?; The first Sarkozy ministry (7 May 2002–30 March 2004)', *Sociologie du Travail*, 48(2): 188–208.

Morin, A. (2003) *Action Collective et Forme de Militantisme des Citoyens Issus de l'Immigration et des Quartiers Populaires. DiverCité à Lyon, Une Tentative de Fédération de la Pluralité.* Master Thesis. Lyon: Institut d'études politiques.

Mouhanna, C. (2000) 'Les services publics et la question jeune: de la crainte au rejet?', in F. Bailleau and C. Gorgeon (eds) *Prévention et Sécurité. Vers un Nouvel Ordre Social?* Paris: Editions de la Délégation interministérielle à la ville.

Mouhanna, C. (2006) 'Young people and police officers in French poor suburbs: the social construction of a conflict', in P. Piotrowski (ed.) *Understanding Problems of Social Pathology.* New York: Éditions Rodopi.

Mouhanna, C. (2008) 'The failure of Ilotage and Police de Proximité systems to withstand the law and order rhetoric in contemporary France', in T. Williamson (ed.) *The Handbook of Knowledge Based Policing: Current Conceptions and Future Directions.* Chichester: John Wiley & Sons.

Mucchielli, L. (2004) 'L'évolution de la délinquance juvenile en France (1980–2000)', *Sociétés Contemporaines*, 53(1): 101–34.

Mucchielli, L. (2009) 'Fall 2005: a review of the most important riots in the history of French contemporary society', *Journal of Ethnic and Migration Studies*, forthcoming.

Muncie, J. (1984) *The Trouble With Kids Today.* London: Hutchinson.

Murdock, G. (1984) 'Reporting the riots: images and impact', in J. Benyon (ed.) *Scarman and After: Essays Reflecting on Lord Scarman's Report, the Riots and their Aftermath.* Oxford: Pergamon Press.

Murray, G. (2006) 'France: the riots and the republic', *Race and Class*, 47(4): 26–45.

Névanen S., Didier E., Zauberman R. and Robert, Ph. (2006) 'Victimization and insecurity in urban areas. The 2005 surveys', *Penal Issues*. http://www.cesdip.org/spip.php?article282.

Noiriel, G. (1996) *The French Melting Pot* (Second edition). Minneapolis: Minnesota Press.

O'Byrne, M. (2006) 'Can Macpherson succeed where Scarman failed?', in A. Marlow and E. McLaughlin (eds) *The New Policing.* London: Sage.

Oberschall, A. (1993) *Social Movements: Ideologies, Interests and Identities.* New Brunswick NJ: Transaction Books.

Oberti, M., (2008) 'Urban riots in France', *EuroTopics*. http://www.eurotopics.net/en/magazin/magazin_aktuell/frankreich-2008-07/oberti/.

Oberwittler, D. (2007) *The Effects of Ethnic and Social Segregation on Children and Adolescents: Recent Research and Results from a German Multilevel Study.* Wissenschaftszentrum Berlin für Sozialforschung: Arbeitsstelle Interkulturelle Konflikte und gesellschaftliche Integration.

Observatoire national des ZUS (2005) *Rapport annuel de l'ONZUS.* La Plaine Saint-Denis: Délégation interministérielle à la Ville.

Observatoire national des ZUS (2007) *Rapport annuel de l'ONZUS*. La Plaine Saint-Denis: Délégation interministérielle à la Ville.

Office for National Statistics (2001) Census: Standard Area Statistics (England and Wales) [computer file]. ESRC/JISC Census Programme, Census Dissemination Unit, Mimas University of Manchester.

Office for National Statistics (2002) *Social Trends*, vol. 32. London: The Stationery Office.

Office for National Statistics (2007) *Social Trends*, vol. 37. London: Palgrave Macmillan.

Ohlemacher, T. (1999) *Empirische Polizeiforschung in der Bundesrepublik Deutschland – Versuch einer Bestandsaufnahme*. Hannover: KFN-Forschungsberichte.

Oldham Independent Review (2001) *One Oldham One Future*. Oldham: Oldham Independent Review.

Osborne, K. (2007) 'A matter of trust', *CityBeat*, 24 January 2007. http://citybeat.com/2007-01-24/cover.shtml.

Ouseley, H (2001) *Community Pride, Not Prejudice (The Ouseley Report)*. Bradford: Bradford Vision.

Pager, D. (2008) 'The Republican ideal? Ethnic minorities and the Criminal Justice System in contemporary France', *Punishment and Society*, 10(4): 375–400.

Pan Ké Shon J.-L. (2004) 'Déterminants de la non-inscription électorale et quartiers sensibles en France', *Population*, 59(1): 147–60.

Péchu, C. (2006) *Droit au Logement. Genèse et Sociologie d'une Mobilisation*. Paris: Dalloz.

Peralva, A. (1997) *L'Incivilité, la Révolte et le Crime. Violences Juvéniles dans la Société du Risque*. Paris: EHESS.

Pfeiffer, C., Kleimann, M., Schott, T. and Petersen, S. (2005) *Migration und Kriminalität. Ein Gutachten für den Zuwanderungsrat der Bundesregierung*. Baden-Baden: Nomos.

Phillips, D. (2006) 'Parallel lives? Challenging discourses of British Muslim self-segregation', *Environment and Planning D: Society and Space*, 24, 25–40.

Phillips, T. (2005) *After 7/7: Sleepwalking to Segregation*. London: CRE.

Pitti, L. (2001) 'Grèves ouvrières *versus* luttes de l'immigration: une controverse entre historiens', *Ethnologie Française*, 31(3): 465–7.

Pitti, L. (2005) 'Catégorisations ethniques au travail', *Histoire et Mesure*, 20: 3–4.

Piven, F. (2008) 'Can power from below change the world?', *American Sociological Review*, 73(1): 1–14.

Piven, F. and Cloward, R. (1972) *Regulating the Poor: The Functions of Public Welfare*. London: Tavistock Publications.

Piven, F. and Cloward, R. (1977) *Poor People's Movements. Why They Succeed, How They Fail*. New York: Pantheon Books.

Piven, F. and Cloward, R. (1991) 'Collective protest. A critique of Resource-Mobilization Theory', *International Journal of Politics, Culture and Society*, 4(4): 435–58.

Polac, C. (1994), 'Quand les immigrés prennent la parole' in P. Perrineau (ed.) *L'Engagement: Déclin ou Mutations*? Paris: Presses de la FNSP.

Power, A. and Tunstall, R. (1997) *Dangerous Disorder: Riots and Violent Disturbances in Thirteen Areas of Britain, 1991–92*. York: York Publishing Services/Joseph Rowntree Foundation.

Proske, M. (1998) 'Ethnische Diskriminierungen durch die polizei: eine kritische relektüre geläufiger selbstbeschreibungen', *Kriminologisches Journal*, 30(3): 162–88.

Putnam, R. (2000) *Bowling Alone – The Collapse and Revival of American Community*. London: Touchstone.

Ramamurthy, A. (2006) 'The Politics of Britain's Asian youth movements', *Race and Class*, 48(2): 38–60.

Ray, L. and Smith, D. (2004) 'Racist offending, policing and community conflict', Sociology, 38(4): 681–99.

Reicher, S.D. (1984) 'The St Pauls riot: an explanation of the limits of crowd action in terms of a social identity model', *European Journal of Social Psychology*, 14: 1–21.

Reicher, S.D. (2001) 'The psychology of crowd dynamics', in M.A. Hogg and R.S. Tindale (eds) *Blackwells Handbook of Social Psychology: Group Processes*. Oxford: Blackwell.

Reiner, R. (1992) *The Politics of the Police*. (Second edition.) London: Harvester Wheatsheaf.

Renton, D. (2003) 'Examining the success of the British National Party, 1999–2003', *Race and Class*, 45(2): 75–85.

Rex, J. (1987) 'Life in the ghetto', in J. Benyon and J. Solomos (eds) *The Roots of Urban Unrest*. Oxford: Pergamon.

Rhodes, J. (2006) 'The 'local' politics of the British National Party (BNP)', *Sage Race Relations Abstracts*, 31(4): 5–20.

Ritchie, D. (2001) *Oldham Independent Review: One Oldham, One Future*. Government Office for the Northwest: Manchester.

Robert, P. (1991) 'The sociology of crime and deviance in France', *British Journal of Criminology*, 31(1): 27–38.

Robert, P. (2008) 'Violence in present-day France: data and sociological analysis', in S. Body-Gendrot and P. Spierenburg (eds) *Violence in Europe: Historical and Contemporary Perspectives*. New York: Springer.

Robert, P. and Pottier, M.-L. (2006) 'Is concern about safety changing?', *Revue Française de Sociologie*, 47(5): 35–63.

Robertson, R. (1995) 'Globalization: time-space and homogeneity-heterogeneity', in M. Featherstone, S. Lash and R. Robertson (eds) *Global Modernities*. London: Sage.

Robinson, D. (2005) 'The search for Community Cohesion: key themes and dominant concepts of the public policy agenda', *Urban Studies*, 42(8): 1411–27.

Roché, S. (2001) *La Délinquance des Jeunes*. Paris: Seuil.

Rothman, J. (2006) 'Identity and conflict: addressing police-community conflict in Cincinnati, Ohio', *Ohio State Journal on Dispute Resolution*, 22(1): 105–32.

Rothman, J. and Land, R. (2004) 'The Cincinatti police-community relations collaborative', *Criminal Justice*, 18(4): 35–42.

Rule, J.B. (1988) *Theories of Civil Violence*. Berkeley: University of California Press.

Sanchez-Jankowski M. (1991) *Islands in the Street*. Berkeley: University of California Press.

Sauer, M. and Goldberg, A. (2006) *Türkeistämmige Migranten in Nordrhein-Westfalen. Ergebnisse der siebten Mehrthemenbefragung*. Essen: Stiftung Zentrum für Türkeistudien.

Sayad, A. (1991) *L'Immigration ou les Paradoxes de l'Altérité*. Bruxelles: De Boeck Université.

Sayad, A. (1999) *La Double Absence, des Illusions de l'Emigré aux Souffrances de l'Immigré*. Paris: Seuil.

Sayad, A. (2002) *Histoire et Recherche Identitaire. Suivi d'un Entretien avec Hassan Harfaoui*. Paris: Éditions Bouchêne.

Scarman, Lord (1981) *A Report into the Brixton Disturbances of 11/12th April 1981*. London: Home Office.

Scarman, Lord (1982) *The Scarman Report: The Brixton Disorders, 10–12 April 1981. Report of an Inquiry*. London: Penguin.

Schell, T., Ridgeway, G., Dixon, T.L., Turner, S. and Riley, J. (2007) *Police-Community Relations in Cincinnati: Year Three Evaluation Report*. Santa Monica, California: The Rand Corporation. http://www.rand.org/pubs/technical_reports/2007/RAND_TR535.pdf.

Schnapper, D. (1998) *La Relation à l'Autre, au Cœur de la Pensée Sociologique*. Paris: Gallimard.

Schneider, C.L. (2008) 'Police power and race riots in Paris', *Politics and Society*, 36(1): 133–59.

Schweer, T. and Strasser, H. (2003) 'Die Polizei – dein Freund und Helfer? Duisburger Polizisten im Konflikt mit ethnischen Minderheiten und sozialen Randgruppen', in A. Groenemeyer and J. Mansel (eds) *Die Ethnisierung von Alltagskonflikten*. Opladen: Leske & Budrich.

Schweer, T. and Zdun, S. (2005) 'Gegenseitige Wahrnehmung von Polizei und Bevölkerung. Polizisten im Konflikt mit ethnischen Minderheiten und sozialen Randgruppen', in H. Groß (ed.) *Innen- und Außenansicht(en) der Polizei*. Frankfurt/M.: Verlag für Polizeiwissenschaft.

Scraton, P. (1985) *The State of the Police*. London: Pluto Press.

Sicot, F. (2000) 'Enfants d'immigrés maghrébins: rapport au quartier et engagement dans la délinquance', *Cahiers de la Sécurité Intérieure*, 42: 87–108.

Siegfried, A. (1913) *Tableau Politique de la France de l'Ouest*. Paris: Armand Colin.

Silverman, J. (1986) *Report of an Independent Inquiry into the Handsworth Disturbances, September 1985*. Birmingham: City of Birmingham.

Siméant, J. (1998) *La Cause des Sans-Papiers*. Paris: Presses de Sciences-Po.

Simon, P. (2008) 'The choice of ignorance. The debate on ethnic and racial statistics in France', *French Politics, Culture & Society*, 26(1): 7–31.

Simpson, L. (2007) 'Ghettos of the mind: the empirical behaviour of indices of segregation and diversity', *Journal of the Royal Statistical Society: Series A Statistics in Society*, 170: 405–424.

Sivanandan, A. (2005) *It's Anti-Racism that has Failed, not Multiculturalism that Failed*. London: Institute of Race Relations.

Skogan, W.G. (1996) 'The police and public opinion in Britain', *American Behavioral Scientist*, 39(4) 421–32.

Skogan, W.G. (2005) 'Citizen satisfaction with police encounters', *Police Quarterly*, 8(3): 298–321.

Skogan, W. G. (2006) *Police and Community in Chicago. A Tale of Three Cities*. Oxford and New York: Oxford University Press.

Smith, D.J. and Gray, J. (1985) *Police and People in London*. (The PSI Report.) Aldershot: Gower.

Smith, S. (2004) *How It Was Done: The Rise of Burnley BNP: The Inside Story*. Burnley: Cliviger Press.

Smith, S.K., Steadman, G.W., Minton, T.D. and Townsend, M. (eds) (1999) *Criminal Victimization and Perceptions of Community Safety in 12 Cities, 1998*. Washington/DC: US Department of Justice.

Snyder, D. (1979) 'Collective violence processes: implications for disaggregated theory and research', in L. Kriesberg (ed.) *Research in Social Movements, Conflicts and Change*. Greenwich: Jai Press.

Sokhey, A.E. (2007) 'From riots to reconciliation: the religious interests involved in healing Cincinatti after civil unrest', in P.A. Djupe and L.R. Olsen (eds) *Religious Interests in Community Conflict: Beyond the Culture Wars*. Waco, Texas: Baylor University Press.

Solomos, J. (2003) *Race and Racism in Britain* (third edition). Basingstoke: Palgrave.

Taj, M. (1995) *A 'Can Do' City. Supplementary Comments and Recommendations to the Bradford Commission Report*. Bradford: Taj.

Taslitz, A.E. (2003) 'Racial auditors and the Fourth Amendment: data with the power to inspire political action', *Law and Contemporary Problems*, 66, 221–98.

Taylor, V. (1989) 'Social movement continuity: the women's movement in abeyance', *American Sociological Review*, 54(5): 761–75.

Thomas, P. (2006) 'The impact of "Community Cohesion" on youth work: a case study from Oldham', *Youth and Policy*, 93: 41–60.

Thomas, P. (2007) 'Moving on from 'anti-racism'? Understandings of Community Cohesion held by youth workers', *Journal of Social Policy*, 36(3): 435–55.

Tiberj, V. (2002) *Vote et Insécurité*. Paris: Ministère de l'Intérieur.

Tilly, Ch. (2003) *The Politics of Collective Violence*. Cambridge: Cambridge University Press.

Tissot, S. (2008) 'French Suburbs: A New Problem or a New Approach to Social Exclusion?', Center for European Studies Working Papers Series, 160.

Travis, A. (2001) Blunkett in race row over culture tests, *Guardian*, 10 December.

Tumber, H. (1982) *Television and the Riots*. London: Broadcasting Research Unit.

Tyler, T.R. (2004) 'Enhancing police legitimacy', *The Annals of the American Academy of Political and Social Science*, 593: 84–99.

UK Indymedia (2005) 'The so-called Lozells riot', 25 November. http://www.indymedia.org.uk/en/2005/11/328123.html.

Waddington, D. (1992) *Contemporary Issues in Public Disorder: A Comparative and Historical Approach*. London: Routledge.

Waddington, D. (2007) *Policing Public Disorder: Theory and Practice*. Cullompton: Willan.

Waddington, D. (2008) 'The madness of the mob? Explaining the "irrationality" and destructiveness of crowd violence', *Sociology Compass*, 2(2): 675–87.

Waddington, D., Jones, K. and Critcher, C. (1989) *Flashpoints. Studies in Public Disorder*. London and New York: Routledge.

Waddington, P.A.J. (1991) *The Strong Arm of the Law: Armed and Public Order Policing*. Oxford: Clarendon Press.

Wallerstein, I. (2005) 'The French riots: rebellion of the underclass', *Commentary*, 174, 1 December.

Watson, C.W. (2000) *Multiculturalism*. Buckingham: Open University Press.

Weaver, R.K. (1986) 'The politics of blame avoidance', *Journal of Public Policy*, 6(4): 371–98.

Webster, C. (2003) 'Race, space and fear: Imagined geographies of racism, crime, violence and disorder in Northern England', *Capital and Class*, 80: 95–121.

Weidacher, A. (ed.) (2000) *In Deutschland zu Hause. Politische Orientierungen griechischer, italienischer, türkischer und deutscher junger Erwachsener im Vergleich*. Opladen: Leske & Budrich.

Weil, P. (2001) 'The politics of immigration', in A. Guyomarch, H. Machin, P. Hall and J. Hayward (eds) *Developments in French Politics*. Basingstoke: Palgrave MacMillan.

Weil, P. and Crowley, J. (1994) 'Integration in theory and practice: a comparison of France and Britain', *West European Politics*, 17(2): 110–26.

West Yorkshire Police (2002) *Chief Constable's Annual Report 2001–2001*. Wakefield: West Yorkshire Police.

West Yorkshire Police (2004) *Bradford Riots*. http://www.westyorkshire.police. uk.

Whyte, W.F. (1996/1943) *Street Corner Society The Social Structure of an Italian Slum*. New York: de Gruyter.

Withol de Wenden, C. (1998) *Les Immigrés et la politique. 150 ans d'Exclusion*. Paris: Presses de la FNSP.

Withol de Wenden, C. and Leveau, R. (2001) *La Beurgeoisie. Les Trois Âges de la Vie Associative Issue de l'Immigration*. Paris: CNRS Éditions.

Wilson, P. (2005) '"Urban terrorism" of gangs', BBC News online, 18 March.

Winfree, T. L. and Curt, T. G. (1971) 'Adolescent attitudes toward the police', in T. Ferdinand (ed.) *Juvenile Delinquency: Little Brother Grows Up*. Newbury Park: Sage.

Yuval-Davis, N. (1997) 'Ethnicity, gender relations and multiculturalism', in T. Modood and P. Werbner (eds) Debating Cultural Hybridity. London: Zed Books.

Zauberman, R. and Levy, R. (2003) 'Police, minorities, and the French republican ideal', *Criminology*, 41(4): 1065–100.

Zedner, L (2006) 'Policing before and after the police: the historical antecedents of contemporary crime control', *British Journal of Criminology*, 46: 78–96.

Index

Cincinnati Black United Front 205, 207
Cincinnati Police Department
  foot-dragging 213
  lawsuit against 205, 207–8
  official investigations into 206–7
Cincinnati riot (2001) 203–15, 231
  causal context of 205–7
  collaborative agreement 207–15
  gentrification of Over-the-Rhine locality 206, 215
  Operation Vortex 212–13
citizenship
  British 41, 87, 236
  French 7, 82, 179, 217
Clancy, A. 219
Clarke, Lord T. 9, 51, 82
Clichy-sous-Bois 3, 29, 148, 149, 150, 151, 152, 153, 159, 232
Cloward, R. 144, 235
Cohen, P. 46
Cole, A. 239
Combat 18 (C18) 9, 54
Commission on Equality and Human Rights 83
Commission on the Future of Multi-Ethnic Britain 2000 82
Commission for Racial Equality (CRE) 7, 83, 86, 236
Commission for Race Relations 165
Community Cohesion 11, 81, 82–93
  as end to multiculturalism 86–90
  as new form of multiculturalism 90–2
  key themes 83–6
  watershed policy 81–2, 230
Contact Theory 91, 92
Copsey, N. 48, 52, 53, 54
'copycat' effect 6, 15, 25, 102, 107
Cottle, M. 206
council estates 8, 22, 23, 60, 62
Council for Community Relations in Lambeth (CCRL) 20
Cox, S.M. 218
crowd behaviour

collective identity 71–2
  diversity of 76–9
Crowley, J. 7
Curt, T.G. 223

Damamme, D. 32
Davies, B. 88
Decker, S.H. 219
de-industrialisation 57, 59, 240
Delon, A. 162–3
Denham, J. 42, 82, 83–4, 88
Denham, L. 9, 41, 42
Développment Social des Quartiers (DSQ) 31, 32
Djaïda, T. 141
Dlott, S. J. 207–8, 209, 210, 213
Donzelot, J. 126, 134
Dormagen, J.-Y. 183
Dosanjh, B. 95, 100–1
double sentence 141, 143, 146n17
Downtown Cincinnati Incorporated (DCI) 206
'dragnet' approach 18
drugs 14, 16, 60, 100, 102, 206, 207, 212, 215
Drury, J. 72, 73
Dubet, F. 137, 219
Dufoix, S. 237
Dufresne, D. 239, 242
Duprez, D. 147

Eatwell, R. 53
Economic and Social Research Council (ESRC) 10
Edelman, M. 243
elections 183–200
  2002 French Presidential 188–9
  2007 French Parliamentary 189–90
  2007 French Presidential 188–97
  impact of 2005 riots on 197
electoral mobilisation campaigns 195
emplois jeunes (state subsidised jobs) 36, 110